W9-DBQ-301

WISCONSIN CHEESE
A Cookbook and Guide to the Cheeses of Wisconsin

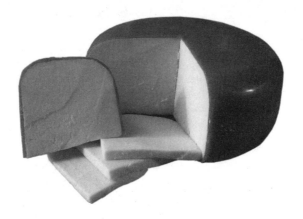

Martin Hintz and Pam Percy

ThreeForks™

GUILFORD, CONNECTICUT
HELENA, MONTANA
AN IMPRINT OF THE GLOBE PEQUOT PRESS

Copyright © 2008 by Morris Book Publishing, LLC

ThreeForks is a trademark of Morris Book Publishing, LLC.

Text design: M.A. Dubé
Unless otherwise credited, spot art © ClipArt.com.

Library of Congress Cataloging-in-Publication Data is available on file.

ISBN: 978-0-7627-4489-3

Printed in the United States of America
10 9 8 7 6 5 4 3 2 1

To the cheesemakers of Wisconsin, for their brilliant, award-winning cheeses.

Contents

Acknowledgments

The authors wish to thank the staff of the Wisconsin Milk Marketing Board and representatives from the state's various cheese and livestock breeder associations, as well as Wisconsin's dairy farmers, chefs, restaurateurs, and retailers who provide this marvelous product and ensure that it gets to the public in many delightful forms, flavors, and presentations. Their suggestions, insights, support, advice, encouragement, tips, and leads were invaluable.

Curious Brown Swiss cattle stand ready for milking. The breed is a high producer praised for its ruggedness and noted for the protein count of its milk. Brown Swiss are among the oldest of all dairy cattle, with origins dating back several thousand years.

Photo by Martin Hintz

A nod also goes to the many fabulous cookbook writers, authors, agriculture specialists, educators, and other cheese experts whose works were inspiring, informative, and thought-provoking.

Special thanks also to our numerous friends and relatives—especially our foodie friends Joan Hummert and Vicki Nelson—who helped test and taste dozens of recipes over glasses of refreshing beverages and endless hours of delightful conversation, serious comparison of notes, and much hilarity to arrive at the selections included in this cookbook.

Plus we'd like to offer a scratch behind the ears to the state's dairy cattle, goats, and sheep. Without them, Wisconsin cheese would not be, well, as udderly delicious as it is.

Preface: Say Cheese!

Wisconsin was made for making cheese. America's Dairyland has been solidifying its destiny for more than 160 years, building its reputation for unparalleled Cheddars and an expansive repertoire that now boasts more than 600 varieties, types, and styles.

Wisconsin's rolling hills, limestone-filtered waters, and rich soils have created the perfect *terroir* for producing cheeses second to none. The state's pastures nurture flavorful alfalfa, grasses, and clover, encouraged by clear northern light and pure rural air. The cows that graze these pastures produce milk that makes richly colored cheeses with herbaceous flavors, reflecting the changing seasons and harvests.

Cheesemakers around the world have long recognized this ideal location, and Wisconsin has welcomed waves of immigrant artisans throughout the years—first from European countries such as Germany, Switzerland, and the Netherlands, and more recently from locales including Italy, France, and Mexico. The result is a bounty of cheeses as different and distinctive as their roots.

But even in a place that's long been synonymous with cheese, change is in the air. Wisconsin is experiencing a renaissance in historic, artisanal techniques, and the result is unbounded creativity and excellence. Wisconsin cheesemakers are still winning awards for their historic versions of Swiss, Muenster, Colby, and Cheddars, but the list now includes French and Italian styles (mascarpone, Asiago, blue, and Gruyère among them) and distinctive twenty-first-century Wisconsin originals, such as Pleasant Ridge Reserve and Gran Canaria, both of which have captured prestigious Best of Show awards from the American Cheese Society. In fact, Wisconsin wins more national and international cheese awards than any other state or country. This book explores the Wisconsin cheese landscape, from everyday family favorites to sophisticated specialty and artisan choices appearing on cheese courses in some of the finest restaurants in the country.

Many of these cheeses are made by craftsmen who've been certified by the three-year Wisconsin

Master cheesemaker Bruce Workman loves his cheese. His Edelweiss Creamery in Monticello is the only plant in the nation making traditional Emmentaler. He uses equipment purchased in Switzerland to produce about 100,000 pounds of cheese a day, made from milk provided by local farmers. Each round of cheese weighs 180 pounds. Photo courtesy of the Wisconsin Milk Marketing Board

Master Cheesemaker program, the only one of its kind outside of Europe. No matter how many cheeses are made here, the commitment to quality is foremost in our cheesemaker community.

So whether you choose a batch of freshly dipped curds or a Caprese salad of Wisconsin fresh mozzarella, tomatoes, and basil, rest assured that you are experiencing the result of years of passionate devotion to making cheese. And the future shows even greater promise for quality innovation.

James Robson
Chief Executive Officer, Wisconsin Milk Marketing Board, Inc.

Numerous notable personalities have helped Wisconsin promote its June Dairy Month. The late comic Joey Bishop posed with this huge wheel of Swiss Colony Swiss cheese in 1968.
Photo courtesy of The Swiss Colony

Photo by Martin Hintz

CHAPTER 1

AN INTRODUCTION TO WISCONSIN CHEESE

THE UBIQUITOUS CHEESE PLATTER, OR ITS ANCIENT equivalent, has been around for at least 5,000 years. To discover how to make cheese, hunters first needed to put down their bows and arrows and pick up a staff with which to herd domesticated goats, sheep, and cows—and a pail to milk them. But what to do with the excess? A solution might have come about with the discovery that milk curdles if it is placed in the sun or heated too long.

Through observation and experimentation, the Mesopotamians in what is today Iraq were among the first to carefully process milk from their flocks. These long-ago people were also among the first brewers. Indeed, portraits in the temple of the goddess Ninhursag demonstrate that beer-and-cheese parties were just as much fun then as now.

Wisconsin's contemporary cheesemakers, using new knowledge and improved techniques, have perfected what those Mesopotamians initially discovered centuries ago. The state's cheese industry now makes numerous exciting specialty and mainline products noted nationally and internationally for their excellent taste, form, and consistency. While these cheeses can stand alone nicely, they're also perfect ingredients in recipes.

It's All in the Moo

The secret to making great cheese is starting with a great milk. For almost two centuries the state's farmers have produced much of the world's best, capitalizing on the geography and climate that produce rich pastureland—and truly contented cows. In its territorial days, almost every crossroads in Wisconsin's major dairy regions boasted

Cow-milking competitions are part of the fun at the Cheese Days celebration held in even years in Monroe, Wisconsin.
Photo by Martin Hintz

its own cheese factory. These local facilities were essential to ensuring a strong farm economy. Before improvements in transportation and storage, such as refrigeration, a perishable commodity like milk needed to be turned into cheese or butter for better preservation and shipping.

Take a look at some little-known milk truths:

- An average dairy cow weighs 1,400 pounds.
- A cow drinks thirty-five gallons of water a day—about how much an average-size bathtub contains.
- Cows can smell feed up to 6 miles away.

- There are about eleven million cows in the United States.
- A typical cow produces 185.5 gallons of milk each month. It takes 340 to 350 udder squirts to make a gallon.
- Milk is 87 percent water.
- Milk products contain a casein protein that clears burning taste buds. That's why a glass of milk is so refreshing after you've eaten something spicy.
- US consumers spend $74.6 billion yearly on dairy products—1.33 percent of our personal income.

Thanks to Cow Parade Facts, Wisconsin State Fair, for many of these factoids!

Wisconsin Cheese Pioneers

Wisconsin cheesemaking got off to a rollicking start with one Mrs. Anne Pickett, who made history in 1841 when she established Wisconsin's first commercial cheese factory, in Fond du Lac County. This feisty female entrepreneur worked out of the tiny kitchen in her log cabin, using milk collected from neighbors' cows. Seventeen years later John J. Smith obtained the first cheese vat and made cheese at his home in Sheboygan County. Smith also reached far beyond the state's borders to peddle his cheese. His brother, Hiram Smith, a farmer on the University of Wisconsin Board of Regents, then established Wisconsin's first full-scale cheese factory. He purchased milk from other dairy farmers or processed their milk in exchange for a percentage of the finished cheese.

"Cheese is probably the friendliest of foods. It endears itself to everything and never tires of showing off to great advantage. Any liquor or, I may say, any potable or any edible loves to be seen in the company of cheese. Naturally, some nationalities choose one type of companion and some other, but you very seldom find clashes of temperament in passing."

—James Beard (1903–1985), American chef and food writer

The Historic Cheesemaking Center in Monroe is located in a restored Chicago, Milwaukee, and St. Paul Railroad Depot built in the mid-1880s. Retired cheesemaker volunteers answer questions about cheesemaking and explain how to use the old cheesemaking tools on display. Photo by Martin Hintz

In 1864 Chester Hazen built a factory in Ladoga, the first such facility not attached to a farm. Initially, critics dubbed the plant "Hazen's Folly" over concerns about mixing milk from several herds. Hazen proved them wrong, however: His operation was a commercial success, with products shipped around the country via railcars.

The industry was helped by influxes of Old World settlers who were already established cheesemakers. Among them were the Swiss, of course. The Italian émigrés favored their *pasta filata* cheeses, such as mozzarella, provolone, and Gorgonzola. The French brought creamy, soft-ripened Camembert and Brie. Germans loved Muenster and Limburger. The English had Cheddar, while the Dutch brought techniques to make Gouda and Edam. Cheeses like Brick, Colby, and cold pack originated in the state.

By 1875 forty-five factories produced two million pounds of cheese a year in Sheboygan County alone. By 1900 the county sported about a hundred plants, churning out eight million pounds. Located in central Sheboygan County, Plymouth became known as the Cheese Factory Capital of the World. To establish uniform grades for Wisconsin cheese, the Dairymen's Association formed a board of trade, based in Watertown in 1872. Much later, in the 1960s, the National Cheese Exchange was sited in Plymouth, setting the price of cheese nationwide.

Dairy farmers and cheesemakers honed their skills through the help of the University of Wisconsin College of Agriculture, which began offering short cheesemaking courses in 1886. In 1890 the university's Stephen Babcock developed a milkfat test to determine which cows produced the richest milk. This test is still used today; the campus's Babcock Hall hosts the Food Sciences Department of the College of Agriculture and Life Sciences.

Several dates are important. In 1921 Wisconsin was the first state to grade its cheese for quality. By 1922 some 2,800 cheese factories existed throughout the state. By the mid-1940s some of these operations had merged or gone out of business, yet there were still more than 1,500 factories manufacturing 515 million pounds of cheese each year.

Today the Wisconsin Milk Marketing Board is proud to note that the state is home to just over one million cows, each producing an average of 17,728 pounds of milk per year. Cheesemakers use approximately 90 percent of this to produce cheese at more than 115 plants. Wisconsin has more licensed cheesemakers than any other state, and each of them must complete a tough curriculum in dairy science and cheesemaking. Many also apprentice under licensed cheesemakers, sometimes for years. Wisconsin is also the only state to offer a Master Cheesemaker program.

More than two billion pounds of cheese are now made in Wisconsin annually, accounting for 25 percent of all manufactured domestic cheese. It's enough to make a Mesopotamian goddess envious.

Every year Wisconsin brings home more cheese awards than any other state at the many cheese contests held across the country. Throughout this book we will highlight the cheeses that have garnered awards. Some prestigious competitions include:

- The Wisconsin Cheese Makers Association hosts both the US and World Championship Cheese Contests during alternating years. More than 1,000 entrants annually vie for these prestigious accolades.
- The Governor's Sweepstakes Cheese & Butter Contest is held at the Wisconsin State Fair in West Allis, Wisconsin.
- The World Dairy Expo Championship Dairy Product Contest takes place in Madison.

- The American Cheese Society Competition, hosted by the American Cheese Society (ACS), was founded in 1982. This annual summer event includes a conference, a world-renowned cheese competition, and a Festival of Cheese. The location varies throughout the country.

Wisconsin Dairy Facts

The Wisconsin Department of Agriculture knows a lot about our state's dairy industry:

> **"The moon really is made of cheese!"**
>
> —El Diablo Yamamoto, character in *A Fireside Chat,* Fireside Dinner Theatre, Fort Atkinson, Wisconsin, June 15, 2006

- Wisconsin agriculture annually creates more than $51.5 billion in economic activity and provides jobs for 420,000 people. About one out of every eight state citizens works in a farm-related job.
- Wisconsin's 19,000 dairy farmers produce more than twenty-three billion pounds of milk a year, more than 14 percent of the entire US milk supply.
- To move all that milk at one time would require a fleet of 500,000 trucks, each carrying 46,000 pounds (or 92,000 glasses) of milk.
- Wisconsin produces enough mozzarella each year to make more than a billion pizzas. In the United States, consumers gobble about ninety football fields of pizza every day. *Abundanza!* That's a lot of cheese.
- Wisconsin is the second leading butter state, producing 290 million pounds annually—25 percent of the total US production, and enough for nearly thirteen billion pieces of toast.

Cheese-Pairing Principles

According to the Wisconsin Milk Marketing Board, lighter beers or lagers pair generally well with lighter cheeses, while ales are a better match with stronger, more assertive-tasting cheeses. Another rule of thumb: Pair lighter cheeses with white wine, and stronger cheeses with red.

Here are some more tips to help you plan your cheese consumption:

Fresh Curds
Wines: fruity white
Beers: lager
Other beverages: sparkling water
Fruits: apples, grapes
Condiments: mustard

Extra Fresh
Wines: fruity wines
Beers: lager
Other beverages: tea
Fruits: plums, peaches
Bread and crackers: brown bread, sourdough bread
Condiments: jams and jelly

Mild
Wines: fruity whites, light reds
Other beverages: sparkling water, hot chocolate
Fruits: apples, grapes, raisins
Bread and crackers: water crackers, melba toast

Medium
Wines: fruity whites, light reds
Beers: bock
Other beverages: cranberry juice
Fruits: apples, grapes, apricots
Bread and crackers: water crackers, flat bread

Aged/Sharp
Wines: dessert wines, hearty reds, Riesling, Sauvignon Blanc, Pinot Gris, Merlot, Cabernet Sauvignon, Sauternes, port, Madeira, rich sherry
Beers: ale, Porter (a dark ale)
Other beverages: apple juice, cider
Fruits: apples, pineapple
Bread and crackers: water crackers, rye bread
Condiments: smoked almonds, pickled onions

Extra Sharp
Wines: hearty reds, fortified wine, Zinfandel, Merlot
Beers: pale ale, stout
Other beverages: coffee
Fruits: pears, apples
Bread and crackers: crusty bread, water crackers
Other foods: dates, spiced apples, onions, tomatoes

Working with Cheese

- When you're microwaving cheese, only use 30 percent (medium-low) to 70 percent (medium-high) power.
- When cooking, heat cheese just long enough for it to melt; cooking too long often toughens it. For more even melting, be sure to chop, dice, shred, grate, or cube the cheese first.

- When you're broiling foods topped by cheese, keep the pan at least 5 inches from the heat to prevent a shoe-leather crusting.
- Cheese must always be refrigerated. The USDA requires a "sell-by" date on all perishable products, usually about three months after packaging. After opening, cheese should be stored under refrigeration for a maximum of twenty-one days.
- Mold on cheese isn't usually a health problem, but it does indicate that harmful bacteria may be starting to grow. Thus, you'll want to pare off any indications of mold from hard cheeses such as Cheddar, Swiss, or Parmesan, as well as from a semi-soft cheese like mozzarella or American. Be sure to cut deeply into the cheese, well beyond the mold. You can then eat the remainder. However, it's best to throw out moldy soft cheeses, including Brie and feta and anything shredded.

Tips courtesy of the Wisconsin Milk Marketing Board

The Top Wisconsin Cheeses

In September 2005 senior editor Mary Van de Kamp Nohl of *Milwaukee Magazine* polled numerous award-winning cheesemakers, cheese sellers, and industry personalities to select the publication's Top 10 Wisconsin specialty cheeses.

1. Uplands Cheese's Pleasant Ridge Reserve. An aged, unpasteurized, washed-rind Beaufort-style cheese inspired by the farmstead cheeses of southeastern France's Alpine provinces (www.uplandscheese.com).
2. Carr Valley's Cave-Aged Cheddar. Cheesemonger Mark Jezo-Sywulka of Sendik's in Brookfield, Wisconsin, says "almost all" of Sid Cook's cheeses "could be on the Top 10 list." This may be his best (www.carrvalleycheese.com).
3. BelGioioso's Creamy Gorgonzola. Italian-born, fourth-generation cheesemaker Errico Auricchio's BelGioioso Cheese produces twelve specialty cheeses, including this gem (www.belgioioso.com).

4. Crave Brothers Farmstead Cheese Classics Marscapone. The James Beard Society's fussy eaters swoon over this mascarpone. The secret to its sweetness is the milk from the 600 cows the four Crave Brothers nurture (www.cravecheese.com).

5. Antigo Cheese's SarVecchio Parmesan. Mark Jezo-Sywulka says it's almost identical in flavor to Italy's famous Red Cow Cheese, which costs almost three times more per pound. Antigo Cheese is now part of Sartori Foods (www.sartorifoods.com).

6. Park Cheese's Sharp Provolone. *Bon Appétit* magazine has for years called this the country's best provolone (www.parkcheese.com).

7. Widmer's Cheese Cellars' Brick. Joe Widmer is still using his Swiss grandfather's bricks to push the whey out of his Brick cheese, a Wisconsin original developed in 1875. No other US plant produces smear-ripened, aged, foil-wrapped, tangy Brick (www.widmerscheese.com).

8. Roth Käse means "good cheese" in German, and the company proves you needn't go to Europe for a great Gruyère. Just head to Monroe (www.rothkase.com).

9. Hook's Cheese Company's Aged Cheddars. Tony and Julie Hook are experts at affinage (cave aging), the process that gives

Master cheesemaker Joseph Widmer grew up in the rooms above his family's Widmer Cheese Cellars plant in Theresa and raised his children there, as well.

Photo courtesy of the Wisconsin Milk Marketing Board, Inc.

a cheese character and produces the crunchy lactic crystals for which their Cheddar is famous (www.cheeseforager.com/hooks.php).

10. Edelweiss Town Hall Cheese Company's Emmentaler. A wonderful old-fashioned "big wheel" Swiss, which many experts say is the most difficult cheese to make (608-938-4094).

Cheese-Speak: How to Talk Like a Cheese Aficionado

Describing cheese is a language in itself. Don't get caught at your next cheese tasting without the proper cheesy vocabulary! Here are a few Wisconsin Milk Marketing Board terms with which to impress your fellow cheese tasters.

> "Wine and cheese are ageless companions, like aspirin and aches, or June and moon, or good people and noble ventures."
>
> —M. F. K. Fisher (1908–1992), US culinary writer and autobiographer, quoted in the introduction to the 1981 classic *Vin et Fromage* by Marylou Scavarda and Kate Sater

If a cheese has a strong, pronounced smell, it is *aromatic*. If the flavor is also strong, words like *assertive, intense, gamey,* or *robust* could describe the cheese. *Sharp* and *piquant* describe the developed flavor of aged cheeses, such as aged Asiago, aged provolone, and blue cheese. Aged Cheddars with a sharp and pepper flavor are sometimes described as *peppery,* as well as piquant or sharp. An example of a *pungent* cheese—one with a very intense aroma—is Limburger, although other descriptors also come to mind (*stinky,* say, or *smelly*). Strong cheese may also be described as *spicy,* with a peppery and herbal flavor.

Mild cheese is light with unpronounced flavors; the term can also refer to young Cheddars. *Faint* or *fleeting* refers to the mildest of cheese, as does *light* or *bland*. Flavors that lie a step above mild, yet a step below intense, are considered *pronounced*.

Cheese terms derived from a particular animal that has a strong farm-related aroma can be described as *cowy, sheepy,* or *goaty,* as well as *barny* or *barnyardy* and *earthy* or *rustic.* All have a hearty or earthy flavor with a distinct aroma.

Cheeses are considered *fruity* if they have a sweet, fragrant flavor or aroma. American Muenster, Baby Swiss, and some Cheddars have a fruity quality.

Mushroomy, or mildly earthy, describes the pleasant fragrance of such cheese as Brie. Some Swiss-type cheeses are *nutty;* Cheddars, too, may smell like walnuts, and fresh goat cheese and Gruyère somewhat resemble the perfume of hazelnuts. *Salty* encompasses many cheeses, although excessive saltiness is not desirable, nor is a cheese with no salt, which is described as *dull* and *flat.* Some cheese is said to have a *grassy* or *weedy* taste. This can result if a cow has eaten silage, bitterweed, leeks, or onions prior to milking.

A cheese is described as *clean* if it has no unpleasant aromas or flavors and a clean finish—that is, no lingering aftertaste.

And of course there are some negative cheese terms that we hope you'll never have to use at a cheese-tasting party. A cheese is *off* if its flavors and odors are not typical of the particular cheese variety. *Astringent* refers to a harsh taste that makes you pucker. *Acrid* and *bitter* are both unpleasant descriptors, with bitterness typified by the aftertaste of eating a grapefruit peel. A cheese might also be described as *fishy* or *ammoniated,* both traits caused by overripeness. Although an unobjectionable hint of ammonia is often found in Brie, Camembert, and chèvres, a heavy smell of ammonia is not. You definitely do not want cheese that is *rancid, soapy,* or excessively *sour.*

In any case, a cheese's *aftertaste*—the last flavor and aroma sensation you experience after tasting it—should not be too pronounced.

For even more cheese-speak, be sure to turn to the glossary at the end of this book.

CHAPTER 2

ARTISAN AND FARMSTEAD CHEESES

ARTISAN AND FARMSTEAD CHEESEMAKING HAS COME full circle in Wisconsin's rich cheese history. Many cheese fans ask us the difference between artisan and farmstead cheeses. Basically, both are handmade, created on a small scale, and in small batches. Artisan cheeses can be made from milk from the farm's herd, but that is not necessarily the case. Farmstead (meaning "from the farm") cheeses are made on a farm from milk produced there. Early cheesemakers all created artisan and farmstead cheese; today Wisconsin prides itself in producing more artisan and farmstead cheeses than any other state.

Wisconsin artisan cheeses are special because cheesemakers follow the French concept of *terroir*. Literally, the word means "soil," yet it also implies that the grazing land of each farm is unique in a way that transfers to the cheese. Important factors in each farm's terroir include its geographic location; the minerals and vitamins in the grasses; the soil; the climate; and the pure, limestone-filtered water that nourishes the land. All these factors shape the flavor of the farm's milk and, later, its cheese. The adage *You are what you eat* pertains here: What the animal eats is a direct link to the quality of the product.

Growing numbers of farmers and cheesemakers have begun to distinguish between pasture-grazed and grain-fed animals. They have found that milk from pasture-grazed livestock creates cheeses that are naturally richer in color, with a slightly more herbaceous and more complex taste. Producers are also experimenting with seasonal milk, some feeling that autumn milk creates a more interesting cheese.

Scientists have contributed to the pasture-versus-grain discussion with discoveries

*Dairy cattle are integral to
Wisconsin's landscape.*
Photo by Martin Hintz

that cheeses from grain-fed cows are very high in the omega-6 fats (the bad kind), yet quite low in important omega-3s. Agriculture experts explain that cheeses from cows' grass-fed counterparts, on the other hand, contain a perfect balance of omega-3 and omega-6 fats. They also have more beta-carotene, vitamin A, vitamin D, vitamin E, and conjugated linoleic acid (CLA)—known to increase muscle mass while reducing body fat. Moreover, CLA is an antioxidant that can enhance the immune system and even fight cancer. Also crucial in making artisan cheese is the *affinage*, or craft of maturing and aging cheeses (you'll sometimes see cheesemakers described as *affineurs*).

In ripening cellars or caves, the cheese may be brushed, bathed (even in wine), and flipped, according to its individual needs. The affineur also has to make certain that the humidity and temperature remain exact as the cheese ages. Innovative caves are being constructed around Wisconsin. Willi Lehner, from Bleu Mont Dairy near Blue Mounds, has created a straw "cave" with thick walls of bales. At LoveTree Farmstead in northern Wisconsin's Burnett County, Mary and Dave Falk age their Trade Lake Cheddar on cedar boughs. The cheese is stored in fresh-air aging caves overlooking one of the property's five-acre ponds.

Wisconsin is also meeting the growing demand for organic cheeses, including feta, Muenster, Parmesan, Colby, Jack, and Cheddar. Organic cheese comes from farms that have avoided the use of pesticides, herbicides, synthetic fertilizers, and food additives. In fact, the state surpasses all others in the number of certified organic dairy farms, with more than 250 in 2006.

Wisconsin also leads the industry in the production of many labor-intensive cheeses. In this process, as the cheese is aged, it is bathed by hand and brushed with a bacterial solution that promotes aging and enhances the flavor. The nutty-sweet Pleasant Ridge Reserve produced by Uplands Cheese Company is made with techniques that date back to the Middle Ages; then and now, the cheese is washed frequently with a brine solution and aged in limestone caves.

Wisconsin excels in artisan Cheddars, with thirteen certified Wisconsin Master Cheesemakers for Cheddar. Some are using the Old World method of "bandaging" their Cheddars in cheesecloth. There are also cheesemakers developing organic and raw-milk Cheddars.

There is a growing demand for nonpasteurized or raw-milk cheese, which must be aged for more than sixty days to ensure that no bacteria exists. The organic milk is cooked at 155°F for fifteen seconds, bringing it to the brink of being pasteurized. Then the cheesemaking process begins, all conducted under the strictest USDA regulations for organic cheese. Organic Valley is one of the companies in Wisconsin making raw-milk cheese, specializing in a Jack-style variety.

Butterfat is the chief natural fatty component of milk. Each breed of cattle, sheep, and goats produces varying amounts of butterfat, which influences the taste of the milk. Artisan cheesemakers prize the resulting variety of flavors with which they can experiment.

Bass Lake Cheese Factory

Bass Lake Cheese Factory is north of Hudson, in the northwest corner of Wisconsin. One of Wisconsin's oldest cheese plants, Bass Lake was established in 1918. After managing the cheese factory for eight years, Julie and Scott Erickson purchased the facility in 1991. Scott is a five-time certified Master Cheesemaker and one of the first to use goat's, sheep's, and cow's milk for his artisan cheeses. He uses generations-old recipes, augmenting them with new skills and techniques to produce innovative Bass Lake originals in more than fifty varieties, types, and styles.

Scott's Canasta Pardo is a rich, award-winning sheep's milk variety. His creamy Country Chèvre, an original slow-made, mild goat cheese, is also a medal winner. His Norwegian heritage emerges in Juusto Leipa, which means "bread cheese," and is based on what is alleged to be a 1,000-year-old Finnish Lapland delight. The cheese has a delightfully squeaky texture and is typically baked with cinnamon or fruit. Lingonberries, cloudberries, cranberries, blueberries, or cherries are options. The cheese is served warm, dipped in maple syrup, honey, jam, or more cinnamon and sugar. Finns love to dip it in coffee in the morning. It's an excellent grilling cheese that holds its shape when heated. Another sweet treat is Scott's Butter Jack with Cinnamon, a delicious dessert cheese when served with pears or apples.

Some Bass Lake cheeses are on the spicy side, such as its Smoked Gouda, Creamy Salsa Gouda (great in spaghetti sauce), Cajun Spiced Colby, and Cheddar Cheese Curds. A few are enhanced with a little vino. Consider trying Bass Lake Merlot Cheddar, an award-winning Cheddar–Merlot blend, or its Goat Cheddar flavored with cranberry wine.

Julie likes to make Juusto Leipa Crescent Rolls. She spreads out a package of Pillsbury crescent roll dough, sprinkles cinnamon sugar on top, and adds a piece of cheese. She rolls them up and bakes according to the directions.

Ultimate Wisconsin Grilled Cheese Sandwich with Jack and Smoked Gouda

This recipe was created by Kenneth Oringer, the executive chef of Clio in Boston (www.cliorestaurant .com). He's also a member of the Wisconsin Milk Marketing Board Ambassador Program, which links the state with chefs from around the country who spread awareness of our wonderful cheeses.

8 slices raisin bread

½ cup (I stick) butter, softened

½ cup honey mustard

4 bread-size slices Bass Lake Jack cheese

8 slices applewood-smoked bacon, fried crisp

I large Granny Smith apple, cored, quartered, each quarter cut into 6 slices (24 in all)

4 bread-size slices Bass Lake Smoked Gouda

1. Spread each slice of the bread on one side with soft butter. Turn them over and generously spread the other side with 1 tablespoon honey mustard.
2. Place a slice of Wisconsin Jack on each of four of the bread slices (mustard-side up), then top with two slices of bacon. Shingle 6 apple slices over the bacon.
3. Top the remaining four bread slices (mustard-side up) with a slice of smoked Gouda.
4. Assemble the sandwiches, pressing them together and leaving the buttered side of the bread exposed.
5. Heat a large heavy-bottomed sauté pan over medium heat.
6. Grill the sandwiches in batches, cooking each until it's golden brown on one side, then flipping it over and browning the other. Repeat with all sandwiches.
7. Place the sandwiches on serving plates, cutting each in half or quarters on the bias. Serve immediately.

SERVES 4

Courtesy of the Wisconsin Milk Marketing Board, Inc.

BelGioioso Cheese, Inc.

Errico Auricchio, the founder of BelGioioso Cheese, Inc., carried on a history of family cheesemaking. His great-grandfather started a cheese company in Italy in the late 1800s. In 1979 Auricchio moved his family from Italy and settled in Denmark, Wisconsin—a small town near Green Bay. There he started up his own cheese company, with the goal of making authentic Italian cheeses using traditional Italian recipes and top-quality Wisconsin milk.

> **"As a chef, I am always overjoyed to find products made in the US that represent the greatest work of artisans in love with their craft. Let Wisconsin cheese surprise you!"**
>
> —Chef Jan Birnbaum, Sazerac, Seattle, Washington, and Epic Roast House, San Francisco, California

Since BelGioioso won the 1982 Provolone World Championship Natural Cheese Contest, its first award, it's gone on to capture dozens of national and regional honors. Its Parmesan was named best Parmesan in the United States in 1986, and the American Cheese Society awarded it Best of Class in 2006. The firm's other Italian cheeses are also prizewinners, including its Asiago, Fontina, Fresh Mozzarella, Gorgonzola, Tiramisu Mascarpone, Vegetarian Parmesan, Pepato, and Romano. BelGioioso has won awards for some of its trademarked cheese: American Grana, a special-reserve Parmesan aged for more than eighteen months; and Italico, a soft, surface-ripened, cream-colored cheese that is hand salted during the aging process.

Other BelGioioso original creations include its Manteche, a handcrafted whole-milk provolone wrapped around sweet cream butter, as well as mascarpone and the spectacular CreamyGorg. Try any of the company's serving suggestions:

- Combine BelGioioso mascarpone with a sweet liqueur. Place alternating layers of fresh fruit and the mascarpone mixture into parfait glasses. Serve with a sweet wine or champagne for an elegant dessert.
- Mix mascarpone with pure maple syrup, spread onto piping-hot French toast, and garnish with fresh berries for an elegant Sunday brunch entrée.
- Serve mascarpone with radishes and a fruity ale beer for an interesting party appetizer.

- For a succulent side dish, combine mascarpone with fresh herbs or vegetables such as basil, spinach, red or yellow peppers, or sun-dried tomatoes. Mix with hot pasta or rice and serve.
- Mix BelGioioso Mascarpone with BelGioioso CreamyGorg. Thinly spread the mixture onto slices of prosciutto. Roll onto breadsticks; pear or apple slices; or zucchini, cucumber, and celery sticks for a mouthwatering appetizer.

Bleu Mont Dairy

Bleu Mont Dairy nestles amid beautiful rolling hills near Blue Mounds, about 25 miles west of Madison. Willi Lehner learned his cheesemaking skills from his father, Bill Lehner, who was a cheesemaker in Switzerland and was honored with a lifetime achievement award for his work making and promoting cheese at the 2006 Monroe Cheese Days.

Willi Lehner started Bleu Mont Dairy more than a decade and a half ago. In 2003 he built a straw "cave" with thick walls of bales coated with a clay mixture of lime and sand. The handmade cavern has an aging room lined with red cedar boards imported from Switzerland and a 14-foot rubber mat roof, topped with straw bales that are turning to sod. The thick walls are crucial in the aging process, because they control humidity and temperature. Recently Lehner added a 24-by-66-foot underground cave, complete with a dome, steel beams, and cement walls and floor. He also produces his own energy by using wind and solar power.

When Lehner learned that the quality of October milk is richer—the butterfat has a higher melting point at that time than it does in spring—he began developing several unique cheeses. To add extra quality, the fall milk is produced by certified organic and grass-fed cows, many of which are mixed breed. Lehner feels that each breed contributes different qualities to the milk and thus makes it superior.

Among Lehner's best-known cheeses are his Bandaged Cheddar and a Swiss cheese that he and his wife, Quitas McKnight, refer to as Nutty Swiss thanks to its rich taste. McKnight loves to cook with their cheese, adding shaved Bandaged Cheddar atop stews and on fresh asparagus spears from their garden. She points out that their Cheddar is also delicious in quesadillas and in quiches.

Cavatappi and Cheese

Bleu Mont Dairy is famed for its humorously named Bandaged Cheddar, which won a first prize at the 2006 American Cheese Society awards. Only the best milk is used in the bandaged ten-pound wheels. No color is added. As the wheels age, they are sprayed with a combination of previous rinds and clean water. The result is a delicious cheese with a clean, nutty, buttery taste that makes this upscale version of mac-and-cheese very special.

5 cups organic whole milk

½ cup (I stick) unsalted butter

6 tablespoons all-purpose flour

Salt and white pepper to taste

Pinch nutmeg

8 ounces Bleu Mont Dairy Bandaged Cheddar, grated

8 ounces Uplands Cheese Pleasant Ridge Reserve, grated

8 ounces Roth Käse Surchoix Gruyère, grated

I pound cavatappi pasta, cooked in sufficient salted water until al dente (slightly undercooked)

1. Preheat the oven to 350°F.
2. Heat the milk in a small saucepan over low heat.
3. In a separate saucepan, melt the butter over medium heat until it begins to foam. Whisk in the flour and cook for approximately 2 minutes, making sure not to let the flour brown. Add the hot milk all at once, and cook, stirring constantly, until the sauce is of medium consistency (approximately 5 minutes). Season to taste. If the sauce is too thick, add a bit more milk.
4. Remove the roux from the heat, adding the nutmeg and all but ¾ cup of the grated cheeses. Combine and stir until completely melted.
5. Toss the sauce with cooked pasta. Pour it into a buttered casserole, top with the remaining cheese, and bake until brown and bubbly (approximately 20 minutes).

SERVES 6 CHILDREN OR 4 ADULTS

Courtesy of Stefano Viglietti, Tratoria Stefano, in Sheboygan, Wisconsin.

Gorgonzola and Pear Pasta

This recipe calls for a creamy—rather than crumbly—Gorgonzola. We recommend BelGioioso's CreamyGorg, a full-flavored, blue-green-veined cheese aged for ninety days.

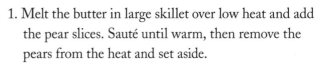

2 tablespoons (¼ stick) butter

2 firm pears, unpeeled, sliced

1 pound rigatoni

8 ounces creamy Italian-style Gorgonzola cheese

1 tablespoon mascarpone

⅓ cup chopped walnuts

1. Melt the butter in large skillet over low heat and add the pear slices. Sauté until warm, then remove the pears from the heat and set aside.
2. Boil the pasta in salted water until al dente, reserving ¼ cup of the pasta water.
3. Cut the Gorgonzola into small cubes and place in large saucepan. Add the reserved ¼ cup of pasta water and heat over a low flame, stirring constantly, until the cheese is melted and has created a sauce.
4. Drain the pasta, return it to the pot, and stir in the mascarpone cheese to coat. Stir in half the sauce, then gently fold in the sautéed pears and most of the walnuts.
5. Place the pasta mixture in a serving bowl and top with the remaining sauce. Garnish with more walnuts and serve immediately.

SERVES 8

Recipe courtesy of Francesca Elfner, BelGioioso Cheese, Inc.

Carr Valley Cheese Factory

The Carr Valley Cheese Factory is now run by Sid Cook, a fourth-generation cheesemaker. Cook was a cheesemaking prodigy who grew up working in his family's plant and began making cheese at the age of ten. At sixteen he earned his Wisconsin cheesemaker's license. Today he is one of Wisconsin's prestigious Master Cheesemakers. Becoming a Master Cheesemaker is a daunting task that involves a rigorous ten-year advanced training and education program.

Carr Valley produces more than fifty different cheeses, many of them award-winning original American artisan varieties. In the early 2000s Carr Valley cheeses captured more than sixty top honors in US and international competitions. Included on the long list of winners are Aged Cheddar, Cocoa Cardona, Gran Canaria, and Mobay cheese.

Cook is also blending cow's, sheep's, and goat's milk in his cheeses. His rich, creamy Benedictine is a washed-rind cheese made with all three milks. The product has an intense flavor after being cellar cured and hand rubbed for twelve weeks before packaging. Gran Canaria, a three-year-old olive-oil-cured mixed-milk cheese, is described as a combination of fruity, nutty, intense, sweet, and pungent.

His prizewinning Cocoa Cardona combines two favorite ingredients: chocolate and goat cheese. It's made in an eight-pound wheel, aged and rubbed with cocoa powder. His Virgin-Pine Native Sheep Blue, made from the milk of pasture-fed sheep, is a blue-veined cheese that's also cave aged for more than eight months.

Mobay cheese, based on the semi-soft Morbier, has French roots. Both feature two layers of cheese divided by a thin layer of vegetable ash. The original uses all cow's milk, while Cook's version is half cow's and half creamy-colored sheep's milk.

Cook is also a certified Master Cheesemaker of Fontina, with its great melting qualities, making it perfect for cooking, as well as for simply eating as a rich, fruity table cheese.

Fennel and Green Apple Salad with Tangerine Vinaigrette

This salad brings together some wonderful autumn ingredients—shaved fennel, julienned green apples, and frissee—all tossed with Carr Valley's Famous Cave Aged Cheddar and a slightly fruity Tangerine Vinaigrette that creates a nice balance with the assertive frissee and fennel.

Salad

1 Granny Smith apple, peeled and julienned

1 fennel bulb, sliced paper thin

1 cup small-diced Carr Valley Cave Aged Cheddar Cheese

1 head frissee lettuce

1 tangerine, seeded, separated into sections

½ cup Tangerine Vinaigrette (recipe follows)

½ cup grated aged Parmesan

Combine all ingredients, finishing with sea salt and freshly ground pepper to taste.

CHEF NOTE:
This recipe yields extra vinaigrette.

Tangerine Vinaigrette

2 cups tangerine juice

½ cup late-harvest Riesling vinegar

½ cup extra-virgin olive oil (preferably Luccini brand)

1 teaspoon roasted garlic paste

1 teaspoon organic honey

1 teaspoon kosher salt

1 teaspoon fresh ground white pepper

Boil the tangerine juice until it is reduced to 1 cup. Let it cool, and whisk together with the remaining ingredients.

MAKES 6 SMALL PORTIONS

Courtesy of Jason Gorman, chef de cuisine, Dream Dance Restaurant at Potawatomi Bingo Casino, Milwaukee, Wisconsin.

Chalet Cheese Cooperative

Chalet Cheese Co-op has the distinction of being the only Limburger-producing cheese plant in the country. Myron Olson, general manager, makes Limburger the old-fashioned way at the small, Alpine-style factory north of Monroe, in the verdant hills of southwest Wisconsin's Green County. A farmer-owned co-op, Chalet was founded in 1885. In 2004 it acquired Deppeler Cheese, another top-quality cheese company in Monroe.

Chalet Cheese has won many awards, including top prizes at the 2006 World Championship Cheese Contest. Chalet's Master Cheesemaker Jamie Fahrney won Best of Class for his Baby Swiss block; the firm's Donald Johnson came in second. Cheesemaker Silvan Blum captured Best of Class for his twenty-pound wheel of Smoked Wisconsin Swiss. Blum also makes Braun Suisse Käse with milk from local Brown Swiss dairy cows, which creates a silky soft and buttery cheese, as well as German Brick and Muenster.

Crave Brothers Farmstead Cheese

The Crave Brothers—Charles, George, Thomas, and Mark—produce farmstead cheese on their farm in Waterloo, Wisconsin. Their farming career started as children on a forty-cow spread near Beloit, where they were raised. In 1978 they all moved to a rented farm near Mount Horeb; they bought their current operation in 1980. Back then, they started dairying with 100 cows. They now have a 600-cow facility.

In addition to their well-known semi-soft Les Frères, the Crave Brothers make a sweet cream mascarpone, fresh mozzarella, and a string cheese called Farmer's Rope, which is stretched and tied in knots, then put in a salty solution that acts as a preservative and flavor enhancer. Their fresh mozzarella is great for salads and appetizers, in addition to bruschetta. Crave Brothers Mozzarella comes in three sizes: *ciliegine* (cherry size), *bocconcini* (ball size), and *ovoline* (egg size).

Petit Frère Puffs

Perhaps the Crave Brothers' signature cheese is the pasteurized cow's milk variety called Les Frères ("the brothers" in French). This is a European-style washed-rind cheese with an earthy, fruity flavor. They also make the smaller eight-ounce wheel known as Petit Frère—"little brother"—featured in this delicious recipe. Both are aged in the affinage cellars of their factory.

1 wheel Petit Frère

2 packages (10 ounces each) puff pastry shells

6 tablespoons minced dried cranberries

¼ cup minced walnuts

6 tablespoons apricot jam

1. Bake the puff pastry shells according to package directions.
2. When the shells are done, pull off the tops and set them aside. Cut a small wedge of Petit Frère and place it in each shell. Divide the cranberries, walnuts, and apricot jam among the 12 shells.
3. Place the reserved tops back on the shells. Return to the oven for 5 to 8 minutes.

SERVES 12

Courtesy of Beth Crave.

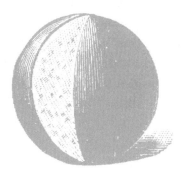

Wisconsin Three-Cheese Soup with Parmesan Croutons

While the Chalet Cheese Co-op's Limburger may be its most unforgettable cheese, the company also makes esteemed Cheddars and Swiss varieties, as you'll taste in this hearty soup. Cheese and beer! It's a great combo.

Three-Cheese Soup

1 cup (2 sticks) butter (clarified optional)

½ cup flour

2 quarts milk

2 tablespoons Tabasco sauce

2 tablespoons Worcestershire sauce

¼ cup chicken soup base

12 ounces Wisconsin beer

1 cup culinary cream or heavy cream

1 tablespoon onion powder

1 tablespoon garlic powder

White pepper to taste

Salt to taste

½ pound shredded Wisconsin Cheddar cheese

½ pound shredded Wisconsin Swiss cheese

½ pound shredded Wisconsin Jalapeño Jack cheese

1. In a 12-inch sauté pan or skillet, melt the butter; remove from the heat. Add the flour and whisk until incorporated. The consistency should be like wet sand. Cook over low heat, stirring occasionally, until just golden. Remove from the heat and set aside.

2. In a large soup pot, heat the milk almost to boiling— DO NOT BOIL. Reduce the heat and add the Tabasco, Worcestershire, soup base, and beer. Incorporate well with a whisk. Add the cream and seasonings, and again heat almost to a boil. Make a roux by slowly incorporating small amounts of the butter–flour mixture until the mixture reaches your desired consistency. Cook for 10 to 15 minutes.

3. Gradually add the cheese in small handfuls, making sure to thoroughly melt and incorporate each handful before adding more. Do not let the soup reach a temperature of more than 150°F or it will separate.

4. Cook over low heat for 15 to 20 minutes, then serve immediately.

Parmesan Croutons

2 loaves bread

2 teaspoons diced garlic

I teaspoon fresh thyme

I teaspoon chopped fresh oregano

¼ teaspoon paprika

I cup (2 sticks) butter or margarine, melted

I cup grated Parmesan

Salt and black pepper to taste

1. Preheat the oven to 350°F.
2. Dice the bread.
3. Mix the seasonings with the butter. Toss this mixture with the croutons until all are coated evenly. Toss the Parmesan and salt and pepper to taste.
4. Place the croutons on a cookie sheet and bake for about 7 to 10 minutes or until crispy.

SERVES 12–14

Courtesy of the American Club in Kohler, Wisconsin.

The American Club in Kohler once provided rooms, food, and recreational facilities for workmen at the Kohler Company. The Immigrant Restaurant, The Winery Bar, The Horse & Plow, The Wisconsin Room, and The Greenhouse are among the complex's award-winning restaurants using high-quality Wisconsin cheese.

Photo courtesy of Kohler Co.

Milk Chocolate Cheesecake

This cheesecake was created by chef Scott Johnson, a graduate of the CIA (Culinary Institute of America) Hyde Park campus who has been the executive chef at the Canoe Bay restaurant since 2001. He is inspired by Alice Waters's tradition of cooking using the freshest possible ingredients with little doctoring, relying on the ingredients to speak for themselves. Chef Johnson has developed an extensive network of local, regional, and other direct suppliers to ensure top quality. We love serving this delicious dessert with fresh raspberries at dinner parties.

Graham Cracker Crust

2 cups graham crackers

2 tablespoons honey

¼ cup melted butter

I teaspoon vanilla extract

1. Preheat the oven to 300°F.
2. In a food processor, combine all the ingredients until moist.
3. Press the mixture into the bottom of a springform pan (see the Chef Note for sizes) and bake until golden brown.

Milk Chocolate Cheesecake

2 tablespoons (¼ stick) butter, softened

¾ cup **Organic Valley Cream Cheese,** softened

¼ cup granulated sugar

¼ cup packed brown sugar

I egg

2 egg yolks

¾ cup **Crave Brothers Mascarpone Cheese**

I teaspoon vanilla extract

2 teaspoons coffee extract

7 ounces milk chocolate, chopped, melted, and cooled

1. Preheat the oven to 300°F.
2. In a food processor, combine the butter, cream cheese, and sugars. Process until smooth. Then add the egg and egg yolks one at a time, followed by the mascarpone.
3. Add the extracts and chocolate, processing until smooth.
4. Pour the mixture into the springform pan. To ensure that the pan does not leak, wrap aluminum foil around the bottom and continue 2 inches up the outside. Place the pan into a water bath and then into the preheated oven; bake until the center of the cheesecake is set (see the Chef Note for baking times).

5. Remove the cheesecake from the oven and let it cool at room temperature for 1 hour. The finished cheesecake must be refrigerated for 2 hours before serving.

SERVES 8

Courtesy of Canoe Bay in Chetek, Wisconsin.

CHEF NOTE:

The cooking time depends on the size of the pan:

Bake a 6x3-inch-deep round pan for 75 to 90 minutes.
Bake an 8x2-inch round for 65 to 75 minutes.
Bake a 9x2-inch round for 55 to 65 minutes.

Do not cook the cheesecake in a convection oven—it dries out the top and leaves the center raw. It is important to use ingredients that are at room temperature when the cake is placed in the oven. Otherwise, the cake will take longer to bake and will be more prone to cracking.

Edelweiss Town Hall Cheese

Edelweiss Town Hall Cheese originated in 1873. In 2004 Wisconsin Master Cheesemaker Bruce Workman reopened the company, renovating a plant that had been left vacant for two and a half years. It took six months of work to transform it into a state-of-the-art high-tech facility.

Workman has a long history in the business, working his way up from washing floors in cheese plants as a youngster. He now is a Master Cheesemaker in Gruyère, Baby Swiss, Butterkäse, Havarti and Raclette, Swiss, and Emmentaler, and was the plant manager and head cheesemaker at Roth Käse for seven years.

His plant is the only factory in North America that can produce the 180-pound Big Wheel Swiss, as well as a Large Wheel Swiss Emmenthaler. He imported from

Switzerland a huge copper-lined vat that can hold 12,000 pounds of milk. Such a container is crucial in the production of real Swiss cheese, because minuscule particles of copper enter the cheese when the milk and curds are being stirred. The subsequent reaction is what creates the rich, nutty flavor of the cheese. He also makes Butterkäse, Lacy Swiss, and Havarti.

> "Have patience. In time, grass becomes milk . . . In time, grass becomes . . . cheese."
>
> —Edelweiss Grazers Co-op

Wisconsin Gruyère Fondue

Edelweiss Master Cheesemaker Bruce Workman is famous for stirring up Wisconsin's largest fondue in a huge pot at the Wisconsin State Fair, Monroe Cheese Days, and other events, where he loves to tell stories about this Swiss dish. Often helping him in the process is Mike Nevil, executive chef of the Chalet Landhaus in New Glarus, Wisconsin. Samples are always served to the delight of fairgoers. Try this home-size version yourself and see!

I large clove garlic, peeled and halved

4 cups (16 ounces) shredded Wisconsin Gruyère cheese

3 tablespoons flour

⅛ teaspoon white pepper

I cup dry white wine

I loaf (16 ounces) French bread, cut into I-inch cubes

Fresh vegetables such as grape tomatoes and broccoli or cauliflower florets

CHEF NOTE:
A few drops of Kirsch will add a little zing.

1. Rub the bottom and inside of a fondue pot with the garlic halves to add flavor; discard the garlic.
2. In a mixing bowl, combine the shredded Wisconsin Gruyère cheese, flour, and pepper. Mix so that the flour coats the cheese, then set aside.
3. Heat the fondue pot to medium. Add the wine and heat until warm; do not boil. Add the cheese, a handful at a time, stirring until the cheese melts and the mixture is a light creamy sauce. Adjust the heat so that the mixture stays fluid (low setting).
4. Spear cubes of French bread or fresh veggies and twirl them in the cheese mixture until coated.

SERVES 8

Courtesy of the Wisconsin Milk Marketing Board, Inc.

Fondue parties were all the rage from the 1950s through much of the 1970s. A fondue evening was usually enhanced by large quantities of inexpensive wine, with the resulting hilarity. After falling out of favor for a time, fondues have been reappearing on the culinary scene, albeit with more refined vintages.

Fondue originated in Switzerland, the word meaning "to melt" in French. Swiss herders are given credit for creating this classic dish. In Alpine pastures the workers' cheese, bread, and wine wound up mixed into the "caquelon," an earthenware pot, and heated. Today's fondue evolved from that classic peasant meal, which was a practical way to use hardened cheese and stale bread. It was discovered by the Swiss aristocracy, who used better cheese and better bread, and subsequently moved on up to become a fine dining item in high-end restaurants.

Fondue-mania kicked off in the States during the 1950s, when chef Konrad Egli of New York's Chalet Swiss Restaurant introduced Fondue Bourguignonne. This was a hearty meal in which speared meat cubes were cooked in hot oil. After that, cheeses quickly made their way into the pot, followed by chocolate fondue around 1964.

According to Hamlyn Press, publishers of *The Fondue Cookbook* (2002), "If a woman drops a cube of bread into the fondue, she has to kiss all the men; if a man drops the bread cube, he has to buy a bottle of wine."

According to fondue etiquette, if an individual drops a cube of bread for the second time, he or she must host the next fondue party.

The world's largest cheese fondue is always a fun feature at the Wisconsin State Fair. Photo by Martin Hintz

Gingerbread Jersey

Carolyn and Virgil Schunk raise Jersey and Holstein cows on the farm Carolyn's grandfather homesteaded in Cadott, Wisconsin. Nearby, in Augusta, they make a variety of cheese using only their own milk. Their "plant" is a converted semi-truck trailer tagged "Cheese on Wheels." They sell their cheese right there from the truck while spectators on an observation deck can watch Virgil make cheese.

Curds are the Schunks' biggest seller, but they also offer a fresh mozzarella line, as well as goat cheeses. The full line of Gingerbread Jersey cheese includes "A Taste of Sicily"—a Monterey Jack with sun-dried tomatoes, basil, and garlic—as well as other flavored jacks. They also make prizewinning goat Gouda, Colby, Cheddar, and Swiss.

Each of the Schunks and their six children, three of whom are dairy farmers, have a favorite cheese recipe. The family loves lasagna and manicotti made with Gingerbread Jersey's own fresh Gouda. Another treat is a grilled-cheese-and-tomato sandwich made with the Taste of Sicily cheese, complemented by a bowl of tomato soup.

> "I am totally committed to using authentic, farm-fresh ingredients that reflect only the finest quality and care at Lola and Lolita. That's why I love using Wisconsin cheeses. I can count on their quality, thanks to Wisconsin's farmers and outstanding cheese artisans."
>
> —Chef Michael Symon, Lola Bistro and Wine Bar, Lolita, Cleveland, Ohio

Henning's Cheese, Inc.

Henning's, a fourth-generation cheese company in Kiel, began operations in 1914 when Otto and Norma Henning purchased an existing cheese factory. Today their grandchildren Kay, Kert, and Kerry Henning manage the plant along with their father Everett and Otto's great-granddaughter. Kerry, a certified Master Cheesemaker in Cheddar and Colby, has captured many awards; his Colby won the 2004 World Championship Cheese Contest, and in 2006 the company took a second place. Famous for its Cheddar, Henning's is also known for fresh cheese curds and string cheese.

Henning's Breakfast Strata

This is a Henning family favorite.

½ cup (1 stick) butter, melted

12 slices white or wheat bread, cubed

8 ounces cooked cubed ham or 19 ounces cooked and crumbled bacon

8 ounces Henning's cheese (your choice), shredded

6 eggs, beaten

2 cups milk

Pour the melted butter on the bottom of a 9x13-inch baking dish. Place half the cubed bread on top of the butter. Cover with the meat and cheese. Top with the remaining bread. Combine the eggs and milk and pour over the bread, covering all the cubes. Cover and refrigerate overnight, or at least 4 hours. Bake at 350°F for 1 hour or until a knife inserted in the center comes out clean.

SERVES 8

Courtesy of Henning's Cheese.

Wisconsin Farmhouse Supper

Henning's Cheese has made wheels of Cheddar weighing up to 12,000 pounds (they've been featured in the Toledo Thanksgiving Parade and other national events). This recipe calls for slightly smaller amounts!

½ cup beer

¼ cup (½ stick) unsalted butter

6 tablespoons flour

I teaspoon salt

½ teaspoon paprika

¼ teaspoon black pepper

¼ teaspoon cayenne pepper

2 cups milk

I½ cups (I2-ounce can) evaporated milk

I cup (4 ounces) shredded Wisconsin
 Sharp Aged Cheddar cheese

I cup (4 ounces) shredded Wisconsin
 Gouda cheese

I cup (4 ounces) shredded Wisconsin Baby
 Swiss cheese

2 tablespoons coarse-grain mustard

I pound mostaccioli, cooked and drained

¾ pound lightly smoked ham, julienned

I½ cups seeded, diced plum
 tomatoes

1. Preheat the oven to 350°F.
2. Simmer the beer in a small saucepan for 3 minutes or until reduced by half. Set aside.
3. Melt the butter in a large saucepan over low heat. Blend in the flour, salt, paprika, black pepper, and cayenne. Cook for 2 minutes, stirring constantly. Gradually add the milk, evaporated milk, and reserved beer. Cook, stirring constantly, until thickened. Remove from the heat; add the cheeses and mustard, stirring until melted.
4. In large bowl, combine the pasta, ham, and tomatoes. Add the sauce; mix well. Pour into a buttered 3-quart casserole.
5. Bake for 25 minutes or until heated through.

SERVES 8

Courtesy of Jellane Henning.

Tony Hook of Hook's Cheese Company proudly shows his award-winning cheese at the Dane County Farmers' Market on Madison's Capitol Square.

Photo by Martin Hintz

Hook's Cheese Company

Tony and Julie Hook opened Hook's Cheese Company in Mineral Point in 1976. The abandoned facility they purchased was built in the 1850s and converted to a cheese plant in 1929 before the Hooks bought and refurbished it. At first they made only Cheddar and Swiss, but in 1980 they expanded their selection to include Colby and various Monterey Jacks. Their Colby won Best of Class in the World Cheese Championship in 1982, making Julie Hook the first (and thus far only) woman to win the World Championship.

In 1997 the Hooks began developing blue-veined cheeses, including Original Blue, the double-cream Blue Paradise, and now Tilston Point—an English-style blue, great for slicing. From 1999 to 2002 the firm held the Grand Champion Cheese title for its Blue Cheese. In 2006 its ten-year Cheddar won first prize in the Cheddar Aged Over 48 Months category at American Cheese Society judging.

Their milk comes from twenty-five small family farms near Mineral Point. You can see them and purchase their popular cheese at Madison's Dane County farmers' market.

LoveTree Farmstead

Mary and David Falk have been farming since 1986 on their 200-acre organic farm in the Grantsburg area of northern Wisconsin. The beautiful glacial terrain and the eight lakes in the Trade Lake region have inspired their award-winning, cave-aged cheeses: Trade Lake Cedar, Big Holmes, Little Holmes, Sumac Holmes, and Gabrielson Lake.

Hook's Blue Cheese Cake

This is a perfect recipe for a large crowd. The cake is very rich, and a small piece is plenty. It is best served with a salad of tender greens tossed with buttermilk dressing; garnish with red-wine-poached pears and spiced pecans.

Crust

2 cups all-purpose flour

I teaspoon kosher salt

¾ cup (1½ sticks) butter

½ cup heavy cream

1. Place the flour, salt, and butter in a food processor and pulse until the butter and flour start to come together. Add the heavy cream. Do not overmix!
2. Take the tart dough out of the food processor; wrap and refrigerate for 30 minutes.
3. Once the dough is cold, roll it out on a floured surface. Fold the dough in half, carefully drape it over a 12-inch tart pan, and refrigerate.

Filling

I pound cream cheese, softened

3 large eggs

¼ cup minced shallots

6 ounces Hook's Blue Cheese

2 tablespoons heavy cream

1. Preheat the oven to 325°F.
2. Place the cream cheese in a mixing bowl. Using the paddle attachment, mix until light and creamy. You may also use a food processor. Make sure to scrape the sides of the bowl.
3. Add the eggs one at a time, followed by the shallots, blue cheese, and heavy cream.
4. Pour the cheesecake batter into the tart crust. Bake for 30 minutes.

SERVES 16 OR MORE

Courtesy of executive chef Chad Kornetzke, Lola's on the Lake, the Osthoff Resort, Elkhart Lake, Wisconsin.

The LoveTree terroir, or sense of place, is marvelous. The farm's livestock graze on the abundant flora in the area. The perfume of wild lilacs, mustard grass, violets, clovers, evergreens, and sweet milkweed seems to flavor even the air. Mary and Dave have developed a cross-breeding program to create Trade Lake Sheep, which can thrive in the harsh northern Wisconsin winters and produce high-butterfat milk.

The couple have been winning awards since 1998, when Mary captured Best of Show in the 1998 American Cheese Society for her Trade Lake Cedar cheese. That was only one year after she earned her cheesemaker's license. In 2002 they were named Food Artisan of the Year by *Bon Appétit*/Food Network. The Falks also swept the Young Sheep Milk Cheese category at the American Cheese Society Conference in 2000 and 2002.

In fall 2000 their Trade Lake Cedar was honored by being inducted onto Slow Foods International Ark of Taste. This Cheddar is their specialty—a natural-rind raw sheep's milk cheese aged on cedar boughs in the farm's fresh-air aging caves for at least two and a half months. Mary describes the cheese as "definitely aromatic," with a beguiling fruity-nutty flavor that ends with a light woodsy undertone. Recommended pairings are champagne, Chardonnay, Syrah, Zinfandel, or Pinot Noir.

Another of their special cheeses is a cow's milk Gabrielson Lake, made from raw milk derived from a single Jersey herd. This is also a natural-rind cheese, aged for more than three months.

There is no lack of creativity in their Holmes series of cheese. All are artisan sheep's milk varieties that are cave aged between four and six weeks. Big Holmes is coated with rosemary, mint, and cedar. Their Little Holmes is dusted with peppermint flakes, aged for about four weeks, and then wrapped in wild nettles soaked in vodka. Holmes Cubs are lightly dusted with herbed charcoal; Black Bears, lightly dusted with herb-free charcoal. The Sumac Holmes is gently rolled in a combination of wild sumac berries and freshly ground peppercorns, creating a fruity taste with a peppery bite.

These young cheese plant workers were probably German or Scandinavian migrant laborers who regularly spent their summers in Green County in the old days.

Photo courtesy of the Thalmann Family

Maple Leaf Cheese Cooperative

Founded in 1910 to establish a consistent market for local farmers' milk, the "small factory" tradition continues at the Maple Leaf Cooperative, with milk still supplied by area dairy farms. Some of the families are now in their second and third generations. The cooperative produces many specialty cheeses under the scrutiny of Jeff Wideman, a Wisconsin Master Cheesemaker.

Maple Leaf makes a wide variety of eclectically delicious cheeses, among which are Cranberry, Blueberry, and Cherry White Cheddar, Bleu (Aged Cheddar with blue Cheese), Naturally Smoked Cheddar, Colby, Jack & Jill (Colby–Monterey Jack), Edam, Gouda, Naturally Smoked Gouda, Monterey Jack and flavored Monterey Jack wheels, Jalapeño, Habanero, Salsa, Chipotle, Yogurt Cheese, and Queso Blanco.

Each has an interesting twist. The Cranberry White Cheddar contains dried Wisconsin cranberries and is aged from six to ten months. Yogurt Cheese comes in a variety of flavors such as Fiesta Pepper, Tomato and Basil, Jalapeño, and Classic Original. True Bleu is a blend of blue cheese and award-winning Cheddar.

Cherry Cheddar Crusted Pork Tenderloin

A sweet cherry flavor combined with a sharp taste of Wisconsin Cheddar raises this pork tenderloin to a new level of deliciousness.

8 ounces crumbled **Maple Leaf Cherry Cheddar Cheese**

I tablespoon diced butter

½ cup bread crumbs (plain or panko)

6 pork tenderloin portions, 6 ounces each

CHEF NOTE:

You can also use 1 cup of dried cherries, chopped in a food processor with 8 ounces of plain Cheddar and bread crumbs.

1. Preheat the oven to 450°F.
2. Combine the cheese, butter, and bread crumbs until the mixture resembles a well-combined dough. The best way to do this is with your hands.
3. Roast the pork in the oven for about 12 to 15 minutes.
4. Remove the pork from the oven and let it rest 10 minutes. Make a ½-inch-deep cut on the top of the tenderloin. Press the crust mixture into the pork.
5. Reduce the heat to 350°F and return the pork to the oven for another 5 to 8 minutes, until the crust is slightly brown.

SERVES 6

Courtesy of chef Wave Kasprzak, The Dining Room at 209 Main, Monticello, Wisconsin.

Meister Cheese Company

Three generations ago a small cheesemaking business began in the southwestern Wisconsin River Valley. The roots of Meister Dairy date back to 1923, when Joseph Meister started this cheese factory. Stanley Meister, Joe's son, consolidated operations in 1981, when the firm's modern manufacturing facilities were built in Muscoda. The colorful little town is called the "Morel Capital of Wisconsin," holding an annual Morel Mushroom Festival the weekend after Mother's Day.

The firm continues to make quality specialty cheeses such as Great Midwest, a line of flavored Monterey Jacks. Capitalizing on the town's mushroom production, the signature Jack flavor, Morel and Leek, is made with locally grown 'shrooms, with each batch of curds hand pressed into wheels. The cheese is a viable complement to any entrée featuring morels, whether it's a hearty stroganoff, pasta with morel mushroom cream sauce, or morels on fettuccine (don't forget to add the Wisconsin Parmesan).

Natural Valley Cheese

Natural Valley Cheese produces select specialty and artisan cheeses at its plant in Hustler, a village (population: 112) in the rolling hills of western Wisconsin. Master Cheesemaker Tom Torkelson works with some eighty nearby Amish dairy farmers to source the highest-quality milk from pasture-fed goats and cows, which he handcrafts into a variety of original cheeses. Farmers bring milk to Torkelson's cheese plant in traditional metal milk cans that have been cold-water cooled. The milk flavor varies with the season and the available pasture.

Torkelson's roots in the Wisconsin dairy world run deep. His father was a dairy farmer in New Glarus; two of his cousins also operate cheese plants in the state. He has been a licensed cheesemaker for more than twenty-five years. Visitors to the Natural Valley plant can watch the cheesemaking from an observation area before visiting the gift store, which sells Amish crafts as well as cheese.

Among Natural Valley's offerings are Castle Rock Reserve and Petenwell, both cave-aged goat's milk cheeses. Torkelson's cave-aged Lemonweir Gold, another goat's milk cheese, has a bright, lemony flavor. Twin Bluffs Select is a robust cow's milk cheese that has been cave aged for full, earthy flavor. Lindina, an aged Brick, is creamy and buttery with that cave-aged earthiness. Plattdeutsch is a pyramid-shaped, 100 percent goat's milk cheese aged two months with a grape-ash covering. Redstone Robust is a goat cheese formed in a wheel and finished in a special curing cellar near the Wisconsin River. It's a semi-soft, rind variety, hand washed for sixty days to produce a red-orange rind with a creamy white interior and robust flavor.

The majority of Natural Valley's cheeses are sold nationally in such markets as El Paso, New York, Denver, and Los Angeles.

North Hendren Cooperative Dairy

The North Hendren Cooperative Dairy in central Wisconsin, a cooperative of thirty-five dairy farmers, has been making cheese since 1923. They started with high-end Cheddars, Colby, and Monterey Jack before moving into specialty cheeses. Over the past few years, the co-op has won numerous prestigious awards. Among the most popular North Hendren cheeses is the classic Black River Blue; its slightly soft texture makes a creamy taste backdrop for the bright blue flavor. The Black River Gorgonzola is sweetly rich and pungent.

Organic Valley Family of Farms

Organic Valley is a farmer-owned cooperative offering award-winning certified organic foods, with one of the largest selections of organic cheeses in the country. Organic Valley cheeses are available in Cheddar, Swiss, and Pepper Jack, among other styles. Cow's Milk Cheddar and Organic Raw Milk Sharp Cheddar are two top-selling products. The company's cheese and butter are regular winners in international competitions. The cheese also comes in reduced-fat and low-sodium varieties, as well as shredded and sliced.

Organic Valley's cheese and butter are made in small batches from milk produced without antibiotics, synthetic hormones, or pesticides. Many of its butters, including its European-Style Cultured Butter, are made at the cooperative's creamery in Chaseburg under the direction of butter maker Tom Tollackson, who belongs to the Coulee Region Organic Produce Pool. This group of organic farmers markets under the label Organic Valley. George Siemon is Organic Valley's chief executive officer and one of the co-op's seven founding farmers.

Roth Käse USA Ltd.

Roth Käse USA Ltd. of Monroe is a world leader in specialty cheese production, with an ever-growing award-winning line. Among the excellent varieties of cheese it produces is a fabulous Grand Cru Gruyère Surchoix, a washed-rind cheese cellar-cured for twelve months or more. Another Roth Käse favorite is Buttermilk Blue, a creamy blue cheese made from fresh raw milk and aged more than sixty days. With a name great for marketing, Vintage Van Gogh is a full-cream Gouda with a smooth, golden body and caramelized flavor. GranQueso, a Roth Käse original, has a snappy, distinctive bite and lingering sweet finish that languishes on the tongue. The firm also makes a unique Fontiago, a blend of Asiago and Fontina.

Swiss-born cheesemaker Bruno Hodel holds up some Roth Käse samples in front of the firm's chalet factory. Photo by Martin Hintz

Roth Käse's chalet factory houses a Swiss-made copper vat for the traditional production of Gruyère. In 2006 it completed a major new culinary center and curing facility. This commitment to excellence has earned Roth Käse cheeses more than 100 awards in regional, national, and international competitions.

In 1863 Oswald Roth began crafting and curing cheese in Uster, Switzerland. In 1911 his son Otto left Switzerland and established Otto Roth & Co., an import business in New York City. By the 1980s this firm was the largest importer of European specialty cheeses in North America and the foundation of the company known now as Roth Käse USA.

Understanding the opportunity to craft excellent specialty

cheeses in America, Fermo Jaeckle, a former executive with Otto Roth & Co. and great-grandson of Oswald Roth, linked with his cousins Felix and Ulrich Roth to found Roth Käse USA Ltd. in 1991. Green County in south-central Wisconsin was selected as the firm's headquarters—a natural choice given the availability of a continuous supply of high-quality milk. It didn't hurt, either, that the area is nicknamed "Little Switzerland" for its Swiss heritage.

Fontiago Polenta with Tomato Basil Concassée

This recipe is good with any of your favorite cheeses.

Fontiago Polenta

3 ½ cups milk (skim is okay)

1 teaspoon garlic powder

1 teaspoon salt

½ teaspoon black pepper

1 ¾ cups coarse polenta

6 ounces Fontiago (a blend of Roth Käse Asiago and Fontina)

Tomato Basil Concassée

4 Roma tomatoes, chopped

1 teaspoon balsamic vinegar

1 tablespoon olive oil

1 tablespoon chopped fresh basil

Salt and pepper to taste

1. In a heavy-bottomed saucepan, bring the milk, garlic powder, salt, and pepper to a boil.
2. Reduce to a simmer and whisk in the polenta. As the mixture thickens, stir with a spoon until it's quite thick.
3. Stir in the Fontiago until melted.
4. Spread on a greased sheet pan and cool completely. Cut in desired shapes and bake or sauté until heated through and browned.

Combine all of the ingredients and spoon over the polenta.

SERVES 8

Courtesy of chef Wave Kasprzak, The Dining Room at 209 Main, Monticello, Wisconsin.

CHEF NOTE:

We usually use a 1-inch-tall baking sheet tray, spreading the polenta on one end even with the sheet's top for uniformity.

Sartori Foods

Sartori Foods, headed by CEO Jim Sartori, is a family-run cheese manufacturer making premium Italian cheese such as SarVecchio Parmesan, which captured a gold medal as Best US Cow's Milk Cheese at the 2006 World Cheese Awards in London. This is a great cheese, one aged for twenty months to give it a creamy, sweet, nutty flavor; it's recognized by cheese experts as one of the Top 10 American-made artisan cheeses. The firm also makes Gorgonzola/Blue, Hispanic, and other specialty varieties.

Sweet Potato SarVecchio Parmesan Soup

Roasting or smoking the sweet potatoes called for in this recipe adds a bold, interesting flavor.

2 cloves garlic, minced

½ cup small-diced celery

½ cup small-diced onion

½ cup small-diced leeks

2 tablespoons (¼ stick) butter

1½ pounds sweet potatoes, medium diced

1 quart chicken stock

¼ teaspoon ground cinnamon

2 tablespoons maple syrup

1 teaspoon salt

1 cup heavy cream

½ cup fresh-grated Sartori Foods
　　SarVecchio Parmesan Cheese

1. Sweat the garlic, celery, onion, and leeks in the butter in a medium saucepan over medium-high heat.
2. Add the sweet potatoes and chicken stock, bring to a boil, reduce the heat, and simmer slowly until the potatoes are tender.
3. Puree the soup until smooth.
4. Return it to the saucepan, adding the cinnamon, maple syrup, salt, heavy cream, and Parmesan.

SERVES 4-6

Courtesy of Sartori Foods, Plymouth, Wisconsin.

Sartori was launched in 1939, earning a strong reputation over the years, one solidified when it purchased Antigo Cheese in 2006. The latter company was noted for excellent Parmesan, Romano, Asiago, and Fontina for more than seventy-five years and was a multiple award winner including its Stravecchio, which was rated one of the Top 12 cheeses by *Bon Appétit* in 2003. It also won best in the Hard Italian category at both the Wisconsin State Fair and the American Cheese Society in 2005.

Awards are nothing new for Sartori, which won the 1995, 1996, 2000, 2002, 2003, and 2005 Wisconsin State Fair First Place Governors Sweepstakes blue ribbon for the entire Italian Grana category of cheese. The company's Joel Pagel was named the 2006 Grand Master Cheese Maker at the Wisconsin State Fair, earning the coveted nod for his Asiago.

Sugar River Cheese Company

The Sugar River Cheese Company was founded in 2002 by Mark Rosen, who wanted to produce top-quality kosher Wisconsin cheeses. The company uses rBGH-free milk from the pastures of southwest Wisconsin to make its cheeses, which are also enhanced by local ingredients. Among Sugar River's specialties are White Cheddar with Chipotle, Monterey Jack with Roasted Garlic and Basil, and Prairie Jack with Parsley and Chive.

Uplands Cheese Company

Mike and Carol Gingrich and Dan and Jeanne Patenaude bought their dairy farm in 1994, raising cows that grazed solely on mixed-species pastureland with its wildflowers, grasses, and herbs. They breed spring calves, which graze when grass growth is optimal. In 2000, the couples decided to make cheese.

Uplands was inspired by the farmstead cheeses from the Alpine provinces of southeastern France, which were nonpasteurized, aged in limestone caves, and washed with a salty brine solution. With that knowledge, the company created its Pleasant Ridge Reserve, reminiscent of a lovely French Gruyère.

Pleasant Ridge Reserve with Warm Rhubarb-Bacon Compote on Pecan Raisin Bread

This recipe is the creation of Tory Miller, executive chef and co-owner of L'Etoile restaurant in Madison. He grew up in the restaurant industry with his sister and business partner, Traci Miller. Tory studied at the French Culinary Institute, leading to jobs at several high-end restaurants in New York, including Eleven Madison Park and Judson Grill. L'Etoile, established in 1976, was named one of the Top 50 Restaurants in the United States by Gourmet *magazine in 2006.*

Chef Miller likes to let great cheeses speak for themselves, so he often serves them uncooked. He pairs Pleasant Ridge Reserve with a combination of rhubarb and bacon, since those strong flavors beautifully accent this strong cheese.

I tablespoon butter

2–4 slices bacon

2 shallots, minced

I clove garlic, minced

¾ cup packed brown sugar

Pinch ground cinnamon

Pinch ground cardamom

Salt and pepper

¼ cup apple cider vinegar

4 stalks rhubarb (preferably red)

16 slices raisin bread or fruit bread

8 ounces Pleasant Ridge Reserve

Parsley leaves, for garnish

1. In a large sauté pan, melt the butter over medium-low heat.
2. Cut or julienne the bacon by cutting it into thin strips, and brown them in the butter. When the bacon is crisp, add the shallots and garlic. Stir and cook for about 2 minutes.
3. Add the brown sugar and spices and stir until smooth. Add the cider vinegar and bring to a simmer.
4. Dice the rhubarb and add it to the pan. Toss through and simmer until tender; be careful not to overcook the rhubarb, as it will become mushy. Taste and adjust the amount of brown sugar based on the tartness of the rhubarb. Place the mixture in a bowl to cool.
5. Cut each slice of bread into the desired serving shape and toast. Place a ½-ounce wedge of Pleasant Ridge Reserve on top, followed by a small spoonful of the compote atop the cheese.
6. Garnish with a parsley leaf and serve.

SERVES 16

Courtesy of chef Tory Miller, L'Etoile Restaurant, Madison.

CHEF NOTE:
L'Etoile uses a house-made pecan and golden raisin bread in this recipe.

Soft, "Sexy" Wisconsin Cheese Grits

This recipe was created by chef Jan Birnbaum from Sazerac in Seattle, Washington—a Wisconsin Milk Marketing Board ambassador-chef. It's a sumptuous dish that can easily be turned into an entrée: Just sauté 1 pound of medium-size peeled, deveined shrimp in butter with a bit of garlic, and use it to top the grits.

5 tablespoons butter

1½ cups chicken broth, homemade or
   prepared

⅓ cup heavy cream

½ teaspoon peeled and chopped garlic

Salt to taste

Pepper to taste

Tabasco sauce to taste

½ cup grits (standard quick grits or stone
   ground)

1½ cups shredded Wisconsin Gouda

1. Bring the butter, broth, cream, garlic, salt, pepper, and Tabasco to a boil. Reduce the heat and simmer until the garlic is soft, about 2 minutes. Add all of the grits, whisking and stirring constantly. Simmer.

2. Continue cooking on low heat, stirring often with a wooden spoon as the mixture thickens and adding more stock if necessary, until the grits are soft and cooked through, about 10 to 15 minutes.

3. Fold in the Gouda cheese, reserving a little for garnish. Serve immediately.

SERVES 4-6

Courtesy of the Wisconsin Milk Marketing Board, Inc.

CHEF NOTE:

Fresh, stone-ground grits have the best flavor; we recommend them over the quick kind in this recipe, although the cooking time will be approximately twice as long. If you do use freshly ground grits, you will want to keep a little extra stock available. Because of the longer cooking time, evaporation occurs.

Their affinage has the same temperature and humidity as French limestone caves. The cheeses are washed with a solution that contains the natural bacteria as found in caverns.

Pleasant Ridge Reserve is a multi-award-winning cheese. It garnered Best of Show from the American Cheese Society in 2001, when it was barely two years old. It won again in 2005. Pleasant Ridge also took top prize at the 2003 US Championship.

Widmer's Cheese Cellars

Widmer's Cheese is located in Theresa, a village in the rolling hills of northeast Dodge County near the northern Kettle Moraine State Forest. The town was founded by the famous French trader Solomon Juneau, whose original home in town still stands on a hill overlooking the Rock River.

The Widmer family has operated the Cheese Cellars since 1922; the firm is now run by Joe Widmer, a third-generation cheesemaker. His grandfather, John Widmer, was a Swiss cheesemaker who came to Wisconsin in the early 1900s and passed along his skills to Joe, who is now a certified Wisconsin Master Cheesemaker. The younger Widmer doesn't have a long commute to work because he lives with his wife, Katie, above the cheese factory.

Widmer's specialty is Brick, a Wisconsin original that's available in both mild and aged versions. The cheese is handmade in small batches. The curd is transferred from the vat to the molds by hand, then each mold is turned three times on the first day. Widmer also produces Cheddar, as well as Colby.

Joe's family loves to make pizza with their young Brick, green peppers, sausage, and sometimes tomatoes.

CHAPTER 3

CHEDDAR AND COLBY CHEESES

CHEDDAR IS REPORTEDLY THE MOST POPULAR CHEESE IN the United States. It originated in England in the 1500s, named for a village called Cheddar Gorge. In America the earliest colonists (usually long-suffering farm wives) continued making Cheddar. Before 1850 nearly all the cheese made in Wisconsin was Cheddar. By 1880, more Cheddar was still being produced in the state than any other variety. Today Wisconsin is the top producer of Cheddar in the United States, although in fact more mozzarella is made here.

Organic Cheddars, raw-milk Cheddars, and Cheddars using seasonal milk from pasture-grazed cows are all being produced in Wisconsin, and all are fine sources of calcium and protein. They're loaded with vitamins B_{12}, A, and B_6, as well as some beneficial fat and riboflavin.

Cheddar comes with its own vocabulary. The term *cheddaring*, for instance, denotes a specific step in the production of Cheddar-style cheese: After heating, the curd is cut into cubes to drain the whey. It's then stacked and turned. You may also have heard of *bandaged Cheddar*, which refers to the traditional English style of wrapping cheddar in cheesecloth. This creates a natural, inedible rind. After being wrapped like a Wisconsin mummy, the cheese is sealed with an exterior wax whose color often represents its flavor. *Mild* generally has a clear wax, red suggests *medium*, and black usually means a *sharp*, aged cheese. Extra-sharp Cheddars also exist.

This range of flavors is a function of a cheese's age. Cheddar generally matures after somewhere between nine months and two years, but it can age for up to twelve years. A young cheese is milder and mellower in flavor and creamier in texture. As it matures, it develops a sharp, nutty flavor. Its texture also changes: What was once smooth and firm becomes more crumbly and granular.

Graphics courtesy of Maple Leaf Cheese

Yellow or White?

The golden hue of Cheddar is created by the addition of annatto—a tasteless, odorless vegetable dye made from the fruit seeds of the tropical achiote tree. The achiote was used by American Indians to make body paint, especially for the lips. It thus was nicknamed "the lipstick tree." These small trees grew well in Latin and South America and were introduced to Southeast Asia by Spanish explorers. The annatto pigment, found in reddish pulp surrounding the seeds, is used for coloring many kinds of foods in addition to cheese.

Only some white Cheddar is made in Wisconsin, but Vermont Cheddar is traditionally white. While we've found both styles equally delicious, we'll still tip our cheesehats toward the Wisconsin version as our favorite.

Big Cheeses

There are many great stories about Cheddar. President Andrew Jackson, a devoted cheese lover, once served a 1,400-pound block of Cheddar cheese at a White House party. It took only two hours for the hundreds of guests to devour the entire chunk. But Wisconsin did even better: A 34,951-pound Wisconsin Cheddar was produced for the New York World's Fair in 1964. The milk of 16,000 cows was needed to create this monster.

Cheddar Pairings

Cheddar is extremely versatile when it comes to serving. The tradition of offering a sharp Cheddar cheese with apple pie dates back to pre-nineteenth-century England. At that time apples weren't as sweet as what you'll eat today; the tartness of the cheese complemented the tartness of the apple. Never ones to leave behind a good thing when they traveled, European settlers continued this tradition in America.

Wisconsin Cheddar also marries well with pears, onions, and tomatoes. It can be flavored with numerous interesting ingredients, such as hot peppers, assorted vegetables, sausage, or even cherries. Many die-hard Cheddar fans opt for the smoked version, especially during winter's snowmobile season. A slice is particularly delicious while pausing on a trail ride for a chili-'n'-cheese lunch in a typical Nort' Woods tavern.

We like to serve red wines such as Zinfandel or Merlot or even offer pale ales or stout beers to friends when putting out a Cheddar-and-crackers platter.

Working with Cheddar, According to the Experts

- If you eat a lot of Cheddar, buy a five-pound block and cut it into smaller chunks. You'll save some money.
- For cooking and convenience, grate the cheese before wrapping it (in 1- or 2-cup portions) for storage.
- Shredded Cheddar can be frozen for three weeks, but it must be packaged properly. Our cheesemaker friends recommend using heavy foil, plastic-coated freezer paper with freezer tape, or freezer bags.
- When you need frozen Cheddar for cooking or eating, thaw it in the refrigerator, then use immediately. It's also okay to cook Cheddar while it's still frozen, although it will be dry and crumbly until it melts.
- If Cheddar is refrigerated in the original wrapper, it can be stored in the fridge for one to two months. Opened and rewrapped properly, it should last for about a month.

> "Serve cheddar any time you feel like adding something wonderful to your life."
>
> —Steve Jenkins, *The Cheese Primer* (Workman Publishing Company, 1996)

- Cheddar, whether mild, medium, or aged, shreds and melts well. This makes for happy chefs at all skill levels. The mild and medium varieties are easier to slice than the aged, which often crumbles. However, remember that, like all cheeses, chilled Cheddar is easier to slice.
- Grating or cutting the cheese into small cubes speeds the melting process. But be sure to cook cheese over a low temperature to avoid it toughening.

Wisconsin Cheddar Scones with Smoked Turkey

We consider this recipe a great way to use leftover Thanksgiving turkey. To round out the flavor, add a dollop of your favorite mustard, cranberry chutney, or cranberry sauce.

4 cups biscuit mix

1½ cups milk

2 eggs

½ cup butter, melted

2½ cups (10 ounces) finely shredded Wisconsin Sharp Cheddar cheese

Smoked turkey, thinly sliced

1. Preheat the oven to 400°F.
2. Combine the biscuit mix, milk, eggs, butter, and cheese; mix well until the ingredients are moistened.
3. Drop the dough by tablespoonfuls onto lightly greased baking sheet. Bake for 12 to 14 minutes or until golden brown.
4. Remove the scones from the oven and let them cool slightly before removing them from the baking sheet.
5. To serve, slice each scone in half and fill with a small slice of turkey. Arrange on a serving tray.

MAKES 32 SCONES

Courtesy of the Wisconsin Milk Marketing Board, Inc.

Santa's Wisconsin Cheese Delight

Santa and his helpers will love this special treat.

3 cups (12 ounces) shredded Wisconsin
    Aged Cheddar

3 cups (12 ounces) shredded Wisconsin
    Gouda

1 cup reduced-calorie Hellman's
    mayonnaise

3 green onions, with tops, finely chopped

⅛ teaspoon hot pepper sauce

¾ cup chopped pecans

¾ cup raspberry or strawberry jam

1. In a large bowl, mix the cheeses, mayonnaise, onions, and pepper sauce. Add the pecans.
2. Press the mixture gently into a 6½- to 7-inch springform pan. Cover and chill for at least 3 hours.
3. Unmold onto a serving plate. Spread the jam on top, and serve with crackers.

SERVES 20

Courtesy of the Wisconsin Milk Marketing Board, Inc.

Wisconsin Chile Relleno Casserole

Move over, brats: Serve this at your next Green Bay Packer party. Your guests will go wild. Don't forget the brewskis!

I pound shredded Wisconsin sharp
    Cheddar cheese

4 cans (4 ounces each) chopped green
    chilies, drained

I pound shredded Wisconsin Monterey
    Jack cheese

4 eggs

3 cups light cream

¼ cup cornmeal

I teaspoon salt

I teaspoon Worcestershire sauce

I cup red picante sauce, cooked and
    thickened with I tablespoon
    cornstarch and I tablespoon water

1. Preheat the oven to 350°F. Butter a 13x9-inch pan.
2. Layer the Cheddar on the bottom of the pan, then the green chilies and Jack cheese.
3. Blend the eggs, cream, cornmeal, salt, and Worcestershire sauce. Pour this mixture over the layers of cheese and chilies.
4. Top with picante sauce, if desired, and bake for 40 minutes. Cut into 12 squares and serve.

SERVES 8–12

Courtesy of the Junior League of Milwaukee cookbook, The Gatherings.

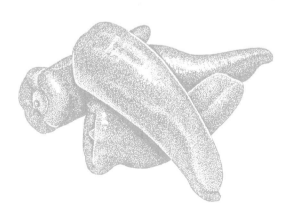

Carrot Muffins with Wisconsin Cheddar, Ginger, and Hazelnuts

What a mix! And healthy, too. The zing of ginger complements this carroty wonder of muffins enhanced by your favorite Cheddar.

1¾ cups flour

⅔ cup packed light brown sugar

1¼ teaspoons ground cinnamon

1 teaspoon baking powder

½ teaspoon baking soda

½ cup natural applesauce

½ cup vegetable oil

1 egg, lightly beaten

1½ tablespoons finely chopped candied ginger

2 cups finely shredded carrots

1½ cups (6 ounces) shredded Wisconsin Cheddar cheese, divided

1 cup chopped hazelnuts or pecans, toasted

½ cup dark seedless raisins

1. Preheat the oven to 400°F.
2. Combine the flour, brown sugar, cinnamon, baking powder, and soda; set aside.
3. In another bowl, combine the applesauce, oil, egg, and ginger. Stir into the dry ingredients; gently mix until just combined. Gently fold in the carrots, 1 cup of the cheese, the nuts, and the raisins.
4. Scoop the mixture into 12 greased muffin cups and bake for 18 to 20 minutes or until baked completely through.
5. Remove the muffins from the oven and sprinkle them evenly with the remaining ½ cup cheese. Let them cool in the pan for 5 minutes, then turn them onto a wire rack.
6. Cool to room temperature and serve.

MAKES 12 MUFFINS

Courtesy of the Wisconsin Milk Marketing Board, Inc.

French-fried Wisconsin Cheese

This treat is a universal favorite at the Wisconsin State Fair.

I pound Wisconsin Cheddar, Muenster,
  Brick, and/or Colby cheese, cut into
  ½-inch cubes

2 eggs, beaten

Seasoned dry bread crumbs or flour

Vegetable oil

1. Dip each cheese cube into the beaten eggs, coat with crumbs, and repeat.
2. Fry the cubes in hot oil (350 to 375°F) until lightly browned. Serve immediately.

SERVES 6

Recipe courtesy of the Wisconsin Milk Marketing Board, Inc.

CHEF NOTE: Cheese curds may be substituted for cheese cubes. You can also coat the cheese ahead of time and refrigerate it until you're ready to fry.

"Hot Cheese!" The Wisconsin State Fair has it all. Photo by Martin Hintz

Smoked Chicken and Sharp Cheddar Panini

Cut these delicious sandwiches in half and serve them with a chilled glass of White Haven Sauvignon Blanc or your favorite Wisconsin beer.

4 boneless smoked chicken breasts

¼ cup sour cream

2 teaspoons mayonnaise

2 tablespoons sugar

I tablespoon apple cider vinegar

2 Granny Smith apples, julienned

I red onion, julienned

8 slices crusty bread

2 cups shredded sharp Cheddar cheese

Extra-virgin olive oil

1. Butterfly each chicken breast by slicing it lengthwise, creating two thin slices. If smoked chicken is unavailable, season breasts with salt and pepper and grill, basting with 1 tablespoon of melted butter.
2. In a mixing bowl, combine the sour cream, mayonnaise, sugar, and apple cider vinegar. Mix until well blended. Toss with the julienned apples and red onions.
3. Top four of the pieces of crusty bread with the sharp Cheddar cheese, then the sliced chicken, then the apple relish, and finally the remaining four slices of bread.
4. Drizzle the top of each sandwich with some extra-virgin olive oil and place that side on a grill or grill pan over medium-low heat. When it's well toasted, drizzle the other side with olive oil and flip.

SERVES 4

Courtesy of chefs Nick Klug and Clinton Del Marcelle, Evensong Spa, Heidel House Resort, Green Lake, Wisconsin.

Clinton Del Marcelle and Nick Klug of the Heidel House Resort in Green Lake.

Photo by Gary Knowles

Apple and Wisconsin Aged Cheddar Bread Pudding

Tart apples and sharp Cheddar create a taste combination that's been enjoyed for centuries. A touch of cayenne gives it a little extra zip.

Custard

4 whole eggs

4 egg yolks

2 tablespoons granulated sugar

2 teaspoons vanilla extract

¼ teaspoon salt

3 cups whole milk

I cup heavy cream

7 cups day-old French bread cubes (1½-inch cubes)

1. In a large bowl, whisk together the eggs, egg yolks, sugar, vanilla, and salt.
2. Stir in the milk and cream. Add the bread cubes and press down, making sure that all of the cubes are covered by custard mixture. Let the bread soak while you turn to the apples.

Apples

4 cups peeled and sliced Granny Smith apples (½-inch wedges)

2 tablespoons lemon juice

½ cup (I stick) unsalted butter

½ cup granulated sugar

½ cup packed light brown sugar

1½ teaspoons ground cinnamon

¼ teaspoon ground cayenne pepper

2 cups (8 ounces) grated Wisconsin Aged Cheddar cheese, divided

1. Toss the wedges with the lemon juice.
2. In a large skillet, melt the butter over medium heat. Add the apples, granulated sugar, brown sugar, cinnamon, and cayenne. Cook until the apples are slightly tender, 8 to 10 minutes, stirring frequently. Cool for 20 minutes.
3. Final preparations: Preheat the oven to 325°F. Generously butter a 9x13-inch casserole dish.
4. Pour half of the bread mixture into the dish. Top with half the cooked apple mixture, then with 1 cup of the cheese. Repeat this layering with the remaining ingredients.

5. Cover the mixture with small piece of waxed or parchment paper. Cover the dish tightly with foil.
6. Bake in a water bath for 60 minutes. Remove the foil and paper, and return the pan to the oven, increasing the temperature to 350°F.
7. Continue to bake the pudding in its water bath for 25 to 35 minutes more or until it's browned and puffed, and a butter knife inserted near the center comes out clean.
8. Remove the dish from the oven and let it rest for 20 minutes before serving. Sprinkle the top with additional cinnamon and cayenne, if desired.

SERVES 8–10

Courtesy of chefs Mary and Greg Sonnier, Gabrielle, New Orleans, and the Wisconsin Milk Marketing Board, Inc.

Wisconsin cheesemakers have captured dozens of top honors for their Cheddars. Among the first-place winners:

- Lil Wils Bandaged Cheddar from Bleu Mont Dairy
- Carr Valley Cheese for its Mammoth Cheddar, Applewood Smoked Cheddar, and 8-Year Cheddar
- Cedar Grove Cheese for Sharp Cheddar
- Hook's Cheese Company for its ten-year Sharp Cheddar
- Land O'Lakes for many Cheddars
- Widmer's Cheese Cellar
- Gibbsville Cheese for its Organic Raw Milk Sharp Cheddar
- Organic Valley for Pasteurized Sharp Cheddar

And that's only a few of them. Other well-praised and -loved Cheddar makers dot the state. Take a look at:

BRUNKOW CHEESE

Typical of longtime Wisconsin Cheddar producers is the Brunkow Cheese Co-op, named for the farmer who donated land in 1899 to build a plant in the rural Darlington area. A close-at-hand cheese factory provided a readily accessible market for milk. The facility was built as a co-op, with participating farmers pledging money or labor for a share in the operations.

Since 1929 the Brunkow Cheese Co-op has been run by the Geissbuhler family, now in its third generation. More than thirty farmers still provide milk for Brunkow's high-end Cheddar and other cheeses. The company is known for its raw-milk Cheddar cold pack spread and also has a popular line of certified organic cheeses.

TIMBER LAKE

Timber Lake makes both traditional Cheddars—including a one-year, a two-year, and a special Private Reserve four-year Cheddar—and flavored varieties such as Chipotle, Tomato & Basil, Mediterranean, and Horseradish. The latter took second place at the World Dairy Expo in 2005. Timber Lake is part of DCI Cheese Company in Richfield, Wisconsin.

ORGANIC VALLEY

Organic Valley Colby was the second-place winner at the American Cheese Society competition, 2006, in the American Originals/Colby category. The year before, Organic Valley Raw Sharp Cheddar likewise took second place at the ASC competition; it also won a bronze medal in London, England, at the World Cheese Awards, and Best of Class at the US Championship Cheese Contest in Milwaukee. *Family Circle* magazine named Organic Valley Cheddar as Top Pick in its Cheddar Cheese Review, 2005.

Colby

Colby Cheese is a Wisconsin original. Inspired by Cheddar, it was created in 1874 in the central Wisconsin town of Colby. Its flavor is reminiscent of a mild Cheddar, but it features a tiny-holed texture and higher moisture content. It's more elastic, too, thanks to the fact that the curds are sprayed with cold water and stirred while still in the vat, which prevents them from bonding.

Colby is delicious plain but also comes in a variety of taste and style options:

- Colby flavors include Cajun spices, caraway, hot pepper, and garlic.
- It can be marbled with Jack or white Cheddar cheese.
- It comes in a certified kosher variety.
- You'll find low-sodium and reduced-fat versions.
- Artisan Colbys include raw milk and organic.

Still, the most common and popular version is the simple thirteen-pound cylinder known as Colby Longhorn. These cylinders are often cut into half-moons or sticks.

Colby is great with chili or sliced in a sandwich such as roast beef, ham, or turkey. It pairs well with apples, tomatoes, pears, and onions.

Indian-Spiced Pumpkin Bread with Wisconsin Colby

This bread is delicious—and spicy! *You might need to serve it with a glass of light beer or light white wine to put out the fire. But it's perfect with a cup of chili on a cold winter's eve, or as an accompaniment to your favorite Indian food.*

2 teaspoons cumin seeds

3 tablespoons butter, divided

½ cup finely chopped onion

2 teaspoons curry powder

¼ teaspoon ground cumin

⅛ teaspoon cayenne pepper

¾ teaspoon salt

¾ cup flour

¾ cup cornmeal

I teaspoon baking powder

½ teaspoon baking soda

I tablespoon sugar

8 ounces (I cup) pumpkin puree, canned or homemade

I½ teaspoons finely diced hot chile, such as jalapeño or serrano

2 eggs, lightly beaten

⅔ cup buttermilk

¾ cup shredded Wisconsin Colby cheese, divided

1. Preheat the oven to 350°F. Butter a 9¼ x 5¼ x 3-inch loaf pan.
2. Heat a small, heavy skillet. Add the cumin seeds and toast just until aromatic. Do not let them scorch or brown. Pour the seeds onto a saucer and set aside.
3. In the same skillet, heat 1 tablespoon of the butter. Add the onion, curry powder, ground cumin, cayenne, and salt. Cook over medium-low heat, stirring frequently, until the onion is soft, about 5 minutes. Let this mixture cool, then stir in the reserved cumin seeds.
4. Sift the flour, cornmeal, baking powder, baking soda, and sugar into a bowl.
5. Melt the remaining 2 tablespoons of butter and set aside.
6. In a large bowl, whisk the pumpkin puree, hot pepper, eggs, buttermilk, onion mixture, and melted butter. Mix just until moistened.
7. Add the flour mixture and stir just until mixed. Fold in ½ cup of the shredded Colby. Spoon the mixture into the prepared loaf pan.

8. Bake for 35 minutes. Remove from the oven and sprinkle the remaining Colby over the top of the loaf.
9. Return the pan to the oven for 5 to 7 minutes more, until the cheese melts and the bread is baked through.

MAKES I LOAF, ABOUT I2 SLICES

Courtesy of the Wisconsin Milk Marketing Board, Inc.

Wisconsin Cojack-and-Ham Panini

Cojack is a marbled cheese blending Colby with Monterey Jack. These delicious panini were created by John Esser.

¼ cup apricot jam
2 tablespoons whole-grain mustard
8 slices marbled rye bread
8 slices Wisconsin Cojack cheese
8 slices deli ham
¼ cup sliced red onions
Soft butter

1. Combine the jam and mustard; spread it evenly on four slices of the bread.
2. Top each of these slices with one slice of Cojack, two slices of ham, a quarter of the onions, and one more slice of Cojack.
3. Top the sandwiches with the remaining slices of bread; spread the outside of each slice with soft butter. Place in a hot panini grill for 1 minute. You can also grill these in a nonstick frying pan if desired.

SERVES 4

Courtesy of John Esser and the Wisconsin Milk Marketing Board, Inc.

CHAPTER 4

SWISS CHEESE

KNOWN AS "AMERICA'S LITTLE SWITZERLAND," GREEN County is the heart of Wisconsin's rich dairy country. The county is home to a vibrant blend of European dairy traditions exemplified by the Swiss immigrants who were attracted to the rolling hills and lush pastures. The new arrivals brought their love of cows, skill at yodeling, and, of course, knowledge of cheesemaking. Cheesemaking remains an important mainstay of the region's economy and rural lifestyle.

Swiss native Nicholas Gerber came to Wisconsin from New York with a profound knowledge of how to make and market cheese. He is considered one of the earliest of Wisconsin's professional cheesemakers, opening the state's first Swiss factory in the 1860s. His plant at the time was located midway between Monticello and New Glarus. Gerber also established the state's first Limburger factory on a farm about 4 miles southwest of New Glarus.

By the late 1870s Green County boasted more than 200 cheese factories. In 1884 Swiss émigré Jacob Regez had become owner of ten plants in the county. Jacob Karlen, also Swiss born, was another major force in the area. He and his wife had eleven children, many of whom became dairy farmers or cheese producers.

Arabut Ludlow was an influential Monroe banker in the later 1800s. He was well aware of the importance of cheese to the Green County economy. When he heard some citizens complain about the aroma of Limburger cheese passing through town on its way to market, Ludlow had producers position several loads of cheese in the town square. He then hosted a meeting, telling those who attended that the cheese was their key to a prosperous future: It was the scent of money. The grumbling quickly ceased, and the cheese wheels continued to roll.

The Southern Wisconsin Cheesemakers Association, which met regularly in Monroe's Turner Hall, became a powerful lobbying group for the state dairy industry in the early 1900s. Harking back to their European heritage, many of the group's early reports and resolutions were given in German. At one session in 1907, the cheesemakers "respectfully asked" the legislature to "enact such laws as will give the people good, safe and permanent highways." It wasn't just for the community's well-being: The manufacturers realized the "urgent need for good roads for all purposes and especially for the successful carrying on of the dairy and cheese industry."

They also recognized the value of continuing education in their chosen field and eagerly took advantage of emerging new technologies. As early as the 1920s, the University of Wisconsin Extension was holding classes and certifying Swiss cheesemakers.

To this day Green County, Wisconsin, retains its central role in the Wisconsin cheese industry and among Wisconsin cheese lovers. This chapter will take you more deeply into the county and into Swiss cheese recipes, lore, and uses.

The Voegeli dairy farm between New Glarus and Monroe has been a family operation for five generations. Current owner Bryan Voegeli milks 140 head of Brown Swiss cows twice a day seven days a week to provide milk for local cheese plants. Photo by Martin Hintz

Big Cheeses

Traditionally Swiss cheese was produced in kettles made of copper—a metal that can be heated quickly and evenly. Most kettles were fashioned of large, heavy riveted copper sheets. The kettle was placed on a steel stand into which steam was piped to heat the milk. Some kettles could be 5 feet in diameter or more and able to contain 2,500 pounds of milk. This was enough to make one 200-pound wheel of Swiss cheese measuring 3 feet in diameter and 6 inches thick.

The practice of making Swiss cheeses in enormous wheels dates back to the Middle Ages, when cheese was taxed per piece, rather than by weight. The tradition continues because it ensures production of excellent cheese in large batches. Edelweiss Creamery of Monticello, Wisconsin, currently makes a 180-pound Big Wheel Emmentaler in a copper vat that holds up to 12,000 pounds of milk.

Swiss Varieties

Swiss cheese is a generic term for the difficult-to-make cheeses that originated in Switzerland and have those trademark holes or eyes. The original and most famous Swiss cheeses are Emmentaler and Gruyère, but many other Swisses have now been added to the mix. The Wisconsin Milk Marketing Board's Cheesecyclopedia, on their Web site www.wisdairy.com, helps explain the varieties.

Emmentaler—also spelled *Emmental* and *Emmenthaler*—originated in the Emmental Valley around 1293. It is touted as Switzerland's oldest and most prestigious cheese. The homeland's Emmentaler is made from part skim, unpasteurized cow's

Wisconsin politician Melvin Laird was joined by Alice in Dairyland (left) and Miss Wisconsin (right) in the early 1960s at the Lions' International Convention at Chicago's Palmer House hotel. The wheel of Swiss cheese was provided by The Swiss Colony. Over his distinguished career, Laird was a United States congressman and later secretary of defense under President Richard Nixon from 1969 to 1973.
Photo courtesy of The Swiss Colony

milk, while Wisconsin versions use pasteurized milk. It's a yellow, medium-hard cheese with large holes and a piquant but not really sharp taste. As with all Swiss cheeses, this variety is great to cook with because it melts easily. Its taste is slightly nutty, mild, and buttery, which allows it to pair well with fruits and nuts.

Gruyère originated in the Gruyère Valley in Fribourg, Switzerland, near the French border. Although Switzerland lays claim to originating this cheese, it has certainly been a part of French cuisine for generations. Gruyère has many subtle differences from Emmentaler. It is made from cow's milk with more fat, so its nutty and buttery flavor has a sweeter taste. Its holes are much smaller and more evenly spaced—sometimes so small, they're almost indistinguishable. Both cheeses, however, are pale yellow in color and have a brownish gold rind. In Wisconsin artisan cheesemakers are creating award-winning Gruyères via age-old techniques in copper vats. The cheese is then aged anywhere from 10 to 12 months to bring out the best flavor.

> "As a buyer of Swiss cheese, it has always bugged me that I am paying full price for the holes and frankly my bread is not being properly covered."
>
> —writer Jeff Wyatt

Gruyère is a delicious appetizer or dessert cheese. It melts easily, making it a perfect addition to an omelet, soufflé, fondue, or bowl of onion soup—it's the classic topping. Fruity white wines such as Gewürztraminer and Sauvignon Blanc pair well with Gruyère, as do red wines like Merlot and Cabernet Franc.

American Swiss is a generic cheese variety first created in the 1950s. Large supermarket corporations and other sales outlets wanted a smaller-holed Swiss cheese that was also rindless for easier handling and better yields. With the development of plastic wrapping, which was able to keep in the moisture while allowing carbon dioxide to escape, cheesemakers were able to create a cheese that could ripen without forming a hard rind.

American Swiss is derived from pasteurized cow's milk that's often partially skimmed. It is aged at least sixty days. Usually made in mass quantities by larger companies, it has a milder flavor than Emmentaler or Gruyère. For convenience, it often comes sliced or grated; you can also find flavored, smoked, aged, low-sodium, reduced-fat, and lacy versions. It goes best with fruity white wines like Riesling or reds such as Merlot and Cabernet Sauvignon.

Baby Swiss is aptly named. It is "younger" than other Swiss varieties—not aged as long. It also has smaller holes and a milder flavor; it usually comes in smaller packages. It's made from whole milk, giving it a creamier texture and more buttery, slightly sweet flavor. Baby Swiss is ideal for melting, great in sandwiches such as ham and corned beef. It enhances omelets, frittatas, and quiches and is delicious with apples and pears. There are many types of Baby Swiss, including smoked, kosher, reduced-fat, organic, and sweet-style.

Sweet Swiss is a Wisconsin-produced rind cheese, a cross between Baby Swiss and **Jarlsberg,** a Norwegian Swiss. The Sweet lies between Swiss and Baby Swiss in flavor, being firmer and fuller than Baby Swiss and softer and milder than traditional Swiss. Like all Swiss cheeses, it melts well and is often served in cubes with fruit.

Raclette is both the name of a cheese and the title of a traditional Swiss dish also popular in France. In fact, *Raclette* comes from the French word *racler,* which means "to scrape off." The preparation of Raclette-the-meal is believed to have been discovered by chance in the Valais region in Switzerland at the end of the nineteenth century by grape pickers eating their dinner before an open hearth. As the legend goes, one worker, wanting to warm himself as he ate, moved too close to the fire while holding a piece of cheese on his knife. He found that in the flames, the cheese melted with a crisp, golden texture. So he scraped the crust off onto a plate and ate it. His friends agreed that this newly found treat was delicious—and thus was Raclette born.

In Wisconsin, Roth Käse offers a delicious Raclette cheese made from pasteurized cow's milk and aged. Like all Raclettes, it's pale yellow with a natural light brown rind. Its texture is smooth and firm, with small holes. It has a bold aromatic flavor that becomes more intense as it heats. For more about Raclette, take a look at the sidebar later in this chapter.

Hol(e)y Cheese!

Q. Why is Swiss cheese served at church?
A. Because it's holy! (Or spell this *holey* for extra spirit.)

So what causes the famous holes in Swiss cheese? The simple answer is that they're created by the expansion of gas within the cheese curd during the ripening period.

VOILÀ! VIVE LE FROMAGE CHAPEAU!

Cheeseheads around the world are fascinated by the Cheesehead hat and all the other accoutrements produced by Ralph Bruno of Foamation. Bruno is tagged "Father of Fromage" for coming up with the idea of turning a cheese wedge into a hat. That 1987 creation was followed by cheese neckties, cheese car dice, and numerous other proclamations of fondness for fromage.

Bruno, from Milwaukee's South Side, agreed that hat wearers tend to have a healthy sense of humor about themselves. He carved up his family's sofa to create his first chapeau.

"The Cheeseheads are a diverse bunch, all bound together by one thing: the cheese," he has emphasized. Hats and related cheese gear are sold internationally.

Tim Merkt of Tim & Tom's Cheese Shop & More in Kenosha models a fabled cheese hat. The store is a popular stop for tourists seeking great cheese and cheese paraphernalia. Photo by Martin Hintz

A more thorough explanation begins by noting that three types of bacteria are used in the production of Emmentaler: *Streptococcus thermophilis*, *Lactobacillus* spp., and *Propionibacterium shermanii*. When the latter (*P. shermanii*) is added to the cheese mixture and heated, carbon dioxide bubbles are created, becoming the traditional holes.

Adjusting the temperature, acidity, and curing time of the mixture controls the dimension of the holes, or "eyes." Larger eyes are formed when the curing time is longer and the temperature higher, factors which punch up the flavor because the acting bacteria and enzymes have more time to mature.

Working with Swiss Cheese

Depending on availability and your taste preference, Emmentaler, Gruyère, traditional Swiss cheese, and Raclette can be used interchangeably in recipes. As with most cheeses, four ounces of Swiss cheese equals one cup shredded.

- If you need to use a low-fat version in a recipe, substitute shredded Monterey Jack cheese.
- Allow Swiss cheese to breathe at room temperature for about thirty minutes before serving as part of a cheese plate.
- When you're melting Swiss, cook it slowly over low heat to avoid a rubbery texture.

"as i was crawling through the holes in a swiss cheese the other day, it occurred to me to wonder what a swiss cheese would think if a swiss cheese could think and after cogitating for some time i said to myself if a swiss cheese could think it would think that a swiss cheese was the most important thing in the world just as everything that can think at all does think about itself."

—Don Marquis, *archygrams* (1933). In this book Archy, a cockroach poet, writes to Mehitabel the cat. Since the roach can't type capital letters as he jumps around the typewriter, letters to his feline friend are written entirely in lowercase.

- To store Swiss cheese, be sure to tightly wrap it. Blocks can be refrigerated for up to two months; sliced, one month. Remember that the cheese will continue to age in the refrigerator and will become increasingly sharper.
- To freeze Swiss cheese, it is best to prepare it in blocks smaller than half a pound. Wrap each block in plastic wrap or foil, place it inside a zip-top bag, and squeeze out as much air as possible. Use within six months.
- Frozen cheese is fine in cooking, although it might be a bit crumbly. After defrosting in the refrigerator, it should be used quickly.

Hasli-Filee

Dinner guests will love this rich, delicious, and elegant way to serve pork.

I large pork tenderloin (1½–2 pounds)

I tablespoon butter, clarified

I cup sliced mushrooms

I medium onion, sliced

I tablespoon chopped parsley

½ cup white wine

¾ cup cream

Salt, pepper, thyme, and mustard to taste

1½ cups grated Gruyère cheese

1. Brown the tenderloin in hot, clarified butter. Add the mushrooms, onion, and parsley. Deglaze with the white wine and simmer for about 15 minutes.
2. Remove the meat. Cut it into 1-inch slices and arrange them artfully around an ovenproof platter. Keep warm.
3. Preheat the broiler. Add the seasonings and cream to the mushroom mixture and bring just to boiling.
4. Pour this mixture over the tenderloin, and cover the meat and sauce with grated cheese.
5. Melt the cheese under the broiler and serve immediately.

SERVES 6

Recipe from Fritzie Meier, Old World Swiss Family Recipes, *second edition, Monroe Swiss Singers, Monroe, Wisconsin (www.MonroeSwissSingers.org).*

Rösti (Swiss Fried Potatoes)

The amounts of potatoes, onion, and cheese in this recipe can easily be varied to suit your taste—and your guests' appetites.

4–6 medium-size potatoes

3 tablespoons butter, melted

½ onion, chopped (optional)

**½ cup shredded Swiss, Gruyère, or
  Emmentaler cheese, divided**

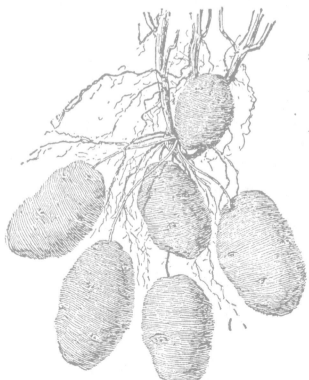

1. The day before: Peel the potatoes and boil or bake them until fork-tender. Refrigerate until you're ready to use them.
2. Shred the potatoes.
3. Melt the butter in a nonstick skillet, adding the onion and frying until translucent.
4. Add the shredded potatoes and about half the cheese. Fry and stir just a bit. Then fry without stirring for 5 to 10 minutes until a golden crust has formed on the bottom. Turn with a spatula. Press down and brown the other side.
5. Season with salt, pepper, and the remaining cheese.

SERVES 6 FOR AN APPETIZER OR 4 AS A MAIN COURSE

Recipe from Pater Waterman and Gloria Jackson, Old World Swiss Family Recipes, *second edition, Monroe Swiss Singers, Monroe, Wisconsin (www.MonroeSwissSingers.org).*

Southern Wisconsin's Green County saw an influx of immigrants in the early 1800s, including migrants from England, Ireland, Germany, and eventually Switzerland. All brought their Old World dairying knowledge with them to their new home. Specialized cheesemakers started operations in the county in the 1850s, with business further spurred by an exploding market for semi-hard cheeses—such as traditional Swiss varieties—in the late 1800s.

MONROE

The town of Monroe became a rail hub for cheese distribution and the focus of wholesale and retail cheese sales. The community—established in 1835—is nicknamed the "Swiss Cheese Capital of the USA."

This hand-cranked butter churn is one of the many milk processing artifacts displayed at the Historic Cheesemaking Center in Monroe.

Photo by Martin Hintz

Monroe's entire central business district, with its courthouse and nineteenth- and twentieth-century commercial buildings, was placed on the National Register of Historic Places in 1982. Two neighborhoods, with some homes dating to 1870, have been designated National Historic Districts.

The town also hosts the Historic Cheesemaking Center, located in the former rail depot through which millions of pounds of cheese were shipped before the advent of trucks. The museum site is easily identifiable because the front door is flanked by two copper cheese kettles, each able to hold 3,200 pounds of milk. Exhibits include old-time cheesemaking equipment, a library, and a photo archive.

NEW GLARUS

Nearby New Glarus was founded in 1845 by pioneers from the Swiss canton of Glarus. Only 1,700 residents live in this charming, rural village reminiscent of a typical Swiss town. Some buildings are more than a century old. There are butchers, bakers, and, yes, cheese shops, many of which showcase cow statues painted by Wisconsin artists outside their doors. A historical village on the west side of town depicts life on the Wisconsin frontier prior to the Civil War. The townsfolk annually stage productions of *Heidi*, a Swiss folk tale about a girl living in the Alps, and *Wilhelm Tell*, of apple-shooting fame. A number of the shows are staged in the traditional Swiss-German dialect.

CHEESE DAYS

Green County Cheese Days began in 1914 when a group of local Monroe businessmen organized a celebration to honor area farmers and cheese producers. They publicized their event by driving a roadster through town with a hand-lettered sign proclaiming FIRST CHEESE DAY COMMITTEE 1914—WE STARTED SOMETHING. Today upward of 80,000 people attend the three-day event held the third weekend in September in even-numbered years.

Festivalgoers can purchase chunks of cheese; dance to polka tunes; enjoy performances by Swiss yodelers, the New Glarus Kinderchor (children's choir), and the Maennerchor (men's choir); and tour the Heart of Cheese Days Exhibit to see traditional *scherenschnitte* (scissor paper cuts) and *bauernmalerei* (folk-art paintings). Cow-milking contests and a huge two-hour parade are also part of the fun. The Berghoff and Blues Festival is held on the grounds of Monroe's century-plus-old Joseph Huber Brewery two blocks south of the courthouse.

The Cheese Days king and queen are crowned at Monroe's Turner Hall on the first day of the celebration. The royal court is

Henry and Melva Tschanz, king and queen of the 2006 Green County Cheese Days, show off their colorful Swiss clothing and smooth dance steps.   Photo courtesy of Green County Cheese Days

introduced, and the Swiss ambassador to the United States comments about the links between Green County and the Alpine homeland. A fountain with cascading Swiss chocolate is a culinary hit. The Cheesemaker's Ball is held on Saturday, drawing cheese producers and dairy farmers, as well as their families, from around the area. Samples of prizewinning cheeses are always offered to the polka-ing partygoers.

Ida's Swiss Zucchini Rounds

When our crop of zucchini arrives, we seem to eat it on a daily basis. We often grill it, baste it with olive oil, and top it with a little Parmesan. But we're always looking for new recipes. This is a good one, and delicious with any of your favorite grilled meats.

⅔ cup Bisquick

½ teaspoon salt

⅛ teaspoon pepper

⅔ cup grated Swiss cheese

1 large egg, beaten

2 cups unpeeled, shredded zucchini (about 2 medium)

2–3 tablespoons butter

1. In a mixing bowl, combine the Bisquick, salt, pepper, and cheese. Stir in the egg until the mixture is moistened. Fold in the zucchini.
2. In a 10-inch skillet, melt the butter over medium heat. Drop in 2 tablespoons of batter for each round.
3. Cook for 2 to 3 minutes on each side or until nicely browned. Serve warm.

MAKES 12 ROUNDS

Recipe from Jocelyn Kline, Old World Swiss Family Recipes, *second edition, Monroe Swiss Singers, Monroe, Wisconsin (www.MonroeSwissSingers.org).*

CHEF NOTE:
This recipe can easily be doubled.

Open-Faced Sandwich Layered with Wisconsin Baby Swiss, Eggplant, and Peppers

Reuben's Deli in New York City was famous for its sandwiches—often named for well-known show business personalities. "The Walter Winchell" consisted of sturgeon, Swiss cheese, and sliced dill pickles on rye. "The Barbara Stanwyck" comprised corned beef, bacon, and melted Swiss on toasted rye. Giving itself a pat on is own back, the deli's trademark sandwich was "The Reuben's," with hearty slices of ham, turkey, and Swiss, augmented by coleslaw and Russian dressing, and served on dark rye bread. These open-faced sandwiches are another way to treat yourself to Wisconsin Swiss on bread—clearly a winning combo.

8 slices eggplant, ¼ inch thick

¼ cup flour

Olive oil

Salt and pepper

4 slices Italian bread

I clove garlic, cut in half

6 ounces thinly sliced Wisconsin Baby Swiss cheese

Fresh basil leaves

¾ cup roasted red peppers (about 2 medium)

6 ounces thinly sliced Wisconsin Monterey Jack cheese with peppers

1. Preheat the oven to 450°F.
2. Coat the eggplant slices with the flour. Cook the eggplant in 2 tablespoons of hot oil over medium-high heat until soft, about 2 minutes on each side, adding more oil as necessary. Or you can grill each side until brown. Season with salt and pepper to taste.
3. Brush one side of each bread slice with more oil; rub with the cut side of the garlic clove. Place the slices directly on an oven rack and bake for 5 minutes or until lightly toasted. Remove (but leave the oven on).
4. On each bread slice, layer Swiss cheese, eggplant, basil, peppers, and Monterey Jack cheese.
5. Place the sandwiches on a baking sheet and bake for 5 minutes or until the cheese is melted.
6. Garnish with additional basil and serve.

SERVES 4

Courtesy of Wisconsin Milk Marketing Board, Inc.

A Raclette party is the trendy alternative to a fondue soiree.

With the advent of Raclette machines, we've found that making these fun dishes is a great way to entertain. There are different varieties of machines. Some have a stainless-steel cheese holder that can accommodate a half round or half square of cheese. These also include a sturdy base and quartz-light mechanism for melting the cheese. The holder swivels and slants downward so the melted cheese can easily be scraped onto a plate.

Other, fancier varieties are small oval or rectangular portable ovens that sit on the table. The upper portion is a nonstick grill to cook meat, fish, vegetables, or bread. Below is a warming oven to heat the Raclette, with individual cooking trays. Choose from the grilled items, putting them on an individual cooking tray and heating it all in the lower oven. You remove your tray when the cheese browns and bubbles (about three to five minutes), scrape the concoction onto a plate with a small wooden or plastic spatula, and top your dish with even more of whatever items you please from the grill.

Having a Raclette party is a fun, casual way to entertain, but organization is the key to a successful soiree! Everything can be cooked, chopped, diced in advance so the host or hostess can enjoy a leisurely evening. Almost any cheese can be used for Raclette—Swiss, Cheddar, Parmesan, Gouda, whatever you're in the mood for. Prepare grilling items and sides beforehand also—steak, seafood, vegetables, bread, gherkins, pickled onions, and so forth. Or you can make your more complex recipes in advance, put them into the individual trays at the last minute, top them with cheese, and bake in the Raclette oven. Shortly before everyone sits down to dinner, preheat the items on the grill; then it's up to your guests to plunge in!

POTATOES AND BRUSSELS SPROUTS

Boil 1 pound each of small, firm potatoes and brussels sprouts until tender, about 20 minutes. Drain and let cool. Cut each in half, and sauté and brown them in a little butter or olive oil. Put them on your Raclette tray topped with grated Raclette cheese and even sautéed onions. Broil until melted, about 3 minutes.

MINI CHEESEBURGERS

We love making tiny cheeseburgers on our Raclette machine. For 1 pound of hamburger, we mix in 2 tablespoons Worcestershire sauce, salt, pepper, and 1 egg. After grilling them on the top of the machine, we add cheese (an aged Cheddar is our favorite) and bake in the Raclette oven for about 3 minutes. These are delicious served with slices of cucumber and a cucumber relish made from 2 small chopped pickling cucumbers, 1 small onion, and ½ cup ketchup. We serve them on mini hamburger buns . . . and don't forget the gherkins!

RACLETTE AND VEGETABLES

Precooked vegetables—sautéed fennel, eggplants, peppers, carrots, onions—are all delicious topped with cheese and baked Raclette-style. Or you can make your favorite ratatouille or spinach dish, top it with Parmesan, and bake in the oven.

FRENCH BREAD, RACLETTE-STYLE

Put a slice of tomato on garlicked French bread (melt chopped garlic together with a bit of butter and spread this on bread). Heat with a piece of Raclette atop and serve with pickles and mustard.

Wisconsin Swiss Rarebit

Welsh rarebit is a recipe that has been around for ages. The Milwaukee Cookbook and Business Directory *(1881) included this recipe from one Mrs. Helmus M. Wells: "Half-pound of cheese, one tablespoon of butter, one teaspoon made mustard, little cayenne pepper, one tablespoon of very fine bread crumbs, soaked in milk. Rub bottom of heated pan with butter; put in cheese, stirring fast; when melted, put in butter, next mustard, pepper; lastly, crumbs pressed dry. Spread smoking hot on toast. Serve at once." Here's an updated version.*

2 tablespoons butter

¾ pound mushrooms, sliced

½ teaspoon salt

3 tablespoons flour

1½ cups dry white wine

½ teaspoon dried tarragon

5 medium scallions, thinly sliced

I cup (4 ounces) Wisconsin Swiss cheese

4 slices pumpernickel or sourdough bread, toasted

Ground nutmeg, to taste

Black pepper, to taste

1. In a large skillet, melt the butter; add the mushrooms and salt. Cook for about 10 minutes over medium heat, stirring frequently.
2. Gradually add the flour, stirring constantly. Cook and stir for about 1 minute.
3. Add the wine and tarragon; cover and simmer for about 15 minutes.
4. Shortly before serving, stir in the scallions and cheese. Cook over low heat until the cheese melts, stirring constantly.
5. To serve, place one bread slice on each serving plate or shallow bowl. Ladle the rarebit over the top. Sprinkle with nutmeg and black pepper. Serve immediately.

SERVES 4

Courtesy of the Wisconsin Milk Marketing Board, Inc.

Today's Wisconsin makers of Swiss cheese, like their compatriots with other varieties, continue to be regular international award winners. The Chalet Cheese Cooperative in Monroe has captured championships with its 20-pound Natural Smoked Swiss Wheel, as well as for other types of cheese. Master Cheesemaker Bruce Workman, owner of Edelweiss Cheese Company, has won international honors for his Emmentaler, as has Jim Klein with Swiss Valley Farms in Platteville, near Green County.

THE VOEGELIS AND THEIR HERD

Bryan and Beth Voegeli own 140 head of Brown Swiss dairy cattle, which are milked twice daily at their farm near Monticello, Wisconsin. The sprawling complex of barns, sheds, lofts, and outbuildings lies between New Glarus and Monroe. The Voegelis' milk is then sold to the nearby Chalet Cheese Company. Voegeli is a fifth-generation dairy farmer who puts in up to fourteen hours a day, seven days a week, working around the 800-acre family farmstead. He also leases another 1,100 acres to grow corn, soybeans, and wheat.

Voegeli, of Swiss heritage, prefers raising the Brown Swiss cow, which he feels "has the best set of feet and legs and is more rugged than Holsteins."

The high protein count in the Brown Swiss milk also makes it good for cheese.

PLATTEVILLE CHEESE

The Platteville Cheese Company in Platteville, Wisconsin, has been producing award-winning cheeses at the state, national, and international levels for about forty years. The plant is famous for the high-quality Swiss cheese, both Emmentaler and Baby Swiss, made by cheesemaker Robert Biddle. In 2005 Platteville's Emmentaler Swiss took second place at the National Milk Producers Federation's annual cheese competition, while its Baby Swiss took third in the 2005 World Dairy Expo Swiss cheese competition.

SWISS COLONY

Mail-order giant Swiss Colony of Monroe, Wisconsin, annually sends millions of catalogs to devoted friends around the country. It was 1926 when Raymond Kubly first got the idea of selling cheese by mail. Using his family's basement and garage, Kubly began by "chunking" cheese—that is, using a butcher knife to cut consumer-size pieces of cheese for wrapping and shipment. It wasn't long before his fledgling firm moved into expanded quarters and branched out into mailing sausages, meats, and pastry desserts.

It took a lot of helping hands to wrap cheese in the early days at The Swiss Colony in Monroe.   Photo courtesy of The Swiss Colony and Green County Cheese Days

Soon Swiss Colony needed extra railcars brought to Monroe to handle the volume of orders prior to the Christmas holidays. In 1948 alone more than one million pounds of cheese were processed, wrapped, and assembled into gift packages. Even now, during the holiday rush, Swiss Colony employs more than 6,000 temporary workers to handle the crunch, augmenting its full-time staff of 1,200.

Today the firm remains one of the largest direct-marketing companies in the United States and now sells many nonfood items, including kitchen appliances, clothing, and furniture. It also has a major Web presence, accounting for 25 percent of sales. Still, cheese remains vital to Swiss Colony, which shipped 1,572,241 pounds in 2006. Medium Cheddar is the most popular.

Bartolotta's Lake Park Bistro Macaroni Gratin

This classy and nourishing version of mac-and-cheese was created by Adam Siegel, executive chef of Bartolotta's Lake Park Bistro in Milwaukee.

¼ cup diced bacon

⅓ cup diced onion

¼ cup diced boiled or baked ham

2 cups heavy whipping cream

¼ cup freshly grated Gruyère cheese

6 cups *cooked* penne pasta

6 tablespoons freshly grated Parmesan cheese, divided

¼ cup panko bread crumbs

1. In a large sauté pan, cook the bacon until crisp. Remove it from the pan; add the onion and cook until soft. Add bacon and ham and heat through.
2. Add the cream and Gruyère and bring the mixture to a boil. Gradually stir in the pasta; return to a boil.
3. Cook over medium heat for 5 to 10 minutes or until the sauce is thickened and coats the pasta. If the mixture is too dry, you can add extra cream.
4. Preheat the broiler.
5. Mix in ¼ cup of the Parmesan cheese. Turn the mixture into a 1½- to 2-quart casserole, top with the bread crumbs, and broil for 2 to 3 minutes or until the top is golden.
6. Serve topped with the remaining 2 tablespoons of Parmesan.

SERVES 4

Courtesy of Adam Siegel, executive chef, Bartolotta's Lake Park Bistro, Milwaukee, Wisconsin.

Jones Canadian Bacon, Spinach, and Swiss Frittata

In 1889 dairyman Milo Jones had a hankering for sausage, the kind his mother used to make. Although he had rheumatoid arthritis and could no longer operate his farm, he did begin making that special sausage, selling it to friends and neighbors. Word of the flavorful product spread, and Jones's new business began to grow. Today, six generations later, the Jones family still operates the original farm as well as producing sausages, bacons, hams, and other packaged meats. These innovative folks were the first meatpackers to quick-freeze sausage and to create "light" sausage products.

1 tablespoon olive oil

⅓ cup thinly sliced sweet onions

10 Jones Canadian bacon slices, sliced into julienne strips (¼ inch thick)

6 large eggs

¼ cup heavy cream or half-and-half

1 cup fresh baby spinach, wilted, or 1 package (10 ounces) frozen spinach, thawed and drained

½ cup bottled roasted red pepper strips, well drained

½ teaspoon salt

¼ teaspoon freshly ground black pepper

¾ cup shredded Swiss cheese

CHEF NOTE:

To turn this into a low-fat, low-carb recipe, substitute 1 percent milk and reduced-fat Swiss cheese for the dairy products; use 3 cups of spinach instead of 1.

1. Pour the olive oil into a 10-inch nonstick skillet over medium heat. Add the sweet onions; cook for 1 minute. Add the Canadian bacon and cook for 3 minutes or until the onions are tender, stirring frequently.
2. Meanwhile, in a large bowl, beat the eggs with the heavy cream or half-and-half. Add the spinach, roasted peppers, salt, and pepper; mix well. Stir this into the cooked Canadian bacon mixture in the skillet, blending well.
3. Cook for 8 minutes or until the bottom of the frittata is golden brown, lifting the edges with a spatula to allow the uncooked eggs to flow underneath.
4. Preheat the broiler. Top the frittata with the cheese and place the skillet under the broiler (or in a hot oven) until the center is set and the cheese is melted. Cut into wedges.

SERVES 4

Courtesy of Jones Dairy Farm, Fort Atkinson, Wisconsin.

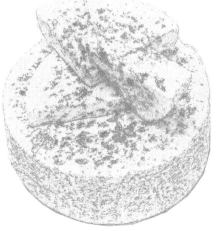

CHAPTER 5

BLUE AND GORGONZOLA CHEESES

BLUES, OR BLEUS, ARE GAINING POPULARITY AROUND the culinary world, often the center of creative cuisine and the darling of trendy chefs. The excitement about blues is their versatility. They are delicious as a stand-alone— no self-respecting cheese plate would be without at least one label. Blues and their cousin Gorgonzola can be crumbled into numerous recipes. They cook well, adding an interesting texture, flavor, and variety to many dishes.

Blue is a marvelous semi-soft cheese variety delicately laced with blue-green veins, the result of mold spores. It's usually made from cow's milk, although goat and sheep varieties are becoming more popular. Today most blue cheeses either are injected with the mold or have it churned with the curds to ensure even distribution. The cheeses are then aged to achieve their piquant flavor, which ranges from very earthy to mild.

Blue cheeses were originally produced in caves where mold is a natural phenomenon. As with many great discoveries, the first blues were probably created by accident when cheese stored in the caves picked up the mold. Someone decided to taste the cheese instead of throwing it out. The resulting strong flavor was of course wonderful, and thus was "blue" born.

The process has come a long way since then. Internationally, there are at least several dozen favorites. Among the most popular are Ireland's mellow Cashel Blue, Germany's smooth Cambozola, Denmark's creamy Danablu, and England's famous Stilton and Shropshire Blue. France gives us Roquefort, Bleu D'Auverge, and Forme d'Ambertpro. Spanish cheesemakers make the knockout foil-wrapped Cabrales and the intense, slightly salty Valdeon.

Back in the States, the famous Maytag Blue Cheese was formalized by researchers at Iowa State University in 1941, utilizing pasteurized milk from Maytag Dairy Farms' prizewinning herd of Holsteins. Initial production was begun by Fred Maytag II of the famed appliance-producing family after he learned of the process. Maytag Blue is also aged in specially designed caves, just like the good old days.

Gorgonzola is named for a village near Milan, Italy, where it was first made in AD 879. In Wisconsin, Gorgonzola is made in two styles: Italian and American. The Italian has an inedible brown rind and a creamy interior, which ripens and becomes earthy tasting. The American style is firmer and more crumbly. Both are creamy in color with bluish green veins.

Pairing wine with blues or Gorgonzola is always a matter of personal choice. The Wisconsin Milk Marketing Board suggests serving a Pinot Noir, Burgundy, port, late-harvest Riesling, red or white sweet, fruity red, or Amarone (full-bodied red) vintage. With blue cheese recipes, however, we have found that crisp white wines, such as Pinot Grigio or Pinot Gris, and dry, sparkling wines like champagne work well.

Wisconsin leads the United States in the production of blue-veined cheeses, in terms of both quantity of cheese and number of blue cheese plants; indeed, our state produces more than 80 percent of the nation's blues. From four Dairy State facilities in the 1980s, there are at least twelve plants today that make an estimated fifty million pounds of blues annually. Creative cheesemakers are making blues in a variety of ways: raw-milk blues, aged and smoked blues, goat's and sheep's milk blues. As usual, Wisconsin is at the forefront of developing new and exciting blues.

Given the tangy taste of blue cheeses, pairing them with a strong beer like Chimay Blue is recommended by folks at our favorite beverage outlets. This beer's yeasty fragrance and hint of roasted malt augment the taste of the cheese.

Working with Blues

- For easier crumbling and to create uniform pieces, place ½-inch slices of blue cheese into the freezer until they're firm—about half an hour. The cheese will be much easier to handle.
- If you're making sauces with blue cheese, slow cooking is required to avoid a grainy melt.
- Because of their high moisture content, blues will reach room temperature faster than many harder cheeses.
- When serving blue cheeses, make sure to wipe down wheels with a disposable towel before cutting—they have a tendency to "weep," or lose moisture.
- To develop more blue veins in a blue cheese that currently has few of them, leave the chunk unwrapped and at room temperature for a short time. Exposure to oxygen will encourage the growth of the blue *Penicillium* mold.

Always refrigerate your blue cheese. After being exposed to air, the blue mold will grow rapidly and cause the flavor and odor to get stronger, according to the Wisconsin Milk Marketing Board.

Dried Fruit and Blue Cheese with Pecans

This is a versatile "one-bite" delicacy, so try using a variety of dried fruits. If they're available, fresh figs make a special treat. As an hors d'oeuvre, pass these treats to party guests or leave them on the buffet table and watch them disappear. You can also serve the dish either as a tasty tidbit at the beginning of the meal or a delicious dessert.

40 dried apricots (or dates, prunes, or fresh figs)

Water

4 teaspoons pure vanilla extract

⅔ cup coarsely chopped pecans

1 cup (4 ounces) cream cheese, cut into chunks, room temperature

3 ounces (¾ cup) crumbled Wisconsin blue cheese

1 tablespoon French brandy

½ tablespoon grated yellow onion

> **CHEF NOTE:**
> We use Calvados as the brandy in this recipe. If you prefer a nonalcoholic mixture, substitute sherry extract. Start with ¼ teaspoon and add to taste.

1. Place the apricots in a saucepan. Add water barely to cover. Stir in the vanilla and bring the apricots to a boil, uncovered. Simmer for about 4 minutes until they're tender but not limp. Drain, dry well, and set aside.
2. Preheat the oven to 375°F. Spread the pecans on a baking sheet and toast them for 4 to 5 minutes, until aromatic. Stir after 2 minutes, and be careful that they do not scorch. Remove and cool. Whirl the pecans in a blender or food processor until they're very fine. Set aside.
3. Place the cream cheese, Wisconsin blue cheese, and brandy in the bowl of a food processor or electric blender. Pulse until all the ingredients are well blended. Add the onion and pulse briefly to incorporate. Remove the mixture to a bowl and refrigerate for at least 2 hours.
4. Place a teaspoon of the mixture atop each apricot, neatly rounding it with a spoon. Dip the top in the pecans.

MAKES ABOUT 40 PIECES

Inspired by a Wisconsin Milk Marketing Board recipe.

Wisconsin Buttermilk Blue and Asian Pear Salad

This mild-tasting blue makes a perfect companion to the sweetness of pears. Who says East and Midwest can't meet?

4 Asian pears

2 tablespoons walnut oil

1 tablespoon rice wine vinegar

3 ounces (¾ cup) crumbled Wisconsin Buttermilk Blue Cheese

½ cup walnut pieces, toasted

2 teaspoons minced fresh chives

Salt and pepper to taste

1. Core and slice each Asian pear and fan it out on an individual plate.
2. Combine the oil and vinegar and drizzle over the pears. Crumble and sprinkle the cheese, toasted walnuts, and minced chives on top. Season to taste with salt and pepper and serve.

SERVES 4

Courtesy of the Wisconsin Milk Marketing Board, Inc.

Endive and Avocado Salad with Wisconsin Blue Cheese

This is a beautiful party salad. Place it on a large round platter to create an eye-pleasing presentation. The mound of colorful carrots is ringed by the endive–blue cheese mixture.

Dressing

½ cup half-and-half (fat-free is great)

¼ cup mayonnaise

1½ tablespoons tarragon vinegar

1 tablespoon grainy mustard

1 teaspoon dried tarragon leaves

1. In a small bowl, stir together the half-and-half, mayonnaise, tarragon vinegar, mustard, and tarragon leaves.

Salad

3 heads Belgian endive

3 large avocados, thinly sliced

4 cups loosely packed, peeled and chopped carrots

6 ounces (1½ cups) crumbled Wisconsin Blue Cheese

¾ cup walnuts, toasted and chopped

1. Trim the endive heads and separate the leaves, arranging them in a circle on the platter. Top each endive leaf with a thin slice of avocado.
2. Toss 6 tablespoons of the dressing with the coarsely shredded carrots. Put the carrot mixture onto the middle of the platter.
3. Strew the crumbled Wisconsin blue cheese over each endive. Sprinkle with the walnuts. Drizzle the salad with the remaining dressing.

SERVES 8

Inspired by a recipe from the Wisconsin Milk Marketing Board, Inc.

Blues pair well with all types of meat. The process can be as simple as creating a supremely juicy Blue Burger by wrapping top-choice ground sirloin hamburger around a clump of blue cheese before cooking. For a special treat, try this using ground buffalo from Battle Creek Bison of Oconomowoc or any other member of the Wisconsin Bison Producers Association. A quality local butcher, such as Blau's Saukville Meats in Saukville, Ozaukee County, can offer both beef and bison for carnivore options.

Or crumble blue on top of high-quality steaks. The cheese can be tenderly melted and slathered across the meat surface after cooking, as is done by chef Chad Kornetzke of the critically acclaimed Lola's on the Lake Restaurant at the Osthoff Resort in Elkhart Lake, Wisconsin. This resort is near the historic Road America race track, regularly frequented by actor Paul Newman and other high-performance sports car fans.

Kornetzke uses four ounces of soft butter and four ounces of crumbled Hook's Blue Cheese, plus one minced shallot, a pinch of fresh thyme, salt, and pepper. He mixes the ingredients thoroughly, forms the butter mixture into a cylinder, and refrigerates. During the last minute of cooking steaks, the chef places two slices of this butter on top of each and then serves.

Or you can sprinkle blue atop a filet and then quickly crust it in the oven. This is the procedure finessed by chef JoLinda Klopp owner of Triskele's in the Walker's Point neighborhood of Milwaukee.

Using Gorgonzola, Klopp salts and peppers, then cooks her top Wisconsin Angus filet mignons to temperature. She mixes a quarter cup of cheese with a tablespoon of panko (Japanese bread crumbs). She then rubs the concoction on a steak during its last minute of cooking. The glaze can also be created under the broiler. If you're grilling, allow at least two minutes with the cheese atop the meat to create the delicious crust.

You can find coarse panko crumbs at specialty food stores, in the Asian section of large grocery outlets, or through the Internet. These crumbs stay crisp much longer than traditional bread crumbs. Tan-colored panko is made from the whole loaf; white panko, from bread minus the crusts.

Klopp also points out that you can make your own bread crumbs at home. First, rough-chop a loaf of dry bread in a blender; mix with the cheese. She suggests experimenting with different kinds of bread: White, wheat, rye, and other breads all add subtle flavor variations.

The Historic Trempealeau Hotel Quiche with Walnut Burger Crust

Walnut Burgers are premade burgers found in the freezer section of quality supermarkets and health food grocery stores throughout Minnesota, Wisconsin, and Iowa. They were developed by Trempealeau Hotel owners Jim and Linda Jenkins. You can use them to make a crust for any quiche—but this particular recipe is one of our favorites. Hotel chef Maximillian Wilda uses Mindoro Blue and Organic Valley Feta: "I like to use cheeses with a little more zip than the traditional American Cheddars," he says.

> **"It's great to see some small Wisconsin cheesemakers producing world-class quality specialty cheeses."**
>
> —Trempealeau Hotel chef Maximillian Wilda, Trempealeau, Wisconsin

I cup Walnut Burgers (4 burgers)

½ cup chopped green peppers

½ cup chopped onions

½ cup chopped mushrooms

6 large eggs

I ½ cups half-and-half

½ teaspoon sea salt

Dash pepper

½ cup chopped tomatoes

4 ounces crumbled **Mindoro Blue Cheese**

I teaspoon chopped fresh oregano or basil

2 ounces grated **Parmesan cheese**

1. Preheat the oven to 350°F.
2. Crumble and press the Walnut Burgers into a greased 10-inch pie plate or quiche pan to form a crust. Place in the oven for 10 to 15 minutes, until the crust begins to firm up and turn golden brown.
3. While the crust is baking, lightly sauté the green peppers, onions, and mushrooms.
4. Beat the eggs lightly and mix with the half-and-half, salt, and pepper.
5. On top of the cooled crust, place the green peppers, onions, mushrooms, tomatoes, and blue cheese. Pour the egg mixture on top.

CHEF NOTE:

This quiche freezes well; it can be warmed in the microwave oven after thawing.

6. Bake at 350°F for 45 minutes, or until the top is browned and a knife inserted into the center of the quiche comes out clean. Top with the Parmesan and chopped herbs.

SERVES 4–6; SERVINGS MAY VARY DEPENDING ON DESIRED THICKNESS OF CRUST

Courtesy of chef Maximillian Wilda, Trempealeau Hotel, Trempealeau, Wisconsin (www.walnutburger.com).

Chef Maximillian Wilda stands outside the Trempealeau Hotel, holding one of his famous quiches made with Mindoro Blue Cheese and Walnut Burgers.
Photo courtesy of the Trempealeau Hotel

Blue Crab Quiche

This is a very easy last-minute recipe, perfect for a lunch or even a light supper. We served this quiche with a hearty green salad, fresh-grilled and peppered zucchini from our garden, and a bottle of quality Pinot Grigio. Although many blues work, we love Salemville Blue with this recipe.

1 piecrust (prepared is fine if you don't have the time to make your own)

1 cup (1 6½-ounce can) lump crabmeat

¼ cup crumbled blue cheese

1 cup chopped or shredded hard mozzarella

1 green onion, chopped fine

⅛ teaspoon pepper

4 eggs

1 cup half-and-half (we prefer fat-free, such as that from Kemps)

¼ cup Parmesan cheese

1. Preheat the oven to 350°F.
2. Mix together the crab, cheeses, and onion and spread on the bottom of the crust.
3. Whisk together the eggs, milk, and pepper and pour this over the crab mixture in the crust. Sprinkle the Parmesan on top.
4. Bake for about 45 minutes. A knife inserted into the quiche about 1 inch from the crust should come out clean.
5. Allow the quiche to set for at least 5 minutes before serving—or serve at room temperature.

SERVES 4-6

CARAMELIZED BLUES

There is something heavenly about the combination of caramelized onions and blue cheese. We prefer using sweet Vidalia onions that caramelize without the addition of sugar.

PIZZA

You can make a delicious pizza with cooked chicken, caramelized onions, blue cheese, and julienned fresh basil sprinkled on top.

GRILLED CHEESE

Try a grilled blue cheese sandwich with caramelized onions on walnut raisin or other rustic country-style bread.

ROASTED ONIONS

Place 1-inch-thick onion slices on a rimmed baking dish, drizzle them with olive oil on both sides, and sprinkle with salt. Bake for about an hour at 400°F, turning a few times to prevent scorching. Place on a platter and top with more olive oil, a splash of sherry wine vinegar, a spoonful of lightly toasted sliced almonds, and a tablespoon of Gorgonzola or your favorite blue.

Pasta with Apples and Black River Gorgonzola

Black River Blue is a classic American blue from the North Hendren Cheese Cooperative in Willard, a hardy Slovenian community in Clark County, Wisconsin. The co-op has been making cheese for eighty years and began specializing in blue-veined cheeses in 2000. Since 2002 its Black River Blue and Black River Gorgonzola have consistently won top prizes across the nation. Both are creamy and exploding with flavor, with consistent veining.

1 cup heavy cream

2 tablespoons dry sherry (optional)

2 cups peeled and chopped apples

1 teaspoon pepper

2 cups crumbled **Black River Gorgonzola** or Blue, divided

1 pound pasta shells, cooked according to package directions and drained

1 cup coarse bread crumbs

½ cup slivered almonds, toasted

1. Preheat the broiler.
2. In a large saucepan, combine the cream, sherry, apples, pepper, and 1½ cups of the cheese. Cook over low heat until the cheese is melted and the sauce thickens, about 5 minutes.
3. Add the cooked pasta shells and mix to combine. Continue cooking on low heat for an additional 2 minutes.
4. Spoon the mixture into a shallow baking dish and sprinkle the top with the crumbs and toasted almonds.
5. Dot with the remaining cheese. Place the dish under the broiler until the crumbs are lightly browned.

SERVES 6

Courtesy of the DCI Cheese Company.

Graphic courtesy of DCI Cheese Company

Frittata I: Wisconsin Gorgonzola, Caramelized Onion, and Potato

What's the difference between a frittata and an omelet? After all, both feature eggs as the basic ingredient—and no self-respecting omelet or frittata would come without cheese. Well, the basic distinction between the frittata, which is from Italy, and the omelet, which originated in France, is the finished form. An omelet is filled with varying ingredients and folded during the cooking process, while a frittata is cooked flat with the ingredients mixed in.

20 small red potatoes

2 large onions, cut ⅛ inch thick

Olive oil

8 eggs

Salt and pepper to taste

4 ounces Wisconsin Gorgonzola cheese

1. Boil the potatoes until they're fork-tender, set them aside until they're just cool enough to handle, and chop them coarsely.
2. Caramelize the onions in the olive oil. Set aside.
3. Heat a heavy ovenproof pan. In it, sauté the chopped potatoes in more olive oil until they're brown, up to 15 minutes.
4. Preheat the broiler.
5. Beat the eggs well, seasoning to taste with salt and pepper. Pour this mixture over the cooked potatoes.
6. Cook the frittata by shaking and tilting the pan. With the aid of a wooden spoon, allow the uncooked eggs to run underneath the potatoes and set on the bottom. Cook for about 5 minutes, until the frittata is nearly set.
7. Sprinkle with the Gorgonzola and the caramelized onions; slide under a preheated broiler for about 2 minutes or until the frittata is set.

SERVES 4–6

Frittata II: Wisconsin Gorgonzola, Tomato, and Spaghetti Squash

This wonderful frittata was created by Wisconsin Milk Marketing Board ambassador chefs Mary and Greg Sonnier of Gabrielle restaurant in New Orleans, Louisiana.

Squash

½ small yellow onion, diced

¼ small red bell pepper, diced

2 tablespoons extra-virgin olive oil

I cup cooked spaghetti squash (see Chef
    Note), completely drained of any liquid

½ teaspoon salt

¼ teaspoon fresh-ground black pepper

1. In a small skillet, sauté the onion and bell pepper in 2 tablespoons of the olive oil until soft, 2 to 3 minutes.
2. Stir in the squash, salt, and pepper.
3. Remove the pan from the heat and set aside to cool.

CHEF NOTE:

To cook the spaghetti squash, preheat the oven to 350°F. Cut the squash straight through the middle; scrape out the seeds with a spoon and discard them. Put the squash halves cut-side down in a baking pan with about 1 to 2 inches of water. Cover with foil and bake for 30 to 50 minutes, depending on the size of the squash, until you can easily insert and remove a knife or fork. Remove from the oven and cool briefly. With a fork, pull the squash strands from the skin and place them on paper towels to absorb moisture.

Frittata

8 large eggs

I teaspoon salt

½ teaspoon fresh-ground black pepper

½ cup heavy cream

1½ teaspoons Worcestershire sauce

4 shakes Tabasco sauce

2 tablespoons extra-virgin olive oil

I medium tomato, thinly sliced

4 ounces Wisconsin Gorgonzola cheese,
    broken into 8 chunks

1. Preheat the oven to 350°F.
2. In a large bowl, whisk together the eggs, salt and pepper, cream, Worcestershire sauce, and Tabasco sauce.
3. Drain any liquid from the squash mixture and stir it into the eggs.
4. In a 10-inch, ovenproof skillet, heat the olive oil until slightly smoking. Pour in the egg–squash mixture. Remove the pan from the heat; top with the tomato slices and cheese.
5. Bake for 25 to 30 minutes or until the custard is set and slightly browned. Let the frittata rest for 10 minutes, then slide it onto a serving plate and cut into wedges.

SERVES 4-6

Courtesy of the Wisconsin Milk Marketing Board, Inc.

Brussels Sprouts with Blue Cheese and Pecans

Add this to your Thanksgiving menu and watch it disappear.

Glazed Pecans

I cup halved pecans

2 tablespoons water

I tablespoon sugar

¼ teaspoon cayenne powder

¼ teaspoon salt

1. Mix all the ingredients and place them on a tinfoil-lined baking sheet. Bake in a preheated 325°F oven for 15 minutes, or until pecans are brown. Remove from oven and let cool.

Vinaigrette Dressing

⅔ cup olive oil

⅓ cup balsamic vinegar

I teaspoon sugar

Salt and pepper to taste

1. Whisk together all the vinaigrette ingredients in a small bowl.

Brussels Sprouts

2 pounds brussels sprouts

3 tablespoons salted butter

Salt and pepper to taste

3 ounces crumbled Wisconsin blue cheese

1. Trim the brussels sprouts and cut an X in the base of each. Boil the brussels sprouts in salted water until they are tender, but still crisp. Heat the butter in a large pan and sauté the brussels sprouts over medium-high heat until golden brown. Season with salt and pepper.
2. Combine the brussels sprouts, blue cheese, and the glazed pecans in a large bowl. Drizzle on desired amount of vinaigrette dressing.

SERVES 8

Recipe inspired by many cheese-loving friends.

Grilled Peaches with Blue Cheese and Honey

Who said you can't add blue cheese to a dessert! All kinds of sweet treats are perfect for the mildly tangy touch of high-end Wisconsin blues and Gorgonzolas. Exquisite sweet white Sauternes or a late-harvest black Muscat adds a touch of extra class—or go all the way with an expensive ice wine. Check with your favorite wine shop for all your options.

2 peaches, cut in half

2 tablespoons olive oil

¼ cup crumbled Wisconsin blue cheese

4 teaspoons Wisconsin honey

1. Preheat the grill to medium high.
2. Brush the flat side of each peach half with olive oil; place them facedown on aluminum foil and grill until soft, about 10 minutes.
3. Serve each peach half with a tablespoon of blue cheese and a teaspoon of honey.

SERVES 2

Wisconsin's blue cheeses are also blue ribboned. First-place winners in the blue cheese category include Wisconsin Farmers Union Specialty Cheese, for both blue and Gorgonzola; Organic Valley; Carr Valley Cheese, for its Virgin-Pine Native Blue; DCI Cheese, for its Black River Blue; and the North Hendren Cooperative Dairy for many of its Black River Blues and Gorgonzola.

WISCONSIN FARMERS UNION

A leader of blue production is the Wisconsin Farmers Union Specialty Cheese Company plant in Montfort, a crossroads hamlet in west-central Wisconsin. The facility produces up to 84,000 pounds weekly, 90 percent of which is blue and 10 percent is Gorgonzola, according to the Wisconsin Cheesemakers Association. That amount is up from 48,000 pounds five years ago, reflecting the growing demand for blue cheeses. Farmers Union milk comes from farms within a 40-mile radius of its plant. Sales soared after its Montforte Gorgonzola Cheese was named the World's Best Gorgonzola Cheese at the 2006 World Championship Cheese Contest in Madison.

ROTH KÄSE

Roth Käse in Monroe is best known for its Gruyère, but the company markets a fantastic Buttermilk Blue, a tangy cow's milk cheese made at a cooperative dairy in Fond du Lac. This is a raw-milk cheese, usually from Jersey cows. It is inoculated with a closely held secret blend of cultures, then salted and cured for two to two and a half months before it leaves the dairy. It is made in five- to six-pound wheels with a foil wrap instead of a natural rind. Buttermilk Blue is creamy with a pungent fragrance and heavily veined with blue-gray.

Roth Käse also makes a Buttermilk Blue Affinee, which is a carefully chosen Buttermilk Blue that is aged in a curing room for at least six months, creating a distinct piquant taste. The company has also partnered with Sweden's VOD Gourmet to produce a Blue cheese with smoky Kentucky whiskey called WhiskeyBLUE, and smooth California port wine WineyBLUE.

SALEMVILLE CHEESE

In addition to its many awards over the years, the Salemville Cheese Cooperative gained international fame when its Gorgonzola was named Best American-Made Blue Cheese at the 2000 World Championship Cheese Contest. The co-op is based in Cambria, a village in Columbia County. The facility was founded in 1984 by thirty-nine area Amish farmers, whose herds range in size from four to about forty. The farmers still hand milk their cows twice daily. The co-op is now owned by DCI Cheese Company.

CARR VALLEY CHEESE

Carr Valley Cheese in La Valle makes a Billy Blue goat's milk cheese, which is aged for four months to give it that special oomph.

The same company's Virgin-Pine Native Blue is a cave-aged blue-veined cheese pierced with needles to allow molds to grow inside. It's made with either cow's or sheep's milk.

DOLCE GORGONZOLA

In 2005 Sartori Foods acquired the Linden Cheese Company. Linden's skill in producing high-end Gorgonzola augmented Sartori's already strong business. The company continued the tradition, making a rich and slightly sweet Dolce Gorgonzola. With its shorter aging time, this variety is a milder cheese than its aged relative. Chefs use the Dolce Gorgonzola on gourmet pizza; it's also great with polenta or risotto. We love it on French bread.

CHÈVRE BLUE

Made in Belmont, Montchevre Betin's Chèvre Blue goat cheese is an aged, crumbly blue that combines sharpness with the tang of a superb goat cheese. It's excellent on salads, but has enough depth to warrant enjoying alone. Or try it with a glass of Pinot Noir.

MINDORO BLUE AND GORGONZOLA

Swiss Family Farms, the maker of Mindoro Blue, is nestled in the hills of southwestern Wisconsin. In 2001 the plant was renovated and expanded due to the growing success of its blues and Gorgonzolas. Mindoro cheesemaker Richard Glick earned his Wisconsin Master Cheesemaker medal for blue cheese in the spring of 2004, the same year Mindoro Blue won a bronze medal at the World Cheese Awards in London. Swiss Family's Mindoro Blue cheese is aged sixty days; Mindoro Gorgonzola more than ninety.

Carr Valley's mouse mascot, Igor, is always ready for a parade. Photo by Martin Hintz

Cantaloupe Carpaccio with Crispy Prosciutto, Wisconsin Virgin-Pine Blue Cheese, and Rosemary Honey

This is a recipe developed by James Campbell, executive chef at the legendary El Farol Restaurant of Santa Fe, New Mexico. Renowned for his "Latino-Mediterranean blend" cuisine, Campbell is also a Wisconsin Milk Marketing Board ambassador.

I cup honey

2 sprigs fresh rosemary

2 cups vegetable oil

8 thin slices prosciutto

2 ripe cantaloupes

¼ cup extra-virgin olive oil

Salt

Black pepper

I cup crumbled Wisconsin Virgin–Pine
    Blue Cheese

1. Warm the honey and rosemary in a small saucepan over low heat for 2 to 3 minutes. Remove from the heat and let the pan rest for 2 to 3 hours. Remove the rosemary sprigs.
2. Heat the vegetable oil in a deep skillet over medium-high heat. Fry the prosciutto until crisp, about 1 minute. Drain and cool on a paper-towel-lined plate.
3. Peel the cantaloupes. Cut them in half and scoop out the seeds. Slice as thinly as possible with a very sharp knife. Arrange 4 or 5 slices on each of eight plates.
4. Drizzle the cantaloupe with the olive oil, then season with salt and pepper. In your hand, crush a piece of prosciutto and sprinkle over each plate. Top with blue cheese.
5. Drizzle with the reserved rosemary honey.

SERVES 8

Courtesy of the Wisconsin Milk Marketing Board, Inc.

Sprinkle your favorite blue on fresh-roasted beets, either the purple or the golden variety. But a caveat: The cheese takes on the beets' coloring, so it's important to serve the vegetables as soon as possible after adding the cheese. As an alternative, place a spoonful of cheese next to the cooked beets, which can be thinly sliced or halved. Garnish with a few leaves of fresh basil.

If fresh beets are not available, you can substitute canned. Drain the can, toss the beets with olive oil, then roast at 350°F for 20 to 30 minutes. Salt and pepper to taste and sprinkle with toasted almonds. Add the crumbled cheese—again, placing it either on top of or next to the beets.

Here are some more Blue Veggie ideas:

- Toss blue cheese with hot green beans and add almonds or cashews.

- Top a steaming baked Wisconsin potato with a crumbled blue.
- Toss blues with cooked corn, cut off the cob. A special treat is combining three ears of corn, cut from the cob, with four slices of cooked bacon, a fresh-chopped red pepper, two pounds of small boiled red potatoes, and three green onions. Make a vinaigrette of three parts olive oil to one part balsamic vinegar, fresh oregano, salt, and pepper. Simply delicious!

> **"Cheese: the adult form of milk."**
>
> —Richard Condon (1915–1996), American satirical novelist, playwright, and crime writer, from *A Talent for Living,* 1961

CHAPTER 6

GOAT AND SHEEP CHEESES

Goat Cheese

Goats are said to be the oldest domesticated farm animals. Most likely, the first cheese was made from goat's milk. According to legend, some long-ago nomad probably inadvertently made cheese when he transported milk in the stomach of a slaughtered animal, later to find that it had coagulated and formed curds. This is due to the reaction of the milk with the stomach enzyme, a natural rennet.

Goat cheese is a significant industry in France and continually gaining popularity in the United States. Most people associate goat cheese with chèvre—the French word for "goat." Actually, goat's milk can be made into a wide variety of cheeses: Cheddar, mozzarella, provolone, feta, Gouda, cottage cheese, and ricotta are among the most prevalent. Boulot is another type, a semi-hard cheese made from raw goat's milk and aged for a minimum of four to six months.

You can substitute goat cheeses for those made from cow's milk in any of the recipes in this book. But remember there is something special about the "goaty" flavor of this style of cheese that will add a unique taste to many recipes.

According to the Dairy Business Innovation Center, a nonprofit Wisconsin organization encouraging the growing specialty and artisan cheese business in the state, goat cheese is among the fastest-growing segments of the state's food industry. The Wisconsin Dairy Goat Association, which began in the 1930s and was later reactivated in 1946, has as its mission to "promote dairy goats, dairy goat products and youth involvement in dairy goats."

The goat's genial nature is another reason goat farming in Wisconsin is gaining popularity. Not only are the does and kids friendly, but they also require less food and

The gal goats at Misty Meadows Farm outside Monroe are an inquisitive lot.
Photo by Martin Hintz

space than other livestock, and can live on more marginal land. They are admirably hardy, doing well in the state's frosty winters. The bucks have a more questionable reputation, due to their randiness and—let's face it—malodor. Pam once had such a billy in the backyard, which ate everything in sight and bleated continuously. After several months, it was shipped off to a farm much more receptive to such creatures. We now have Thelma and Louise, two delightful Saanen does. Each has a distinct personality, as appropriate to their "Queens of the Dairy Goats" designation, with Thelma being the more outgoing and Louise of a more coquettish persuasion.

Goats are bred between August and March, with a gestation period of five months. They give birth to between one to four kids, after which they produce between half a gallon and three gallons of milk a day for about ten months.

Six types of dairy goats are recognized by the American Dairy Goat Association: Nubians, LaManchas, Alpines, Oberhaslis, Toggenbergs, and Saanens.

WHAT'S THE HEALTH BREAKOUT?

Milk Variety	Goat	Cow	Human
Protein	3.0	3.0	1.1
Fat (percent)	3.8	3.6	4.0
Calories per 100ml	70	69	68
Vitamin A	39	21	32
Vitamin B	68	45	17
Riboflavin	210	159	26
Vitamin C	2	2	3
Vitamin D	0.7	0.7	0.3
Calcium	0.19	0.18	0.04
Iron	0.07	0.06	0.2
Phosphorus	0.27	0.23	0.06
Cholesterol	12	15	20

FRESH CHÈVRE VERSUS CREAM CHEESE

Per ounce	Chèvre	Cream Cheese
Calories	69.4	99.5
Protein	4	2.1
Fat (grams)	5.5	10.0
Cholesterol (mg)	17.6	30.5
Sodium (mg)	83.4	84.5
Calories from fat (percent)	70.4	95.0

Tables courtesy of the Wisconsin Dairy Goat Association (www.wdga.org)

In the United States we have grown up on cow's milk, although many colicky babies found relief drinking goat's milk because it's easier to digest—in fact, its buffering qualities are perfect for treating ulcers. Surprisingly, as much as 70 percent of the world's population relies on goat's milk. Without maligning the cow industry, goat's milk is healthier in many ways, although it's still uncommon in mainline grocery stores.

After California, Wisconsin is now the second largest producer of goat milk. In 2006, according to the Wisconsin Agricultural Statistics Service, the number of goat dairy herds rose to 165, producing 27.6 million pounds of milk. In 2005, there were

142 licensed goat dairies in the state, with twelve plants making goat milk cheeses or blended cheeses.

What to pair with goat cheeses? While this depends on age of the cheese and the depth of its flavor, white wines usually link better than reds with salty goat cheese. And fresh chèvre with champagne is a marriage made in tasting heaven.

Making Goat Cheese

Making soft goat cheese is relatively easy, as explained by Wisconsin Dairy Goat Association members (who can provide numerous recipes). You simply need pasteurized goat's milk, a starter, liquid rennet, and salt. For chèvre, the first step is pasteurizing fresh goat's milk by heating it at 150°F for thirty minutes. Slowly and gently stir it to keep the fat molecules whole. Next, add a lactic culture with select bacteria, because pasteurization destroys bacteria. Then add a small amount of rennet. The cheese is drained for about twenty-four hours. It is weighed, salted (at 1 percent), and hand mixed. This fresh cheese should be eaten within two weeks.

Working with Goat Cheese

- Mild goat cheeses should be kept cold, tightly wrapped.
- Since goat cheeses are more delicate than cow, they should not be overbeaten or heated too quickly or they will become watery.
- Goat Cheddars are more flavorful; a lesser amount is needed for recipes.
- According to Katie Hedrich in *Moving Dairy Goats Forward*, the best way to cut soft goat cheese is with a piece of unflavored dental floss.

Spinach Salad with Strawberries and Warm Goat Cheese Rounds

Warm goat cheese rounds are a delicious addition to any salad, especially this one. The combination of the tart balsamic dressing and smooth goat cheese is fantastic. You can also bake goat cheese and serve it with a salad—that's what we do with our garden-fresh ingredients.

½ cup pine nuts

½ cup olive oil

3 tablespoons balsamic vinegar

2 teaspoons Dijon mustard

I teaspoon sugar

I teaspoon freshly ground black pepper

3 large egg whites

I teaspoon water

2 logs (3.2 ounces each) soft mild goat cheese

½ cup dry bread crumbs, plain or Japanese panko

2 tablespoons olive oil

I package (12 ounces) fresh spinach, washed, with stems removed

2 cups sliced strawberries

1. Sauté the pine nuts in an ungreased pan until they are golden, about 2 to 3 minutes. Set aside.
2. Combine ½ cup of the oil with the vinegar, mustard, sugar, and pepper; whisk well and set aside.
3. Whisk the egg whites and water. Cut the cold chèvre into slices about ⅓ inch thick. Dip each slice in the egg whites, shake off the excess, and coat both sides with the bread crumbs. The slices may be prepared ahead and cooked at the last minute.
4. Heat 2 tablespoons of olive oil and sauté the cheese rounds until golden, about 30 seconds per side.
5. Toss the spinach and pine nuts with the vinaigrette dressing. Place on individual plates. Top with a few goat cheese rounds and strawberry slices.

SERVES 4

Recipe inspired by Veronica Kozlowski and Katie Hedrich, courtesy of Moving Dairy Goats Forward *by the Wisconsin Dairy Goat Association (www.wdga.org).*

CHEF NOTE:
Another way to bake goat cheese for salads is to brush a 6-ounce round of Wisconsin goat cheese with 3 tablespoons of melted butter and roll it with ½ cup of plain bread crumbs mixed with a tablespoon of your favorite herbs (basil, oregano, parsley, salt). Bake in a preheated 400°F oven for 10 minutes. Serve with your favorite salad.

Grilled Tomato and Goat Cheese Napoleon with Cilantro Dressing

Chef Michael Feker, who originated this superb recipe, was born in Iran and grew up in Switzerland. He trained in France and in Southern California.

Tomatoes

4 tomatoes, sliced thick

Olive oil

Salt and pepper to taste

1. Brush the tomatoes with olive oil, salt, and pepper, and grill lightly. They should be soft but not mushy. Set them aside to cool.

Cilantro Dressing

2 cloves fresh-peeled garlic

2 cups extra-virgin olive oil (approximately)

I bunch cilantro, bigger stems removed

½ cup rice wine vinegar

Salt and white pepper to taste

1. In a blender, puree the garlic until smooth by adding a small amount of olive oil.
2. Slowly add cilantro and more oil until the cilantro is gone and you have a thick, smooth paste. Add the vinegar, salt, and pepper to taste.

Salad

¼ pound of your favorite goat cheese, room temperature

I bunch mixed greens

I red onion, thinly sliced

1. Arrange one piece of tomato in the center of the plate and top with a small spoonful of goat cheese. Place a small amount of cilantro dressing on top of the goat cheese. Top with another slice of tomato and repeat to form a small tower (about three or four slices).
2. On the side, prepare the mixed greens salad by tossing the greens, thinly sliced red onion, and remaining cilantro dressing. Arrange the greens around the tower as a garnish salad.
3. Serve immediately.

SERVES 4

Courtesy of Chef Michael Feker, Il Mito Restaurant, Milwaukee, Wisconsin.

CHEF NOTE:

Our other salad favorites include asparagus, goat cheese, and walnut pieces with salad greens. Red potatoes are also delicious with goat cheese.

Black Bean and Goat Cheese Tortas

Great for all ages, there's nothing b-a-a-a-d about this recipe.

2 cans (15 ounces each) black beans,
    drained

3 tablespoons ground cumin

1 teaspoon freshly ground black pepper

15 large flour tortillas

3 cups grated Cheddar cheese

12 ounces fresh goat cheese

Olive oil

Chili powder

Salsa

1. Preheat the oven to 475°F.
2. Place the beans, cumin, and pepper into a food processor; process until smooth.
3. Make three piles of five tortillas on your work surface. Divide the bean puree, Cheddar, and crumbled goat cheese on one tortilla. Place another tortilla on top, pressing down gently, and repeat the process until you have four layers. Place a tortilla on top. Repeat the entire layering process with the remaining bean puree, Cheddar, goat cheese, and tortillas. (You will have three tortas.)
4. Place the tortas on cookie sheets. Brush the top of each with olive oil and sprinkle lightly with chili powder.
5. Bake for about 5 minutes, or until the tortillas are softened and just starting to brown. Cut each into four wedges and serve with salsa.

SERVES 8

Recipe by Diana Murphy, courtesy of Moving Dairy Goats Forward *by the Wisconsin Dairy Goat Association (www.wdga .org).*

Mini Cheese Soufflés in Tomato Shells

When the bountiful summer crop of tomatoes arrives, this is an elegant way to use up some of the supply.

6 large tomatoes, firm and ripe

Salt

2 tablespoons unsalted butter

2 tablespoons finely chopped
    shallots

2 tablespoons flour

6 tablespoons heavy cream

4 egg whites

Pinch cream of tartar

6 egg yolks

½ teaspoon salt

½ teaspoon Emeril's Original
    Essence (or combination of
    your favorite herbs)

I cup finely crumbled fresh goat
    cheese or feta

I tablespoon finely grated
    Romano cheese

1. Preheat the oven to 400°F.
2. Cut the upper half from each tomato and scoop out the seeds and pulp.
3. Sprinkle the insides of the tomatoes lightly with salt and invert them on paper towel for 20 minutes.
4. In a small, heavy saucepan, melt the butter. Add the shallots and cook, stirring, for 2 minutes. Stir in the flour and cook, stirring, for 3 minutes.
5. Whisk in the cream and simmer, stirring constantly, for 5 minutes.
6. Using an electric mixer, beat the egg whites, adding a pinch of cream of tartar, until stiff peaks form.
7. Remove the cream sauce from the heat and whisk in the egg yolks, salt, Essence, and goat cheese.
8. Fold a quarter of the egg whites into the cheese–egg yolk mixture. Gently add the remaining egg whites.
9. Fill the tomato shells with batter until three-quarters full.
10. Place the tomatoes in a baking dish and sprinkle ½ teaspoon of Romano cheese over each. Place the tomatoes in the oven and immediately reduce the heat to 375°F.
11. Bake until the soufflés have risen and are golden brown on top, about 20 to 25 minutes. Do not open the door during baking. Remove and serve immediately.

SERVES 6

Recipe by Anna Hedrich from La Clare Farm, Chilton, Wisconsin, courtesy of Moving Dairy Goats Forward *by the Wisconsin Dairy Goat Association (www.wdga.org).*

CAPRI CHEESE

Capri Cheese is made from registered Nubian goat milk on the Thalhammer family's organic farm in Blue River, the heart of Wisconsin's Driftless area. They specialize in organic feta with milk pumped fresh from the parlor to the cheese vat at their cheese facility, which officially opened in 2001. Felix Thalhammer, the proprietor, is often seen at the Madison farmers' market. His favorite way to enjoy his feta year-round is to cut it into ¼-inch slabs and lay it on a cookie sheet that has been brushed with olive oil. He then tops it with ground black pepper and heats it in a 400°F oven for about 5 to 10 minutes, until it begins to brown around the edges. He serves it on lightly toasted rye sourdough or whole-grain bread.

DREAMFARM

Diana and Jim Murphy and their family live on an idyllic twenty-five-acre farm in Cross Plains, where they raise goats and chickens. After they fell in love with dairy goats, they decided to produce cheese; Diana subsequently became a licensed cheesemaker in 2004. The twenty milking dairy goats at Dreamfarm are pasture raised and supplemented with certified organic grain during lactation. Diana makes chèvre in a variety of flavors. She has two French

blends: Herbes de Provence with rosemary, thyme, savory, fennel seed, basil, lavender, and marjoram; and French Herb with chive, parsley, basil, tarragon, rosemary, and marjoram. She also makes plain chèvre and an Italian blend with tomato, onion, garlic, and fresh ground peppercorns. Other favorites are feta and Rosebud, a fresh cheese that can be sliced.

FANTOME FARM

Anne Topham, considered a pioneer of making French-style chèvre in Wisconsin, has been making farmstead goat cheese at Fantome Farm for twenty years. She and Judy Borree moved to Wisconsin from Iowa and bought a fifty-acre farm that sits high on a hill 40 miles west of Madison. With the help of friends, they built a barn for the goats and converted a garage into a small cheese factory they call a "cheeserie."

At Fantome Farm, Topham and Borree handcraft cheese in small batches with milk from about a dozen goats. It's not found at retail outlets, but you can see the two cheesemakers every Saturday during the growing season at the farmers' market on Madison's Capitol Square. Their deliciously delicate chèvre is made with pasteurized milk from their own herd. It's occasionally marinated and herbed, as well as providing a base for their Thyme Logs, which are dusted with herbs and cave aged for one to two weeks.

They also make small quantities of Boulot, a raw-milk semi-hard cheese that's aged for four to six months. Another new cheese is the farm's award-winning Fleuri, a round cave-aged cheese dusted with clean ash. This cheese, based on a variety Topham and Borree discovered in France, won second place at the 2006 American Cheese Society competition.

MISTY MEADOWS FARM

Laura Doll Jay and her husband, Antony, raise 200 milk goats on their Misty Meadows Farm north of Monroe, Wisconsin. Their days consist of 5:00 a.m. and 5:00 p.m. milkings of Nubians, LaManchas, Alpines, and Saanens they have raised from babies—or "kids" in goat-farmer language.

The young couple then sell the butterfat-rich milk to the Montchevre Betin dairy in Belmont (see below), where it's processed into various cheeses for grocery stores and specialty shops.

"I got my first goat, Misty, as a pet," says Laura. "We then named the farm, Misty Meadows, after her," she explains.

The couple began dairying in 2003, building milking stalls that handle eight animals at a time. "I started milking goats by hand and that got pretty tiring," Laura recalls of their start-up operations. "So we figured we needed a better

Laura and Antony Jay raise dairy goats north of Monroe. Shown with them is Misty, the farm's namesake. Photo by Martin Hintz

system." The flock now produces around 600 pounds of milk a day, and it's hard to keep up with the demand.

Antony's dad, Jeff—a design consultant for cheese factories in the United States, Mexico, and Latin America—helped in the construction of their milking parlor. A native of Bath, England, the elder Jay acted as immigration sponsor for his son, who met Laura seven years ago while the two worked at the Jung Garden Center in Madison. Laura is from Fox Point, a suburb of Milwaukee.

MONTCHEVRE BETIN

Located in the tiny town of Belmont, Wisconsin, Montchevre Betin was established in 1988. The company offers handcrafted goat cheeses containing no hormones, additives, or preservatives. Jean Rossard, the owner, mastered the art of cheesemaking in France and has cheesemaking in his genes. Both his grandmother and father made goat cheese in France. He is from Deux-Sevre, a wine and goat's milk region not far from Cognac in the southwest of France.

The company has an extensive list of goat cheeses. Among its award-winning products is a traditional aged Crottin, the winner of the gold medal at the 2002 World Cheese Competition. They also make a line of fresh Chèvre Logs in a variety of flavors: Plain, Garlic, Herb & 4 Peppers, Lemon Zest, Sun-Dried Tomato Basil, and Cranberry/Cinnamon, which took second prize at the 2002 Wisconsin State Fair. Other treats include goat Cheddars, goat fetas, aged chèvres, and a blue goat cheese called Chèvre in Blue. The newest addition to their line is called Darsonval, a semi-soft washed-rind goat cheese aged for ninety days. Its mild and sweet flavor makes it a great table cheese, or it can be substituted for Raclette in recipes.

MOUNT STERLING CHEESE COOPERATIVE

The Mount Sterling Cheese Cooperative is located in tiny Mount Sterling, Wisconsin (population: 217). It's the last working cheese plant in picturesque Crawford County but the country's largest goat's milk cheese co-op. Members hail from Wisconsin, Iowa, and Minnesota. The plant, incorporated in 1976, isn't far from the tourist mecca of Gays Mills and its fabled apple orchards. Many visitors there enjoy the tradition of loading up on Mount Sterling cheese before heading home.

The co-op specializes in Raw Milk Mild Cheddar; Raw Milk Sharp Cheddar; Pasteurized Cheddar; No-Salt Cheddar; Greek Style Feta; Fresh Jack; and Fresh Jack with Dill, Garlic, Onion, Chives, Jalapeño Peppers, and Tomato and Basil. The firm has also developed a smoked, raw-milk mild Cheddar. In addition, the Whey-Cream Goat Butter is recommended for anyone who can't have cow's milk.

Baked Goat Cheese with Sofrite

This recipe was created by Jack Kaestner, the executive chef at the Oconomowoc Lake Club and a part-time culinary instructor at Waukesha County Technical College.

About I pound Spanish onions

7 cloves garlic, divided

½ cup extra-virgin olive oil, divided

I teaspoon sea salt or kosher salt

28 ounces chopped plum tomatoes with juice

½ teaspoon ground black pepper

3 teaspoons herbes de Provence, divided

I teaspoon honey or sugar (optional)

12 ounces fresh Fantome Farm goat cheese

¼ cup (½ stick) salted butter

¼ cup grated Parmesan cheese

I or 2 baguettes

1. Preheat the oven to 350°F.
2. Cut the onions in half through the core end. Remove the core, set the onions cut-side down, and slice ¼ inch thick. You want about 5 cups of slices.
3. Finely chop 4 cloves of the garlic.
4. In a heavy 2-quart nonreactive saucepan, heat ¼ cup of the olive oil over medium heat. Add the onions and cook, uncovered, stirring every 5 minutes or so, for about half an hour. Steam should build up and sweat the onions. Liquid should build in the bottom of the pan as well. If the onions are dry, you can cover them and add a bit of water to build up steam.
5. Add the garlic and salt.
6. Reduce the heat and cook, stirring often, for 40 minutes or until the liquid is syrupy. The onions should have a golden hue to them.
7. Add the tomatoes, pepper, 1 teaspoon of herbes de Provence, and the sugar or honey if desired.
8. Cook over medium heat until the sauce thickens. Adjust the seasoning and cool.
9. Place the tomato mixture in the bottom of a 10x12-inch casserole and scatter walnut-size pieces of fresh goat cheese across the top. Splash the dish with a bit of olive oil if desired.

10. Place in the preheated oven and bake for 15 minutes. The cheese should just hold its shape after baking but will slightly fall apart. It should not brown.

11. While the goat cheese bakes, prepare the bread. You'll be baking it during the last 8 minutes alongside the cheese. Start by mincing the remaining garlic.

12. Melt the butter and mix in the Parmesan, remaining ¼ cup olive oil, and garlic.

13. Split the baguette and spread with the butter mixture. Sprinkle on the remaining herbes de Provence and toast in the oven for 8 minutes.

14. Turn the sofrite onto a plate or leave it in its casserole dish. Decorate with olives if desired. Slice the baguette into 2-inch pieces and serve warm with the sofrite.

FEEDS 8 HUNGRY GUESTS AS AN HORS D'OEUVRE

Courtesy of Jack Kaestner, executive chef at the Oconomowoc Lake Club.

Orange Curry Chicken Stuffed with Chèvre

The sauce created in this recipe is also wonderful on roasted or stuffed pork.

Orange Curry Sauce

½ cup maple syrup

2 tablespoons soy sauce

2 tablespoons ketchup

1 tablespoon Dijon mustard

2 teaspoons orange zest

1½ teaspoons curry powder

1 teaspoon Worcestershire sauce

2 cloves garlic, minced

1. In a medium-size bowl, mix all the ingredients with a whisk; set aside.

Chicken

4 boneless, skinless chicken breasts

5 ounces Woolwich Dairy Chevrai Goat Cheese, mini log (plain)

2 ounces vegetable oil (for frying)

1 ounce white flour (for dusting)

1. Preheat the oven to 350°F.
2. Slice a pocket into each breast lengthwise along the thicker inside.
3. Cut the Chevrai into four even portions, and place them inside the chicken pockets.
4. With two toothpicks, sew the pockets closed.
5. Heat the oil. Dredge the chicken in the flour to coat.
6. Place the breasts into the moderately hot oil and lightly brown on both sides. Transfer to a casserole dish, pouring the sauce atop.
7. Bake for 30 minutes, or until the breasts are no longer pink inside (the time varies with the thickness of the breasts). Baste the chicken with the sauce four or five times as it bakes.

SERVES 4

Recipe from Woolwich Dairy, courtesy of Moving Dairy Goats Forward *by the Wisconsin Dairy Goat Association (www.wdga.org).*

Goat Cheese and Fennel

Fennel lovers will delight in pairing fennel with a delicious goat cheese.

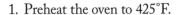

3 medium fennel bulbs, cut lengthwise in eighths, tops removed

Salt and pepper to taste

1 large egg yolk

½ cup crème fraîche

1 6-ounce log chèvre, sliced into ¾-inch rounds

2 tablespoons olive oil

1. Preheat the oven to 425°F.
2. Cook the fennel in boiling water seasoned with salt and pepper until it's tender, about 20 minutes.
3. Combine the egg yolk and crème fraîche with a pinch more salt and pepper.
4. Arrange the fennel in the bottom of an 8x8-inch baking dish or the equivalent.
5. Pour the crème fraîche mixture over the fennel. Place the chèvre rounds on top and drizzle with the olive oil.
6. Bake for about 20 minutes, until the cheese has just started to brown.

SERVES 4-6

THE FINICKY DAIRY GOAT?

We've all laughed at the joke that goats will eat anything, even cans. Actually, that fable, the staple of comics and cartoons for generations, might have started when someone saw a goat gnawing on a can's label—the paper and paste taste good to these critters.

While dairy goats need a constant supply of roughage, tin is not on the menu. They do love a rich pasture where they can happily browse, however. Crisp, dried hay can also be on their diet if they are penned. Offering them alfalfa is like presenting a fervent chocoholic with a tray of Valrhona bonbons made from premier Venezuelan cacao. A balanced grain ration and mineral supplements are especially beneficial to keep milkers healthy. Dairy goats also appreciate salt as their "condiment" of choice and demand fresh, clean water in their troughs.

Dairy goats have good table manners, at least for the animal world, and are picky about their foods. If served something they haven't tried before, they snuffle and sniff around the edges before sampling. Even a curious goat will turn up its nose at anything that doesn't meet its taste standards.

> **"Goats are not like cows. They won't run to the farthest end of the farm when you want to catch them. Goats will stampede into the barn with the first two drops of rain. They don't even like a sprinkle."**
>
> —Larry Hedrich, president, Wisconsin Dairy Goat Association

> **"Goats have distinct personalities. It's like living with a whole lot of teenagers. You don't know what's going to happen next, except that you know they're going to get out of their pen. They are looking for a chance to explore and prove they can do it. They won't run away but stand just 6 inches out of reach. But once you grab their collars, they amble back to the enclosure. It's all just a game with them."**
>
> —Larry Hedrich, president, Wisconsin Dairy Goat Association

Fried Green Tomatoes with Fresh Goat Cheese and Sun-dried Tomato Vinaigrette

This recipe comes to us thanks to chef David Swanson of Braise on the Go Culinary School—a facility that makes learning fun and easy. After all, Swanson is showcasing food. He presents his programs at a variety of locations, including under the open canopy of sky on the same farms that also provide fresh produce for his recipes.

Vinaigrette

1 cup sun-dried tomatoes (drained)

4 ounces rice wine vinegar

8 ounces grape seed oil

2 teaspoons salt

1. Place the sun-dried tomatoes in the blender and add the vinegar.
2. While the blender is running, slowly add the oil to form an emulsification. Season with salt. Set aside.

Tomatoes

4 large, unripe green tomatoes, cut into 4 slices each

½ cup milk

½ cup cornmeal

1 teaspoon coriander

1 teaspoon cumin

¼ teaspoon cayenne pepper

2 tablespoons salt

Vegetable oil, for frying

1. Place the thick-sliced tomatoes in the milk. Set them aside to soak for a few minutes.
2. Mix the cornmeal with the spices. Remove the green tomato slices from the milk. Dredge them in the cornmeal, then fry them in vegetable oil in a skillet over medium heat on both sides until golden brown.

Final Assembly

6 ounces fresh Fantome Farm goat cheese

2 ounces basil, torn

1. Top the fried tomatoes with the goat cheese and basil.
2. Drizzle with vinaigrette and serve.

SERVES 4

Recipe courtesy of chef David Swanson, Braise on the Go Culinary School, Milwaukee, Wisconsin.

Grilled Summer Vegetables with Spiced Goat Cheese

Living in Wisconsin, grilling vegetables is something we dream about all winter. Especially when we can pick them from our garden a few hours before dinner. There are a few tricks to perfectly grilled vegetables. Each vegetable should be cut uniformly, about ½ inch horizontally. We usually lay them on a large tray and sprinkle or brush on a marinade. Cook the veggies on a preheated grill, at medium heat. Larger vegetables can be grilled directly on the grate; use a grilling basket for the smaller pieces. Be sure to keep an eye on the vegetables, turning them frequently. If necessary, add a little oil if they seem too dry. Be sure to avoid charring. Depending upon what we have in the garden, we can lay out a real feast.

I large onion

I red pepper

I medium zucchini

I2 asparagus spears

I yellow pepper

I small eggplant

I2 cherry tomatoes

II ounces goat cheese, such as Woolwich Dairy's Madam Chèvre or Gourmet Goat, cut into small pieces

Marinade

½ cup lemon olive oil

I tablespoon Dijon mustard

I tablespoon chopped fresh oregano

I tablespoon champagne vinegar

Salt and pepper to taste

1. Prepare all of the veggies for grilling.
2. Whisk the marinade ingredients together and brush on the vegetables.
3. Warm the barbecue, then roast the vegetables, brushing with the remaining marinade as they grill.
4. Transfer them to a salad bowl and top with the goat cheese.

SERVES 4

Goat Cheese Dessert Dip

This easy recipe is a mellow way to wind down a meal, regardless of the season.

8 ounces plain fresh goat cheese

¼ cup packed brown sugar

2 tablespoons powdered sugar

1 teaspoon vanilla extract

1 teaspoon almond extract

1. In a bowl, mix the ingredients together gently but thoroughly to remove any lumps.
2. Serve with sliced fruit.

MAKES ABOUT 1 CUP

Recipe courtesy of Diana Murphy, Dreamfarm.

Goat Cheese Fudge

This recipe was created by Gerald Carey of Careys Briarwood Farm in Stratford, Wisconsin.

4 cups powdered sugar

8 ounces chèvre, softened

4 ounces unsweetened chocolate, melted

1 teaspoon vanilla extract

Dash salt

¾ cup chopped walnuts (optional)

1. Gradually add the sugar to the chèvre, mixing well after each addition.
2. Add the melted chocolate, vanilla, and salt.
3. Spread the fudge into a greased 8x8-inch pan and chill.

MAKES 16 2-INCH PIECES

Courtesy of Moving Dairy Goats Forward *by the Wisconsin Dairy Goat Association (www.wdga.org).*

Iced Goat Cheese Carrot Cookies

These cookies provide a healthy blend of vegetable and cheese. Watch them disappear!

Cookies

½ cup soft chèvre

½ cup (I stick) butter, melted

¾ cup sugar

I cup mashed cooked carrots

2 eggs

2 cups flour

2 teaspoons baking powder

½ teaspoon salt

1. Preheat the oven to 400°F.
2. In a large bowl, combine the chèvre, butter, sugar, carrots, and eggs. Mix thoroughly and set aside.
3. In another bowl, sift together the flour, baking powder, and salt. Stir the butter mixture together with the flour mixture.
4. Drop the cookie dough by spoonfuls approximately 2 inches apart on a lightly greased baking sheet.
5. Bake for 8 to 10 minutes or until no imprint remains when you touch a cookie lightly with your finger.

Icing

¼ cup (½ stick) butter, softened

2 cups powdered sugar

¼ teaspoon salt

¼ cup whole milk

½ teaspoon vanilla extract

1. In a large bowl, cream the butter until smooth.
2. Add the powdered sugar, salt, milk, and vanilla; mix until smooth and creamy.

MAKES ABOUT 4 DOZEN

Recipe courtesy of Linda Campbell, Khamiara, courtesy of Moving Dairy Goats Forward *by the Wisconsin Dairy Goat Association (www.wdga.org).*

Sheep Cheese

Although sheep's milk cheese is harder to find than that from goats or cows, interest in it is continually expanding, and Wisconsin is on the cutting edge of its development. The Wisconsin Sheep Dairy Cooperative (WSDC), one of the largest sheep organizations in the United States, is also the largest producer of high-quality sheep's milk in the United States. There are fifteen co-op members milking between 100 and 400 sheep.

In 2006 the co-op won the top prize for its Dante cheese at the annual American Cheese Society (ACS) Competition in Portland, Oregon. Created by cheesemaker Dane Huebner, Dante was rated the best aged sheep's milk cheese, based on both technical and aesthetic traits. The product came from Cedar Grove Cheese in Plain, Wisconsin, and was marketed by WSDC. Dante, made from 100 percent sheep's milk, is aged a minimum of six months. With a firm, dry texture, it has a rich nutty flavor. Making the cheese is labor intensive: It's produced one vat at a time, and only during the grazing season. It's then cave aged, hand turned, and salted daily. The milk comes from pasture-fed sheep in the Eau Claire area of northwest Wisconsin.

Dante sheep's milk cheese took five years to develop, beginning at the University of Wisconsin–Madison, which has the only dairy sheep research program in North America. The researchers produced a new crossbreed of East Friesian and Lacaune, which is now the state's main dairy stock. The university also worked to improve the milk composition and yield of dairy sheep, as well as designing new production methods. These included modifications to milk storage and handling. In the field, Cedar Grove further refined the process.

Mona, another Cedar Grove specialty, is made from a blend of sheep's and cow's milk and aged at least six months. It's moister in texture and milder than Dante. A cheese called Faarko—*faar* means "sheep" and *ko* is "cow" in Danish—is an American original created by Dane Huebner. Faarko is a semi-soft, creamy, and buttery cousin of Havarti. Both the Dante and Mona labels were inspired by great artists. Rodin's *The Thinker*, with the head of a sheep, was the inspiration for Dante. Da Vinci's *Mona Lisa* has morphed into a sheep on the Mona label.

Dane Huebner recommends pairing port wine with Dante; with Mona, serve a demi-sec white wine.

Founded in 1878, Cedar Grove Cheese buys milk from more than twenty local farmers. Much of it is organic, and all is free from rBGH—the genetically engineered bovine growth hormone injected into lactating cows so that they produce more milk. The firm produces more than 3.5 million pounds of cheese a year. In addition to its award-winning sheep's milk cheese, you can purchase organic cheeses such as Cheddars, from mild to aged, as well as squeaky organic cheese curds.

According to Huebner, sheep's milk is functionally and chemically ideal for cheese. The milk is flavorful with a high butterfat content.

According to Julie Daniluk, a registered holistic nutritionist (RHN), sheep's milk has many health advantages. It contains almost twice the percentage of calcium, phosphorus, iron, and zinc as cow's milk. It also has more of vitamins A, E, C, and B complex than cow's milk offers—sometimes twice as much. Sheep's milk contains 5.5 percent protein compared with 3.7 percent in cow's milk. Plus, its milkfat comprises 25 percent medium chain triglycerides (MCTs)—healthy fatty acids that are easily digested. MCTs aren't stored in the body as fat, and they don't raise LDL (bad) cholesterol.

A study by Dr. Leonard S. Girsh found that 99 percent of his patients were tolerant to sheep's milk versus a 34 percent toleration for soy, goat's, and rice milks. When these folks switched to sheep's milk, health issues including diarrhea, nausea, vomiting, headaches, sinus congestion, migraines, and skin rashes were relieved.

In recipes, sheep cheeses can be substituted for any cheese. It is delicious atop pasta marinara, potatoes, or grilled vegetables, as well as in sandwiches. It's also a great stand-alone served with crackers or bread, olives, and salami.

WINNING AND WORTHY WISCONSIN SHEEP CHEESES

CARR VALLEY CHEESE

Carr Valley Cheese is a name that has cropped up many times already in these pages. Among its innumerable awards, the firm took second place at the 2004 American Cheese Society Competition for River Bend cheese made from pasture-grazed sheep's milk. This smoothly delicious washed-rind cheese has been cellar cured for twelve weeks.

Carr Valley creates other prizewinning sheep cheeses, including both Marisa and Cave Aged Marisa. The former won first place at the 2004 American Cheese Society Competition and took second at the 2004 Wisconsin State Fair. Cheesemaker Sid Cook describes it as mellow, complex, and sweet—so he named it for his daughter Marisa, who has similar traits. Cave Aged Marisa is a white, seasonal product made with milk from pastured Wisconsin sheep and aged in an open-air cave. It captured first place at the 2005 American Cheese Society Competition, was a blue-ribbon winner at the 2005 Wisconsin State Fair, and took second place in its class at the World Cheese Competition.

Other brands in the Carr Valley sheep repertoire include a feta—a strong Greek sheep's milk cheese with a chalky body and crumbly texture—and Virgin-Pine Native Sheep Blue. This is similar to the firm's Virgin-Pine Native Blue cow's milk cheese, but sweeter and harder. It is made from 100 percent pasture-fed sheep, bandaged and cave aged for more than eight months.

HIDDEN SPRINGS FARM

At Hidden Springs Farm, Brenda and Dean Jensen craft artisan sheep's milk cheeses from their herd of more than a hundred Lacaune and East Friesian dairy sheep. They like that combination, Friesians being more prolific producers and the Lacaunes adding more fat and protein. Their western Wisconsin property, seventy-six acres in the Driftless area, inspired the name of their Driftless sheep cheese, a rich, soft, and creamy cheese made in their creamery. It comes both plain and with fresh basil, extra-virgin olive oil, and sea salt.

Brenda loves to experiment with sheep cheese and came up with a delicious honey lavender as well as a pumpkin-flavored variety, perfect for pumpkin cheesecake. She is also experimenting with maple syrup from her Amish neighbors.

BUTLER FARMS

Bill and Janet Butler moved to Wisconsin from upstate New York in 1993 to start a sheep dairy farm. Their Butler Farms now averages about seventy-five ewes and produces several farmstead cheeses. Their 100 percent sheep's milk cheeses include an Aged Tomme, which has a white mold rind; Fresh Brebis, a mild and creamy variety similar to goat chèvre; and a fresh Bulgarian-style feta. The couple also makes a rich and creamy Camembert from sheep's milk and cow's cream. Butler Farms is the first licensed Grade A sheep dairy in the United States.

Bacchus—A Bartolotta Restaurant Sheep Cheese Wontons with Sweet Potato Puree, Crispy Sage, and Parmigiano-Reggiano

These wonderful wontons were created by Adam Siegel, executive chef of Bartolotta's Lake Park Bistro and of Bacchus—A Bartolotta Restaurant. Both are found in Milwaukee, Wisconsin. Chef Siegel was nominated for a James Beard Award as Best Midwest Chef in 2007.

Sweet Potato Puree

4 medium sweet potatoes

½ cup cream

Salt and pepper to taste

1. Wrap the potatoes in foil, place them in a 350°F oven, and bake until very tender—an hour or more.
2. Remove the meat from the skins and place in a food processor along with the cream, salt, and pepper. Puree until smooth. Set this aside until you're ready to serve.

Filling

¾ pound Hidden Springs Driftless sheep cheese

¼ pound mascarpone

I tablespoon chopped Italian parsley

I tablespoon chopped fresh basil

I tablespoon chopped fresh thyme

Salt, white pepper, and nutmeg to taste

2 ounces Parmigiano-Reggiano cheese, grated

1. In a large mixing bowl, add all of the filling ingredients except the Parmigiano. Mix thoroughly. At the end, fold in the Parmigiano. Wrap and refrigerate until needed.

Wontons

40 wonton wrappers

Cornstarch

Water

1. Put a teaspoon of the filling mixture in the center of a small wonton wrapper. Make a mixture of equal parts cornstarch and water. Dip a finger into the mixture and rub it around the edges of the filling.
2. Now take the wonton and fold it over to form a triangle, pressing the edges together. Use scissors to trim the edges, if desired.

3. Cook the wontons in boiling salted water for about 1 minute or until the dough is tender.

Sauce and Final Assembly

3 tablespoons unsalted butter

20 small sage leaves

3 tablespoons grated Parmigiano-Reggiano cheese

1. Brown the butter in a pan on the stove. When it's browned, take it off the heat and add the sage leaves.
2. Add the cooked wontons, season with a little salt and pepper, and toss with the grated Parmigiano-Reggiano.
3. To serve, place each wonton on a spoonful of sweet potato puree and top with a piece of sage.

Bacchus—A Bartolotta Restaurant Sheep Cheese Ravioli

If you have a ravioli-making pasta machine, you can follow the basic recipe below to create your own ravioli.

I pound all-purpose flour

I teaspoon salt

4 eggs

I egg yolk

1. In the bowl of an electric mixer with a hook attachment, combine the flour and salt.
2. Turn the mixer on at slow speed. Slowly, one by one, add the eggs and egg yolk.
3. After a couple of minutes, a dough should be formed; if not, add some drops of water to help it along. Turn the mixer to medium and let it run for about 3 minutes to work the dough.
4. Take out the dough, cover it with plastic wrap, and let rest for at least half an hour.
5. To make the ravioli, follow the instructions on your ravioli maker pasta machine.

SERVES 12 AS AN APPETIZER OR 8 FOR A MAIN COURSE

Courtesy of Adam Siegel, executive chef of Bacchus—A Bartolotta Restaurant, Milwaukee, Wisconsin.

Roasted Beet Salad with Sheep Cheese Croquettes

This recipe calls for a chioggia, which is a beautiful heirloom beet with alternating rings of white and bright pink.

I large red beet, peeled

I large yellow beet, peeled

I large chioggia, peeled

½ cup olive oil

Salt and fresh-ground black pepper

¼ cup pistachio oil

Juice of ½ lemon

I ounce chopped fresh herbs (such as parsley, tarragon, chives, dill, chervil)

12 ounces Driftless fresh sheep cheese

4 eggs, beaten

4 cups panko bread crumbs

2 quarts canola oil, for deep-frying

I cup micro arugula

1. Toss the beets in the olive oil with salt and pepper. Wrap each one in aluminum foil and roast in a 350°F oven for 1 to 1½ hours. While they're still warm, peel the beets and cut them into a small dice.
2. Mix the diced beets with the pistachio oil, lemon juice, herbs, and more salt and pepper.
3. To make the croquettes, roll the cheese into 1-ounce balls. Roll these in the egg wash, then the panko; repeat. Deep-fry in canola oil at 360°F. Season with salt and pepper.
4. To serve, divide the beet mixture among four plates. Place three croquettes on each plate, then sprinkle the micro arugula over the top.

SERVES 4

Courtesy of executive chef Justin Carlisle, Harvest Restaurant, Madison, Wisconsin.

Fettuccine with Spinach, Tomatoes, and Butler Farms Cheese

This is one of Janet Butler's favorite recipes, created by Robin Worth and published in Madison Magazine, *August 1997. Brebis is a soft, mild sheep's milk cheese with a creamy spreadability.*

2 tablespoons olive oil

I medium red onion, finely chopped

2 ounces ham, diced (optional)

2 cloves garlic, minced

I pound fresh spinach, washed, large stems removed, *or* I package (I0 ounces) frozen chopped spinach, thawed and squeezed to remove excess water

4 ripe plum tomatoes, chopped

I teaspoon chopped fresh thyme

Salt and pepper to taste

I pound spinach fettuccine

I container (6 ounces) Butler Farms Brebis

1. In a large saucepan or Dutch oven, heat the olive oil over a medium flame; add the onion and sauté until slightly softened. Add the ham (if desired); stir and sauté for one minute. Add the garlic, spinach, tomatoes, and thyme and sauté for 3 to 4 minutes or until the tomatoes are softened and the spinach has wilted down. Season to taste with salt and pepper.

2. Meanwhile, bring a large pot of water to a boil. Cook the spinach fettuccine according to package directions. Drain the pasta and toss it with spinach mixture and Butler Farms cheese to coat. Serve immediately.

SERVES 4-6

CHAPTER 7

ITALIAN CHEESES

THERE HAS LONG BEEN AN ITALIAN PRESENCE IN Wisconsin. The picturesque village of Genoa was settled in the 1850s by Italian immigrants, many of whom worked in nearby lead mines. The iron mines of northern Wisconsin also drew their share of Italian laborers. Lured by the promise of jobs in the mills and the woodworking and stonecutting shops of Milwaukee, the numbers of Italians continued to grow through the 1920s. The city's Third Ward hosted numerous Sicilian families, with hundreds of skilled workers from northern Italy living in the Bay View neighborhood south of downtown. Madison's Italian community is centered a few blocks south of the Capitol and the University of Wisconsin campus.

The Italians brought their love of cooking and their cheesemaking skills to Wisconsin. Asiago, mascarpone, mozzarella, Parmesan, provolone, ricotta, and Romano became staples in many a household. Cheese was always an important ingredient in Mama's kitchen and in the many Italian restaurants that eventually popped up around the state. The numerous varieties of Italian cheese continue to enhance the flavor of luscious sauces and blend well with the meats, vegetables, and spices in the innumerable pastas, pizzas, and other favorite dishes in Italian cuisine. As always, the Wisconsin Milk Marketing Board has plenty of colorful information describing the many delectable varieties (www.wisdairy.com).

Buon appetito!

Asiago

Asiago hails from a region in the Alps of northern Italy known as the Asiago High Plateau. Food historians conjecture that farmers there developed this variety around AD 1000. Italian Asiago is milder than its Wisconsin counterpart. Stateside, it is aged, evolving from mild to a richer, more nutty and buttery flavor. Asiago also hardens with age and becomes more granular, with tiny holes. It is described as a cross between sharp white Cheddar and Parmesan. As with other cheeses, the wax color indicates its age: Clear or white suggests mild; brown suggests medium; and black indicates aged. Asiago should also have tiny holes within its shape.

Asiago is a great table cheese, delicious with nuts, particularly walnuts and pecans, along with fruit such as grapes, apples, figs, pears, and dried apricots. We also like it grated in salads, paired with a balsamic vinaigrette.

Shredded or grated, it cooks well in baked dishes including pasta and soups, or on vegetables, in seafood dishes, and with pizza. It can be melted on lavosh, an Armenian unleavened bread. It's often used with focaccia, a flat Italian bread seasoned with olive oil and herbs, topped with meat or vegetables along with cheese.

According to recent studies, Asiago cheese is low in fat and rich in protein, with one cube, or approximately one ounce, having 110 calories.

Chef Wave Kasprzak of the Dining Room in downtown Monticello whips up a cheese dish at the Green County Cheese Days. Photo by Martin Hintz

Asiago Cheese Puffs

These treats will be the hit of any cocktail party. They pair perfectly with a cold glass of champagne.

I tablespoon butter

I tablespoon olive oil

½ teaspoon salt

Dash cayenne pepper

I cup water

I cup flour

4 eggs (for lighter puffs, use 2 whole eggs and 4 egg whites)

½ cup shredded BelGioioso Asiago

½ cup grated BelGioioso Parmesan

1. Preheat the oven to 400°F.
2. In a small saucepan, combine the butter, olive oil, salt, cayenne, and water; bring to a boil.
3. Add the flour all at once; stir until the mixture forms a smooth ball. Cook over low heat until the mixture is drier but still smooth.
4. Put the mixture into a mixing bowl and beat in the eggs, one at a time. Stir in the cheeses.
5. Drop spoonfuls of batter onto a greased cookie sheet. Bake for 20 minutes or until the puffs are slightly browned and firm. Serve immediately.

MAKES 30 PUFFS

Courtesy of BelGioioso Cheese, Denmark, Wisconsin.

Homestyle Meat Loaf with Asiago Spinach Filling

This is not your typical meat loaf recipe! It lifts the loaf to a new level of sophistication. Sartori cheesemaker Joel Pagel, competing against twenty-one other Wisconsin cheesemakers, was named the 2006 Grand Master Cheese Maker for his Asiago.

½ cup ketchup

¼ cup packed brown sugar

1½ tablespoons cider vinegar

1 medium onion, chopped

2 cloves garlic, minced

1 tablespoon vegetable oil

2 large eggs

1 tablespoon fresh thyme

1 teaspoon salt

½ teaspoon fresh-ground black pepper

1 tablespoon Dijon mustard

1 tablespoon Worcestershire sauce

¼ teaspoon hot sauce

½ cup milk

1½ pounds ground chuck

½ pound ground pork

⅔ cup crushed saltine crackers

¼ cup minced fresh parsley

1 cup fresh spinach, steamed and drained (*or* a 10-ounce package frozen spinach, thawed and squeezed)

1½ cups shredded Sartori Foods Asiago

1. Preheat the oven to 350°F.
2. Combine the ketchup, brown sugar, and cider vinegar. Reserve glaze.
3. Sauté the onion and garlic in the oil until softened and set aside. Combine the eggs, thyme, salt, pepper, Dijon, Worcestershire, hot sauce, and milk. Mix this with the ground chuck, ground pork, cracker crumbs, parsley, and onion–garlic mixture until well combined.
4. Flatten the mixture into a rectangle and spread it with the spinach and Asiago up to 1 inch from the edge. Roll, forming a loaf.
5. Brush the loaf with half of the glaze. Place in a draining 9x5-inch meat loaf pan and bake until the internal temperature reaches 160°F, about 1 hour. Cool for 20 minutes, then slice and serve with the remaining glaze.

SERVES 8

Courtesy of Sartori Foods, Plymouth, Wisconsin.

In the fiercely competitive 2006 World Championship, Earl Wilson of Burnett Dairy Cooperative in Grantsburg, Wisconsin, won Best of Class for his Provolone. Steven Tollers, also from Burnett, took second.

Wisconsin Parmesans have also seen competitive success. In 2006 BelGioioso's version won top honors in American Cheese Society competitions. The prior year, Sartori (then the Antigo Cheese Company) earned honors for its Stravecchio; BelGioioso Cheese claimed second for its American Grana; and Sartori (then Antigo) took third for Parmesan, as well as earning a gold medal as Best US Cow's Milk Cheese at the 2006 World Cheese Awards in London. Judges cited its "piquant, nutty flavor and extra-aged character."

SARTORI FOODS

The Sartori family emigrated to the United States from northern Italy in the early 1930s. Family patriarch Paul Sartori wanted to utilize his knowledge of producing exceptional Italian cheeses in America. Settling in Plymouth, he founded S&R Cheese, now Sartori Foods, in 1939. The Kettle Moraine region of east-central Wisconsin was ideal for Sartori's traditional cheesemaking process because its climate and landscape were similar to those in the Old World.

Paul's grandson, Jim Sartori, has continued the Sartori Foods tradition as a family-owned manufacturer. Capitalizing on the area's rich farmland, Sartori Foods works with local farmers who supply quality milk. The Sartori team of Master Cheesemakers, product developers, and culinary specialists closely collaborate to ensure consistency and quality.

In 2005 Sartori Foods acquired the Glacier Point Artisan Cheese Company, which produces

the award-winning, blue-veined Dolcina Gorgonzola, in addition to traditional blue and Gorgonzola. In 2007 the former Antigo Cheese Company was added to the Sartori family, which now creates the award-winning SarVecchio Parmesan, SarVecchio Asiago, and other Italian-style cheeses.

EAU GALLE

Eau Galle (pronounced *O Galley*), nestled in the rolling hills of western Wisconsin, began as a milk-processing plant in the mid-1800s. Leo Buhlman, founder of the Eau Galle Cheese Company, apprenticed for eight years as a cheesemaker in Switzerland before coming to the United States in 1926.

He worked in several Wisconsin cheese factories, learning English along the way, before purchasing the then-closed cheese plant in Eau Galle in 1945. Buhlman kept the Eau Galle Cheese Factory name and went on to make and market award-winning Swiss cheese for about thirteen years. In 1958 he switched to Cheddar to accommodate a changing market. A few years after that, the plant changed product lines again and began making hard Italian cheese.

In 1964 Buhlman's son John took over plant

Because small dairy facilities like the Foley cheese plant could supply high quality milk for cheese, farms in early 20th century Green County had one of the largest gross incomes of any county in Wisconsin during this time.

Photo courtesy of The Swiss Colony

operations—though Leo continued working until he was eighty-nine years old, despite having to walk with two canes. In 1986 the Eau Galle Cheese Factory kept the village name when it moved to a modern plant 4 miles east of town.

The factory added new automated equipment in 2005 and became organically certified in the production of hard Italian cheeses. The Buhlman family still operates the plant.

SARGENTO

Sargento Foods is a family-owned company founded in 1953 when Leonard Gentine, described as an "enterprising young man who loved cheese," teamed with Joseph Sartori. In the mid-1950s Gentine developed a vacuum package that helped preserve cheese quality, establishing a national standard. In 1958 Sargento became the first US company to sell shredded cheese. In 1969 it introduced a peg bar holder for grocery stores to better display its offerings.

The company's Food Service Division now produces custom cheese products according to the specifications of many national restaurant chains. These include natural sliced and shredded cheeses and breaded appetizers. Its Food Ingredients Division provides custom cheese products for other food manufacturers—sliced, shredded, and diced cheeses, portion control packs, fillings, and assorted sauces.

The company employs about 1,300 workers in plants in Plymouth, Kiel, Hilbert, and Elkhart Lake. In 2006 a hundred workers at the Plymouth operation won $208.6 million in the Wisconsin State Lottery—its largest payout ever. Most of them continued working.

PARK CHEESE

Park Cheese of Fond du Lac, Wisconsin, has been making cheese for a hundred years. Owned by the Liebetrau family since 1975—Eric Liebetrau is now at the helm—the company began as a small farm cooperative producing brick cheese in the 1890s. Cheesemaker Armando Ferrari and his wife, Lina, left their hometown of Piacenza, Italy, in 1960 to work Park Cheese. Ferrari, a fourth-generation cheesemaker, learned his skills at the age of ten from his father and grandfather. In the 1940s the company began making Italian cheese; it now produces about nine million pounds a year in eight varieties, sold under the Casaro brand.

In 2003 *Bon Appétit* magazine named the company's Casaro Aged Provolone as one of the Top 10 American-made artisan cheeses.

Mascarpone

Mascarpone originated in the Lombardy region of Italy. This rich, creamy white cheese conjures up images of mouthwatering desserts—especially the popular tiramisu, with its sweetened mascarpone and ladyfingers soaked in espresso and cognac. Mascarpone has a buttery taste with a smooth, thick texture. It contains 70 percent milkfat, which makes it a triple crème. This cheese is extremely versatile in cooking and used far beyond desserts. It pairs well with dry sparkling wines or champagne.

Because mascarpone is a fresh, delicate cheese, keep it well chilled and be sure to eat it soon after purchasing. Do not overwhip or overprocess mascarpone if you're using it in frosting or dips—it'll turn into butter and become clumpy.

Since 2004 Crave Brothers Farmstead Cheese in Waterloo, Wisconsin, has consistently won major awards for its delicious mascarpone. The cheesemakers there have all kinds of suggestions for serving this specialty of their house:

- Blend mascarpone with interesting dessert toppings such as powdered chocolate, coffee, fruit, or even liqueurs.
- Season and use in place of mayonnaise in chicken or tuna salad.
- Mix mascarpone with honey or maple syrup for a nice fruit dip.
- Season with lemon juice, lemon peel, and sugar, then fill individual tart shells and top with raspberries.
- Mix an eight-ounce container of mascarpone with sugar to taste. Whip one cup of heavy cream and add it to the cheese. Layer this mixture with fresh fruit in parfait glasses for a light summer dessert.

Stuffed Vegetable Cannelloni

To be sure, this is Italian! Mamas everywhere love this flavorful combo.

I6 cannelloni pasta shells

I ½ cups BelGioioso Ricotta con Latte, well drained

I large egg, beaten

I ⅓ cups grated BelGioioso American Grana, divided (if this is unavailable, the company's Parmesan makes a fine alternative)

I cup seeded and diced fresh tomatoes (about 2 medium), drained

⅔ cups cooked chopped broccoli

¼ cup minced fresh parsley

I teaspoon grated lemon zest

Salt and pepper to taste

½ cup (I stick) butter, melted (optional)

1. Preheat the oven to 350°F. Butter a 9x12-inch baking dish.
2. Cook the pasta according to directions until al dente. Be sure to place the individual cannelloni into the boiling water gently or they will clump together. Set aside.
3. In a large bowl, combine the ricotta, egg, and ½ cup of the BelGioioso American Grana; mix well. Add the tomatoes, broccoli, parsley, lemon zest, salt, and pepper, again mixing well.
4. Stuff about 2 tablespoons of the filling into each cannelloni. Place them in a single layer in the buttered dish. Drizzle melted butter over the pasta, if you like, and sprinkle with the remaining cheese.
5. Bake for 15 to 20 minutes, until the cheese is melted and slightly browned. Serve immediately.

SERVES 6-8

Courtesy of BelGioioso Cheese, Denmark, Wisconsin.

Char-Grilled Peaches with Mascarpone Soup

This extraordinary dish is the brainchild of Sanford D'Amato, the chef-owner of Sanford, Coquette Café, and Harlequin Bakery, all found in Milwaukee, Wisconsin.

Peaches

4 large or 8 small freestone peaches, washed, cut in half, stones removed

⅛ teaspoon ground cardamom

⅛ teaspoon ground black pepper

1½ tablespoons melted butter

1 tablespoon honey

1. Heat the grill.
2. Toss the peach halves with the cardamom, black pepper, melted butter, and honey. Mix well.
3. Place the peaches, cut-side down, on the hot grill and cook for about 3 minutes, until the fruit is well caramelized. Turn the fruit over onto the skin side and grill, covered, for about 3 to 4 minutes; the peach halves should be cooked and just yielding, but not soft. (Grilling times will vary depending on the sizes of peaches.) Remove the fruit from the grill and let it cool to room temperature.

Mascarpone Soup

8 ounces (1 cup) mascarpone cheese

¼ cup milk

1 tablespoon honey

⅛ teaspoon ground cardamom

Pinch kosher salt

¼ cup whole hazelnuts, toasted, salted, and chopped coarsely (for garnish)

1. Mix all the soup ingredients together until smooth. Add any accumulated juices from the grilled peaches and divide among four bowls.
2. Divide the peach halves on top of the soup and garnish with the toasted hazelnuts.

SERVES 4

Courtesy of chef Sanford D'Amato, chef-owner Sanford, Coquette Café, and Harlequin Bakery, Milwaukee, Wisconsin.

Chocolate Wisconsin Mascarpone Fondue

This recipe (created by Trey Foshee, the chef of George's at the Cove Restaurant in La Jolla, California) is perfect for a dinner party. We put all the ingredients into a double boiler before the guests arrive and cook at the last minute. Out of this world!

½ pound bittersweet chocolate, chopped
½ pound milk chocolate, chopped
1¼ cups cream
⅓ cup sugar
8 ounces Wisconsin Mascarpone cheese
**2 ounces bourbon, orange liqueur, or
   another favorite liqueur**
1 cinnamon stick

1. Combine all the ingredients in a medium bowl (or the top of a double boiler). Place over a pot of simmering water on the stove burner. Do not allow the bowl to touch the water.
2. Heat until the mixture is melted, smooth, and warm, stirring often. Remove from the heat.
3. Pour the mixture into a fondue or other pot and keep it warm. Serve immediately, dipping the accompaniments of your choice: cubed pound cake; assorted fresh fruits such as strawberries, apple chunks, or banana chunks; or marshmallows.

SERVES 6-8

Courtesy of the Wisconsin Milk Marketing Board, Inc.

Mozzarella

Mozzarella is a generic term for the several kinds of Italian fresh cheese made by a process called *pasta filata*, where the curds are dipped in hot water and then stretched, kneaded, and cut to form balls or logs.

Fresh mozzarella was first made near Naples from the milk of water buffalo—originally it was called Buffalo Mozzarella or Mozzarella Fresca. At the time neither pasteurization nor refrigeration existed, so it was intended to be eaten almost immediately. This soft, slightly elastic cheese has a mild, milky flavor and is delicious in salads, sandwiches, and appetizers.

The mozzarella that most Americans are familiar with is a low-moisture variety made from cow's milk, once called *Fior di Latte*. This cheese became popular after

Phyllis Giovanelli has been working at Bobby Nelson's Cheese Mart since she was ten years old. Now she owns it.

Photo by Martin Hintz

World War II, when pizza was "discovered" by ravenous American GIs in Italy weary of mess hall cooking. This variety also contains more fat than other mozzarellas, which makes it better for cooking and gives it a longer shelf life.

Today mozzarella is the second most popular cheese in the United States. Wisconsin makes more of it than any other cheese—close to 650 million pounds a year!—in a variety of styles, including reduced-fat, organic, whole-milk, low-moisture whole-milk, part-skim, and low-moisture part-skim versions. The various mozzarellas have different cooking properties. The part-skim kind browns better and faster and shreds and slices easier, whereas a mozzarella made with whole milk has a creamy texture and melts better, especially when covering a pizza. Don't forget the anchovies.

Mozzarella is an integral part of an Italian antipasto platter, which we make with tomatoes, olives, roasted peppers, and anchovies, as well as capicola, salami, or prosciutto. We favor Milwaukee's own Usinger's Famous Sausage—and especially that firm's scrumptious Genoa salami, replete with pork, beef, and plenty of garlic, a perfect addition to anything antipasto. Mozzarella is also fantastic with pesto—which we make from our own fresh basil—with sun-dried tomatoes, and in sandwiches.

Other serving ideas to try:

- The classic way to serve mozzarella is with sliced tomatoes and chopped fresh basil, drizzled with a premium extra-virgin olive oil, and seasoned with freshly ground pepper. We usually present this version as an appetizer, along with French bread or mixed with fresh greens.
- For a simple appetizer, place a slice of mozzarella atop roasted or grilled eggplant slices and broil briefly.
- Or slice a baguette, brush it with garlic oil, and top with a slice of fresh mozzarella with chopped sun-dried tomatoes. Bake for about 3 minutes in a 400°F oven.

Light red wines such as Beaujolais Nouveau or Bartolinos—or white wines including Chardonnay, Pinot Grigio, Semillon, and Sauvignon Blanc—all pair well with mozzarella.

Crave Brothers Farmstead Classics Marinated Herbed Tomato Salad

Mozzarella is traditionally sold in the form of a 10-ounce ball, ⅓-ounce ciliegine, 1¾-ounce bocconcini, 4-ounce ovolini, or 1-pound log. This delicious Mediterranean dish uses the little ciliegine—each about the size of a cherry.

Salad

6 ripe tomatoes, cut into wedges

3 sweet peppers, sliced (use a combination of green, red, and yellow)

1 sweet Spanish onion, sliced (white or red)

1 cup pitted black olives, drained

2 containers (8 ounces each) Crave Brothers Farmstead Classics Fresh Mozzarella *ciliegine* (cherry-size balls)

1. Slice the vegetables into glass serving bowl. Add the olives and cheese.

Dressing

⅔ cup vegetable oil

¼ cup red wine vinegar

¼ cup snipped fresh parsley or cilantro

¼ cup snipped green onions with tops

1 teaspoon salt

¼ teaspoon pepper

1 teaspoon sugar

½ teaspoon dried basil *or* 1 tablespoon fresh basil, if available

½ teaspoon dried marjoram

1. Combine all of the dressing ingredients in a screw-top jar and shake well.
2. Pour the dressing over the salad, cover, and refrigerate for 3 to 4 hours before serving.

SERVES 6-8

Courtesy of Janet Crave, Crave Brothers Farmstead.

Parmesan

The history of Parmesan cheese dates back to the twelfth century, when it was developed by Benedictine and Cistercian monks of Italy's Po River Valley—known ever since as the Cradle of Parmigiano-Reggiano. At that time the pastures of Emilia and Lombardy were carpeted with clover and lucerne, a delicious grassy perennial with perky blue blooms. Both quickly fattened cows and were credited with increasing the volume of milk. These two forages were important in the production of Parmesan. The monks found that by double heating the cow's milk, a paste-like substance formed, which they turned into what may be the world's most famous cheese.

Parmesan quickly became the stuff of legend, renowned for its taste and adaptability. English king Henry VIII once received some top-flight Parmesan as a gift from Pope Julius II to secure his aid in a war against France. In the 1400s Italian poet Giovanni Boccaccio wrote in his *Decameron* about a mythological kingdom based atop a pile of Parmigiano wheels. It has also been a practice of northern Italian banks over the generations to hold wheels of high-quality Parmigiano as collateral on loans. Cookbook author Maria Liberati considers Parmigiano-Reggiano a food for truly refined sensibilities, much like a Cuban cigar for a captain of industry or a sleek Ferrari for a race driver.

Parmesan is pale yellow with a sweet, nutty flavor that intensifies with aging, which can take up to ten months. It is made from part-skim milk and thus is naturally low in fat. Its hard, granular texture is perfect for grating or shredding over everything from pasta to soups and salads.

Parmesan has become very popular with cooks in the United States. We use it regularly for many of our favorite dishes. The folks at BelGioioso Cheese offer many serving suggestions:

- Stir Parmesan into mashed potatoes for extra flavor.
- Top fresh asparagus with Parmesan and butter, then bake.
- Add grilled chicken and fresh spinach leaves to hot pasta, then sprinkle with grated Parmesan.

- Grill portobello mushroom caps until soft. Sprinkle with shredded Parmesan and broil until the cheese is melted.
- Serve cubes of Parmesan with fresh grapes, fresh strawberries, dried figs, and walnuts for an appetizer or light dessert.
- Parmesan pieces drizzled with aged balsamic vinegar make a wonderful way to finish a meal.

> **"Why, my cheese, my digestion, why hast thou not served thyself in to my table, so many meals?"**
>
> —William Shakespeare, from *Troilus and Cressida,* Achilles speaking

Parmesan also pairs beautifully with wine. Try it alongside Chardonnay, Riesling, Sauvignon Blanc, Pinot Blanc, Burgundy, Merlot, Dolcetto, Barolo, or Vin Santo.

We can't resist adding the following recipe quickie from Julie Ansfield of Milwaukee: In a buttered 9½-inch oval gratin dish, create a bed of cooked asparagus stalks. Top these with two fried eggs—undercooked and seasoned with salt and pepper. Sprinkle with grated Parmesan and bake at 425°F until the cheese is melted. *Fabuloso!*

Spinach and Artichokes Adored

This is one of our favorite dishes—a perfect companion to roast beef or lamb, especially for holidays. Using fresh artichokes is preferred, but you can substitute canned or frozen if you chop them into bite-size pieces.

4 fresh artichoke hearts, *or* I can (8–14 ounces) artichoke hearts, drained and quartered

4 packages (10 ounces each) chopped spinach

½ pound mushrooms, sliced

6 tablespoons butter, divided

¾ cup mayonnaise

¾ cup grated Parmesan cheese

Salt and pepper to taste

3 medium tomatoes

½ cup dry seasoned bread crumbs

1. If you're using fresh artichokes, steam them or cook them in boiling water until tender, about 45 minutes. When they're cool enough to handle, remove the leaves and choke and chop the hearts into pieces.
2. Preheat the oven to 325°F.
3. Cook the spinach according to package instructions. Strain well in a fine sieve.
4. Sauté the mushrooms in 2 tablespoons of the butter until slightly brown.
5. Combine the mayonnaise and cheese. Add the artichoke hearts, mushrooms, and spinach. Season to taste with salt and pepper.
6. Pour the mixture into a 13x9-inch baking dish.
7. Slice the tomatoes ½-inch thick and place them atop the spinach mixture.
8. Sauté the crumbs in the remaining ¼ cup butter until they're brown. Place a spoonful on each tomato.
9. Bake for 20 minutes.

SERVES 8–10

Courtesy of the Junior League of Milwaukee cookbook, Be Our Guest.

Morels and Eggs "En Cocotte" with Parmesan Cheese

Morels are a much-prized delicacy in the mushroom world. Each spring morel hunting is a time-honored activity all over Wisconsin.

I cup vegetable stock

2 cloves garlic, crushed

I tablespoon truffle oil (optional)

¼ cup cream

Salt and pepper to taste

¼ cup (½ stick) butter, divided

2 cups morels, cleaned and cut in bite-size pieces

8 extra-large eggs

½ cup shaved Crave Brothers Parmesan Cheese

1. Combine the stock, garlic, truffle oil (if desired), cream, salt, pepper, and 2 tablespoons of the butter in a saucepan. Bring the mixture to a boil, then let it simmer for 15 minutes. Remove the pan from the heat and let the broth cool.
2. Sauté the morels in the remaining 2 tablespoons of butter over medium-high heat. Season to taste with more salt and pepper, and set them aside to cool.
3. Preheat the oven to 325°F.
4. Place the cooled morels into eight ramekins. Crack an egg into each ramekin, seasoning with salt and pepper. Top each ramekin with broth.
5. Bake for 7 to 10 minutes or until the egg is slightly underdone. Remove the ramekins from the oven, sprinkle on the Parmesan, and serve immediately.

SERVES 8

Courtesy of chef David Swanson, Braise on the Go Traveling Culinary School.

WISCONSIN'S ITALIAN CHEESEMONGERS

Great Italian cheeses are made all over Wisconsin—but where to buy them? The following are among the best Italian cheesemongers statewide. We love shopping in these outlets because each store has friendly staff who really know their cheese . . . and olives . . . and everything Italian.

- Glorioso's Grocery, Milwaukee.
- Groppi's Food Market, Bay View.
- Tenuta's Italian Grocery & Delicatessen, Kenosha.

West Allis Cheese & Sausage Shoppe (in the downtown Milwaukee Public Market); Whole Foods Market (in Madison and Milwaukee); and Market Square Cheese (in Wisconsin Dells) also offer extensive selections of Italian cheeses amid their array of other state-made varieties.

"It is not a matter of choosing the right cheese, but of being chosen. There is a reciprocal relationship between cheese and customer: Each cheese awaits its customer, poses so as to attract him, with a firmness or a somewhat haughty graininess, or, on the contrary, by melting in submissive abandon."

—Italo Calvino (1923–1985), Italian novelist, describing a cheese shop visited by the main character in his critically acclaimed novel *Mr. Palomar*. The protagonist was seeking a semblance of order and reason in what he saw was "a chaotic and unreasonable world." The cheese shop was his salvation.

Zesty Wisconsin Parmesan Popcorn

Movie theater popcorn just won't taste the same after you try this recipe at home. A bowl is best along with sips of cold Wisconsin cranberry juice.

½ cup unpopped popcorn

3 tablespoons oil

3 tablespoons butter, melted

¼ cup (I ounce) grated Wisconsin Parmesan cheese

I teaspoon oregano

½ teaspoon salt

1. In large covered saucepan (3 quarts or larger), heat one kernel of popcorn in the oil. When the kernel pops, add the remaining popcorn.
2. Cover and cook over medium-high heat, shaking the pan often. When the popping stops, put the popcorn into a large bowl and drizzle the melted butter atop.
3. Toss lightly. Quickly stir in cheese and seasonings. Toss to mix.

SERVES 2

Courtesy of the Wisconsin Milk Marketing Board, Inc.

Shrimp and Olive Pasta with Wisconsin Parmesan Cheese

This colorful and tasty pasta dish is a meal in itself. All you need is a glass of Pinot Grigio and a loaf of Italian bread.

I pound large raw shrimp, shelled and deveined

¼ cup olive oil, divided

I ½ cups diced onions

3 cloves garlic, minced

I can (I6 ounces) diced tomatoes with juice

I cup diced fresh asparagus

⅓ cup dry white wine

I cup black olives, halved

I pound rotini pasta, cooked and drained

I ½ cups (6 ounces) grated Wisconsin Parmesan cheese

¼ cup chopped fresh parsley

¼ cup julienned fresh basil

I teaspoon salt

½ teaspoon pepper

1. In a large skillet over medium heat, cook the shrimp in 2 tablespoons of the oil for about 3 minutes or until opaque, stirring often. Remove the shrimp from the skillet; set aside.
2. In same skillet, cook the onions and garlic in the remaining oil for 3 minutes.
3. Add the tomatoes, asparagus, and wine; heat to a boil. Reduce the heat to low and simmer for 5 minutes. Add the cooked shrimp and olives; heat through.
4. In a large bowl, gently combine the cooked pasta, shrimp–vegetable mixture, cheese, parsley, basil, salt, and pepper. Serve immediately.

SERVES 10

Courtesy of the Wisconsin Milk Marketing Board, Inc.

Provolone

Provolone is very similar to mozzarella in the way it's made, but it is aged. Originally it was bound with a string and hung from the ceiling in curing rooms. Young provolone is *dolce,* or sweet, aged up to two or three months. After it ages and becomes spicier and more granular, the cheese is called *picante.* Sometimes it's waxed in different shapes. Traditionally, provolone had a slightly smoky flavor, a result of the wood fires used in Italian curing rooms. Wisconsin cheese factories make both smoked and unsmoked provolone.

Provolone comes in all shapes and sizes. A 600-pound, 7-foot-long Giant Provolone called a Giganti is available for those with hearty appetites. If that's a bit much, a 200-pound Giganti can be purchased. We like to visit Tenuta's Italian Grocery & Delicatessen in Kenosha, Wisconsin, which has some of these monsters on display. One dangling from the ceiling tops 250 pounds; slices are carefully cut off with a special piano wire device and "lots of experience," according to Ralph Tenuta. His dad, John, started the store in 1950, drawing shoppers from around southeastern Wisconsin and northern Illinois. Tenuta's now stocks around a hundred varieties of Italian cheese, many Wisconsin made.

BelGioioso, one of Wisconsin's major producers of Italian cheeses, makes provolone in a variety of ways. The firm's Rindless Provolone, which has won the title of World's Best, is made with whole cow's milk and aged at least sixty days. Unsmoked, it's an excellent melting cheese and easy to slice. BelGioioso Small Style Provolone is also made from whole cow's milk and aged at least sixty days. The firm's Aged Provolone—also rated World's Best—is aged from five to twelve months, the oldest having an extra sharp, piquant flavor. BelGioioso Italian Extra Sharp Provolone is made the true Italian way: roped, dipped into a plastic coating, and aged for twelve months. And BelGioioso makes a provolone called Manteche, sometimes called Burrini in Italy. It's created by wrapping mild Provolone around sweet cream butter, which takes on the flavor of cheese as it ages.

For cooking, Provolone is multipurpose. It can be used on pizzas, in lasagnas, and for flavorful casseroles. It goes well with tomatoes and fruits such as pears, grapes, and figs.

This cheese pairs well with Beaujolais, late-harvest Gewürztraminer, Italian beers, and any sort of lager—which Wisconsin has in wonderful abundance. Marty favors Berghoff's Original Lager Beer from the Joseph Huber Brewery in Monroe or Capital Brewery's award-winning Bavarian Lager, brewed in Middleton.

Orchiette Pasta with Park Cheese

Lina Ferrari, who loves to cook, uses Park Cheese Provolone in this delicious pasta recipe—her own creation. She points out that the cheese intensifies when aged, becoming pungent and full flavored.

½ pound asparagus spears, tough ends discarded

2 shallots, diced

I clove garlic, diced

2 tablespoons extra-virgin olive oil

2 large ripe yellow tomatoes, peeled and chopped

½ cup Italian white wine, preferably Orvieto

½ cup chicken stock

½ cup fresh basil chiffonade

½ pounds orchiette (little ears) pasta, cooked al dente

I cup shredded Park Cheese Provolone

2 tablespoons grated Park Cheese Parmesan

1. Pour boiling water over the asparagus; cover and let this sit for 3 minutes. Drain. Grill the spears on a lightly oiled griddle or sauté it in a skillet over high heat until it's al dente and somewhat browned. Set aside. When the spears are cool, cut them into 3- to 4-inch pieces.

2. Sauté the shallots and garlic in the olive oil until translucent. Add the tomatoes; sauté until they're soft and give up their juices. Add the wine and chicken stock. Boil this mixture over high heat until it's reduced by one-quarter.

3. Add the asparagus pieces and basil to the pan and mix.

4. Add the freshly cooked pasta; stir to coat.

5. Add the cheeses and toss to melt. Serve immediately.

SERVES 4

Romano

Romano cheese is named for the city of its origin: Rome. There are different types. Pecorino Romano is made from sheep's milk with a sharp and tangy taste; Caprino Romano, made from goat's milk, is extremely sharp; Vacchino Romano is a very mild cow's milk cheese. In Wisconsin most Romanos are made of cow's milk or a combination of cow's and goat's or sheep's milk. Like Parmesan, this cheese must age at least five months, but Romano has a slightly higher fat content and a sharper taste than its counterpart.

In cooking, Romano can be substituted for Parmesan in most recipes if you're looking for a more assertive flavor. Freshly grated Romano is great with pasta and soups, cooked vegetables, on pizza, in quiches or frittatas. It pairs well with apples, pears, tomatoes, and olives.

Try red wines such as Merlot, Cabernet Sauvignon, Zinfandel, or Chianti or beer with your Romano.

Ricotta

Ricotta is an Italian cheese made from the whey remaining after mozzarella or provolone is produced. The name *ricotta*—which means "cooked twice" in Italian—refers to the second processing of the liquid, when cheesemakers add lactic acid or vinegar and reheat it to almost the boiling point.

The resulting ricotta is a fresh, soft, snowy white cheese that's similar in texture to cottage cheese though considerably lighter. It's naturally low in fat, with a content ranging from 4 to 10 percent. It also has less salt than cottage cheese. The flavor is rich but mild and slightly sweet.

Ricotta is an excellent cooking cheese that binds ingredients because of its cohesive texture. It's a must in classic Italian dishes including lasagna, manicotti, and cannelloni. It appears in Italian desserts such as cannoli—deep-fried Sicilian pastries—and *cassata* cakes. Traditionalists love *pastiera*, a typical Neapolitan Easter dessert, often served simply by marrying ricotta with sugar, cinnamon, and—occasionally—chocolate shavings. Ricotta also makes a tasty low-fat cheesecake, either sweet or savory.

The Viglietti Family's Pasta Christina

Stefano Viglietti of Sheboygan's Tratoria Stefano developed this pasta dish and named it for his mother, Christine, whose own pasta creations were among his childhood favorites. It was a hit at one of our cheese parties. To add a little zip, use a hot Italian sausage.

3 tablespoons olive oil

I pound (about 4 links, or use bulk) Italian sausage, crumbled

4 cups quartered button mushrooms

4 cloves garlic, minced

¼ cup chopped parsley, divided

⅓ cup white wine

I cup chicken stock

¼ cup (½ stick) butter

I2 cherry tomatoes, quartered

I pound spaghetti

3 large pasteurized eggs

½ cup grated Parmesan cheese

½ cup pecorino Romano

1. In a medium sauté pan, heat the oil over a medium flame. Add the sausage and brown, turning and breaking up as needed.
2. Add the mushrooms and sauté until lightly browned, about 5 minutes.
3. Add the garlic and 2 tablespoons of the parsley. Sauté briefly.
4. Add the wine and stock; cook until the liquid is reduced by half, 5 to 10 minutes.
5. Add the butter and tomatoes and turn off the heat, allowing the butter to melt.
6. In abundant salted boiling water, cook the spaghetti.
7. In a small bowl, beat together the eggs, cheeses, and remaining 2 tablespoons of parsley.
8. In a large serving bowl, combine the hot pasta, hot sauce, and egg–cheese mixture. Quickly toss to coat the pasta evenly.

SERVES 6

Courtesy of Stefano Viglietti, Tratoria Stefano, Sheboygan, Wisconsin.

Blueberry Ricotta Coffee Cake

A great way to start the day, but delicious anytime, especially with a steaming-hot cup of coffee.

I cup flour

½ cup oat bran

½ cup plus 2 tablespoons packed light brown sugar, divided

2 teaspoons baking powder

½ teaspoon baking soda

¼ teaspoon ground cinnamon

¼ teaspoon salt

I cup (8 ounces) low-fat Wisconsin ricotta cheese

½ cup plain, fat-free yogurt

2 eggs, beaten

¼ cup (½ stick) butter, melted

½ teaspoon vanilla extract

½ cup fresh or frozen blueberries

1. Preheat the oven to 350°F. Butter an 8x8-inch baking pan.
2. Stir together all of the dry ingredients except 2 tablespoons of the brown sugar. Set aside.
3. Mix the cheese, yogurt, eggs, melted butter, vanilla, and blueberries. Stir into dry ingredients until just mixed.
4. Pour the batter into the prepared pan and sprinkle it with the remaining 2 tablespoons of brown sugar.
5. Bake until just firm to the touch, about 40 minutes.

SERVES 6

Courtesy of the Wisconsin Milk Marketing Board, Inc.

We know, we know: You saw the word *Italian* in this chapter's title, and you immediately started thumbing through, looking for the pizza part. We understand. Here it is.

Ironically, pizza didn't actually originate in Italy. Instead, the early Greeks baked large, round flat bread accessorized with olive oil, potatoes, and spices. It was the Italians, however, who named these round breads "pizza," at first eaten *au naturel*. History tells us that in the late 1800s, Queen Margherita of Savoy had taken a shine to this tasty treat. She ordered Rafaelle Esposito, a street vendor, to create a few pizzas for her. Flattered, he concocted a special dish with tomatoes, mozzarella, and fresh basil . . . thus inventing the famous cheese pizza that we know today. The dish became the rage in the United States after World War II, when returning Yanks craved the dish they had grown to love while in Europe.

Today the choice of pizza toppings is seemingly limitless, although a cheeseless pizza seems almost a sacrilege. Any combination of various meats, fruits, vegetables, spices, and even nuts can create a gourmet delight. Pizzas are great in the morning as leftovers, as Mart will attest, as well as for hors d'oeuvres, lunch, dinner, and even dessert.

The following suggestions are for a 12-inch pizza, made with your own or a purchased pizza crust. In general, pizza should be cooked in a 450°F oven for 12 to 15 minutes. Some fans prefer a lower temperature, such as 375°F, for 20 to 25 minutes or until the cheese topping is bubbly.

Sartori Roasted Vegetable Pizza with Asiago and Fontina Cheese

l tablespoon garlic-infused olive oil

2 tablespoons portobello mushroom, sliced

2 tablespoons red onion, sliced

2 tablespoons yellow pepper, cut into thin strips

2 tablespoons orange pepper, cut into thin strips

¼ cup cherry tomatoes, cut in half

⅓ cup grated Sartori Foods Fontina cheese

⅔ cup grated Sartori Foods Asiago cheese

l cup grated Sartori Foods mozzarella cheese

2 tablespoons fresh basil, chiffonade

1. Preheat oven to 375°F.
2. Grill vegetables until parcooked; brush the pizza crust with the olive oil; then top with the grilled vegetables and cheeses.
3. Bake 20 to 25 minutes until golden brown, top with the fresh basil, and serve.

Courtesy of Sartori Foods.

Salemville Gorgonzola and Caramelized Onion Pizza

2 tablespoons olive oil

2 tablespoons butter

4 large Vidalia or other sweet onions, sliced, browned and caramelized

4 ounces Auricchio Americano Mascarpone cheese

3 ounces Salemville Gorgonzola cheese, cubed or crumbled

¼ cup chopped pecans

Salt and pepper to taste

1. Cook onions in olive oil and butter over low heat until browned and caramelized, approximately 1 hour.
2. Spread onion mixture on a 12-inch pizza crust.
3. Sprinkle cheese and pecans on top of onion mixture.
4. Bake at 475° for 10 to 12 minutes or until cheese melts.

Courtesy of the DCI Cheese Company.

Wisconsin Gruyère, Asparagus, and Prosciutto Pizza

1 ½ teaspoons chopped garlic

1 teaspoon olive oil

2 cups (8 ounces) shredded Wisconsin Gruyère cheese

3 ounces prosciutto, julienned

3 ounces (5 spears) asparagus, trimmed, blanched, and cut into 1-inch pieces

½ cup (2 ounces) julienned red onion

1. Combine the garlic and olive oil and spread on a 12-inch pizza crust. Add the rest of ingredients.
2. Bake in a 450° oven for 15 to 20 minutes or until cheese melts.

Courtesy of the Wisconsin Milk Marketing Board, Inc.

Oriental Stir-Fry Pizza

14 ounces chicken breast, cut into strips

1 cup snow peas

¾ cup red pepper strips

½ cup diced celery

½ cup diced green onions

¾ cup baby corn ears

½ cup hot stir-fry oil

1 cup Peanut Satay Sauce (recipe follows)

2 tablespoons toasted sesame seeds

2 cups Wisconsin Hot Pepper Monterey Jack
  cheese, shredded

¾ cup honey-roasted peanuts, crushed

½ cup rice noodles

1. Preheat oven to 375°.
2. Pre-bake 12-inch pizza shell for 10 minutes.
3. Sauté the chicken strips, snow peas, red peppers, celery, green onions, and baby corn in the stir-fry oil until crisp. Set aside to cool.
4. Brush the pizza shell with the Peanut Satay Sauce and strew with the sesame seeds. Arrange the sautéed chicken and vegetables on the crust. Top with the Wisconsin cheese and peanuts.
5. Bake at 375° for 12 to 18 minutes.
6. Top with rice noodles for crunch.

Peanut Satay Sauce

6 cloves garlic, pounded

3 shallots, minced

2 teaspoons powdered hot cayenne pepper

1 teaspoon grated lemon peel

2 tablespoons stir-fry oil

1 tablespoon lemon juice

1 jar (12 ounces) crunchy peanut butter

15 ounces water

½ cup sugar

1–2 teaspoons salt, to taste

1. Stir-fry the garlic, shallots, cayenne, and lemon peel in the oil. Remove the lemon peel.
2. Add the lemon juice and simmer for a minute.
3. Add the peanut butter and water. Bring to a boil.
4. Add the sugar and salt. Boil until thickened.

Courtesy of the Wisconsin Milk Marketing Board, Inc., and chef Phillip Koenig.

Oliveto Pizza with Wisconsin Brick Cheese

3 spring garlic bulbs (up to 6 inches), slit and sliced
    fine

5 asparagus spears, parboiled, thinly sliced

3 small red potatoes, parboiled, thinly sliced

3 ounces baby pancetta, julienned, sautéed over
    low heat, and drained on paper towels

7 ounces Wisconsin Surface-Ripened Brick
    cheese, cut into slices

I tablespoon fresh thyme *or* I teaspoon dried thyme

I tablespoon red pepper flakes

Salt and pepper to taste

1. Preheat oven to 475°
2. Top a 12-inch pizza crust with the
   ingredients in the order listed. Drizzle with a
   small amount of olive oil.
3. Bake on lower rack of oven for 12 to 15
   minutes or until golden brown.

*Recipe by Curt Clingman, chef and co-owner of JoJo's
Restaurant, San Francisco, courtesy of the Wisconsin Milk
Marketing Board, Inc.*

Fiesta Pizza with Wisconsin Queso Blanco

I can (I6 ounces) vegetarian refried beans

¾ cup prepared salsa (medium or hot)

I yellow or red bell pepper, julienned to make I cup

I cup (4 ounces) crumbled Wisconsin Queso
    Blanco or Queso Fresco

¼ cup sliced scallions

1. Preheat oven to 450°.
2. Spread all ingredients on a 12-inch pizza
   crust.
3. Bake for 8 to 10 minutes or until cheese is
   melted.

Courtesy of the Wisconsin Milk Marketing Board, Inc.

Bananas Foster Pizza

4 ounces Wisconsin cream cheese, softened

I teaspoon vanilla extract

3 tablespoons maple syrup, divided

4 large bananas

2 tablespoons chopped hazelnuts

3 ounces Wisconsin mascarpone

Chocolate shavings (optional)

1. Combine the cream cheese, vanilla, 2 tablespoons of the maple syrup, and 2 of the bananas (sliced) in a bowl. Mix well.
2. Spread the banana–cheese mixture evenly over a 12-inch pizza crust. Top with the remaining bananas (sliced) and the chopped nuts.
3. Lightly spread the remaining maple syrup on filling.
4. Bake in a 450° oven for 12 to 15 minutes.
5. Garnish with mascarpone and chocolate shavings.

Courtesy of the Wisconsin Milk Marketing Board, Inc.

"I had no idea so many great cheeses were being made in Wisconsin. It's a beautiful state that reminds me in many ways of my home in Piedmont [Italy]."

—Chef Roberto Donna, Galileo da Roberto Donna, Washington, DC

S^tGENIX
maison 60%.
16,70^F pièce

St FELICIEN
maison 50%
8,90^F

CHAPTER 8

FRENCH CHEESES

FRANCE, LIKE WISCONSIN, IS A PARADISE FOR CHEESE lovers. The estimated number of cheese varieties in France ranges between 350 and 500, and more than forty of them are AOC—*Appellation d'Origine Contrôlée.* This designation guarantees the origin of the cheese, the milk used, and the length of aging, as well as ensuring that the cheese is produced by an established method. Roquefort was the first cheese awarded this status, in 1925.

French regions also have their specialties. Normandy is famous for its Camembert; the Loire Valley and Provence, for their goat's milk cheeses; Alsace, for its robust Muenster, where the cheese originated; the Paris area, for delicious Brie. The caves of Roquefort-sur-Soulzon—a village in the Pyrennées—are the official home of Roquefort.

Classic French Dishes

French cuisine is known for its creativity, diversity, and emphasis on natural products, and cheese plays an integral role. Both the formal haute cuisine and the regional cuisine of rural France use cheese as an ingredient and a stand-alone. No self-respecting French dinner would omit a cheese course, which usually follows the main course and precedes dessert. We cheese lovers are indebted to the French for their innovation and mastery of such marvelous dishes as soufflés, crepes, quiches, Croque Monsieurs, and many more.

Quiche: Quiche has been a culinary delight for thousands of years. It dates back to the Middle Ages, originating in the Lorraine region of France, then a Germanic kingdom called Lothringen that later changed its name under French rule. The word *quiche* is derived from the German *Kuchen,* meaning "cake." In Nancy, France, a quiche-like recipe called *félouse* was developed in the sixteenth century. At first, quiche included only eggs, cream, and smoked bacon; the bottom crust was made from bread dough. Cheese was added later—all kinds of cheese, with Gruyère, Swiss, hard mozzarella, Parmesan, and blue cheeses most common.

Although quiche became known in the United States in the 1950s, it wasn't until the late 1970s that it became all the rage. It was popular in restaurants as lunch, dinner, or hors d'oeuvre fare because it was relatively simple to make, held up well, and offered seemingly unlimited possibilities for the creative cook. Chopped vegetables, such as broccoli and mushrooms, meats like ham and bacon, and shellfish including crab, lobster, and shrimp all make excellent additions.

Quiche became the butt of jokes after Bruce Feirstein's *Real Men Don't Eat Quiche: A Guidebook to All That Is Truly Masculine* came out in 1982. It was touted as unmanly because of its dainty reputation. Today quiche has regained its popularity, according to Steve Ehlers, owner of Larry's Brown Deer Market, in Brown Deer Wisconsin, north of Milwaukee.

Omelets: The word *omelet* is thought to have originated in a recipe found in a Roman cookbook titled *Apicius,* dating to around the late fourth or early fifth century AD. The compilation is considered the "first" cookbook, possibly assembled by a cook or epicure of the same name. The dish was called "overmele," made with eggs, honey, and pepper.

We have been making cheese omelets for years. In fact, Pam learned how to make an *omelette au fromage* in France in 1970. Recently a young French exchange student who stayed with us ate an omelet every day and loved them so much he wanted our

> *"Comment voulez-vous gouverner un pays qui a deux cent quarante-six variétés de fromage?"*
>
> **("How can you govern a country which has two hundred and forty-six varieties of cheese?")**
>
> —Charles de Gaulle, from *Les Mots du Général,* Ernest Mignon (1962)

Wisconsin's rolling hills, covered with lush grass, are heaven for contented cows.

recipe to take back home! We admit that our omelets are enhanced by selecting the best fresh eggs from our chicken coop each morning. Short of that luxury, the fresher the egg, the better.

Soufflés: The word *soufflé* means "breath" or "puff" in French—a reference to the amount of time they will hold their shape. The first recipe for soufflé is thought to have appeared in *Le Cuisinier Moderne* (1742) by Vincent La Chapelle. In *The French Cook* (1813) by Louis Ude, the word *soufflé* first appeared in English. By the mid-1800s the dish had become very common. A cheese soufflé recipe was included in *The Settlement Cookbook (The Way to a Man's Heart)* in 1903.

Quiche Alsacienne

This is perfect for a light summer meal, either for lunch or dinner. For a summer dinner on the back deck, we like to serve it with a salade Niçoise and fruit, as well as a glass or two of Sancerre. If you omit the onions, by the way, this dish becomes Quiche Lorraine.

I piecrust (homemade pastry is best, but a ready-made crust can be used in a pinch)

6 strips bacon

I onion, chopped

I cup cubed Gruyère

¼ cup grated Parmesan

4 large eggs

1½ cups cream (or substitute fat-free half-and-half)

¼ teaspoon ground nutmeg

½ teaspoon salt

¼ teaspoon pepper

1. Preheat the oven to 450°F.
2. Cook the bacon until crisp. Pour off all but 1 tablespoon of the grease. Cook the onion in the bacon fat until slightly brown.
3. Strew the crumbled bacon, onion, and cheeses in the bottom of the pastry shell.
4. Beat the eggs with a whisk; add the half-and-half and spices. Pour this mixture over the bacon, onion, and cheese mixture.
5. Bake for 15 minutes, then reduce the oven temperature to 350°F and continue baking the quiche until it's done, about 30 more minutes. You can tell that it's ready when you insert a knife about an inch from the crust and it comes out clean.

SERVES 4

The Perfect Cheese Omelet

Pam prefers the simplicity of a cheese omelet, while Marty loves the addition of everything from mushrooms to chives, caramelized onions, bacon, and even potatoes. Add these at the same time as the cheese. Gruyère remains our favorite in cheese omelets.

3 fresh eggs

2 tablespoons sweet butter

Salt and pepper to taste

3 tablespoons grated Wisconsin cheese

1. Beat the eggs until frothy.
2. Melt the butter in an omelet pan. The melted butter should be hot but not too hot (enough to sizzle a drop of water). If the butter has browned, toss it out and start over.
3. Add the eggs and let them begin to cook.
4. To create a light and airy omelet, tilt and shake the pan, using a fork or spatula to allow the uncooked portion to settle and cook on the hot surface.
5. When the eggs are almost cooked, add salt and pepper and the cheese. Sometimes it is necessary to cover the pan with a lid for a few minutes to melt the cheese.
6. When it's finished, carefully fold the omelet in half and slide it onto a plate.

SERVES 1 HUNGRY PERSON

Cheese Soufflé

Don't be intimidated by the thought of making a soufflé. They aren't as daunting as they appear, and they make perfect party fare with a glass of champagne.

3 tablespoons sweet butter, plus extra to grease the soufflé dish

3 tablespoons unbleached flour

I cup whole milk, room temperature

I teaspoon ground nutmeg

I teaspoon salt

I teaspoon white pepper

⅓–⅔ cups grated cheese of your choice; we prefer Gruyère or a sharp Cheddar

4 egg yolks

5 egg whites, room temperature

Pinch cream of tartar

¼ cup finely grated Parmesan or bread crumbs

CHEF NOTE:
This is a recipe for a 6-cup soufflé dish or four 8-ounce ramekins. For an 8-cup soufflé dish, use 6 or 7 egg whites.

1. Preheat the oven to 425°F. Butter the soufflé dish and dust it with Parmesan.
2. Melt 3 tablespoons of butter over medium-low heat, add the flour, and cook for 5 minutes, stirring constantly. Add the milk and continue stirring until thickened. Mix in the nutmeg, salt, and pepper, and then stir in the cheese. When it is melted and thoroughly mixed in, add the egg yolks, then set aside.
3. Beat the egg whites (room temperature), adding the cream of tartar as you do so. Do not overbeat. If the peaks hold their shape when you lift the beaters, they are perfect.
4. Fold a third of the egg whites into the sauce mixture and mix thoroughly. Then add the rest and mix very gently to keep as much air as possible in the mixture.
5. Gently move the soufflé mixture to the buttered soufflé dish. It should be about three-quarters filled. For a top-hat appearance, make a 1-inch groove around the edge of the soufflé with your finger.
6. Put the soufflé in the oven and reduce the temperature to 375°F.
7. Bake for 40 to 45 minutes. Don't peek for at least 20 minutes. Serve immediately.

SERVES 4

Artichoke Hearts and Mushrooms

Perfect for an appetizer or served along with your favorite steak, this trio of tastes makes an elegant addition to any meal.

4 fresh artichokes

2 tablespoons butter

¼ cup grated Gruyère cheese

½ pound mushrooms, chopped finely

1. Steam the artichokes until the leaf comes out easily, about half an hour. Peel the leaves, remove the choke, and keep the artichoke bottoms whole.
2. Lightly sauté the artichoke bottoms in the butter. Remove them from the pan and keep them warm.
3. Preheat the broiler.
4. Sauté the mushrooms in the same pan as the artichokes until they're browned.
5. Fill the artichoke hearts with the mushrooms and top with the cheese.
6. Heat under the broiler for a few minutes until the cheese is melted and slightly brown.

SERVES 4

Croque Monsieur

What would a French bistro be without a Croque Monsieur? Originally served in 1910 in a Paris cafe, this standard remains popular throughout France and Switzerland as a casual meal. You can even purchase a special sandwich grilling iron with two hinged metal plates to facilitate the making of these treats.

2 slices bread

1 teaspoon salted butter

1 teaspoon Dijon mustard

2 slices thinly sliced ham

**2 tablespoons (or more) finely grated
    Gruyère cheese**

1. Butter one side of the bread and put a layer of mustard on the other. Put the grated cheese and sliced ham on the mustard side and place the other bread slice on top, butter-side up.
2. Heat a pan and grill the sandwich for about 4 minutes on each side, until golden brown.

SERVES 1

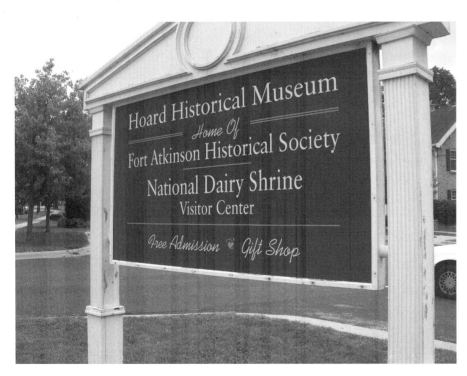

The National Dairy Shrine, founded in 1949, honors dairy leaders, retains archives on the dairy world, and promotes the industry. Photo by Martin Hintz

Croque Monsieur Variations:

- When served with a fried egg, a Croque Monsieur becomes a Croque Madame.
- Dip the entire sandwich in beaten eggs and grill in melted butter.
- Turn your sandwich into a delicious casserole by topping it with 2 cups of a rich Mornay Sauce and baking at 375°F until browned, about 20 to 30 minutes.

Mornay Sauce (Cheese Sauce)

1. Make a basic white sauce by melting ¼ cup (½ stick) of butter in a saucepan over medium-low heat. Add ¼ cup of all-purpose flour and whisk well. Remove the pan from the heat and add 2 cups of milk; return it to the heat and whisk for a few minutes, until the sauce has thickened and is smooth.
2. Reduce the heat and add ½ cup of grated and firmly packed cheese. To avoid stringiness, don't overcook. If the cheese does become stringy, you can add a little white wine.

CHEF NOTE:
Mornay sauce made with Cheddar is great on steamed broccoli. Put the broccoli and sauce in a casserole dish, top with 2 tablespoons of bread crumbs, and bake for 20 minutes at 425°F.

Camembert and Brie

Camembert is often considered the national cheese of France. In Wisconsin, French cheesemakers are making Camembert with rich Wisconsin milk that has a compositional resemblance to French milk. Camembert is distinguished by an edible bloomy rind, which is due to a white mold called *Penicillium candidum* that is applied to the surface. The cheese ripens from the outside in a few weeks and ages to a more pungent taste.

Camembert and Brie are almost identical and can be used interchangeably in recipes. Both should be served at room temperature. They can be baked briefly or heated in a microwave oven.

One of Wisconsin's most notable Brie makers has roots that stretch back to France. That country's giant dairy company Groupe Lactalis—founded in 1933 by the Besnier family—bought a plant in Belmont, Wisconsin, in 1981. In 1995 it expanded its facility to become the largest and most technologically advanced soft-ripened cheese manufacturing facility in the United States. Groupe Lactalis's President Brie took top honors at the American Cheese Society's 2005 competition in the Brie Made from Cow's Milk category. President Brie with Herbs, President Pepper Brie, and plain and herbed Bries have won many awards nationally and internationally. Groupe Lactalis also owns the Rondelé Specialty Foods in Merrill, Wisconsin.

Camembert and Brie are very versatile cheeses:

- They're delicious in sandwiches with a cranberry sauce and turkey.
- Create an easy hors d'oeuvre by topping either cheese with chutney.
- For a quick and elegant appetizer, wrap Camembert or Brie in puff pastry, brush on an egg wash, and bake.
- Put a piece of either cheese (rind removed) on a thinly sliced baguette and serve with a salad of mixed greens, apple wedges, candied pecans, and balsamic vinaigrette.
- Grill slices of fennel, onion wedges, and asparagus. Add cubes of Camembert or Brie; drizzle on a balsamic vinaigrette and add pine nuts. This is delicious with couscous.

- Add cubes to penne pasta mixed with cooked asparagus tips, sautéed shallots, prosciutto, and snipped chives. Drizzle with olive oil and grind over plenty of black pepper.
- Groupe Lactalis suggests a Brie and Bacon Salad: To 12 ounces of mixed lettuce leaves, add 15 ounces of President Brie cut into pieces, 8 slices of cooked and crumbled bacon, and 1 avocado cut into bite-size pieces. Toss with croutons and your favorite vinaigrette.

Sparkling wines, champagnes, and Pinot Noir are all wonderful companions for Camembert and Brie.

Brie and Chutney Melt

Try serving this treat with apple wedges, or topped with almonds or walnuts. You can also substitute strawberry or raspberry preserves for the chutney and bacon.

6 slices bacon

1 8-ounce round President Brie

⅓ cup chutney

1. Grill the bacon, drain it on paper towels, and break it into small pieces.
2. Trim the top off the Brie and place the cheese on a microwave-safe plate. Top with the chutney. Microwave on high for 1 minute.
3. Sprinkle with the bacon pieces and serve with crackers.

SERVES 8 AS AN APPETIZER

Courtesy of Groupe Lactalis, Belmont, Wisconsin.

Brie and Turkey Croissants

These easily prepared croissants make for great picnic dining or holiday parties when the family gathers to celebrate good times.

2 croissants

4 ounces turkey, thinly sliced

4 thin slices red and green pepper, roasted or sautéed in a pan

2 thin slices red onion

4 ounces President Brie

2 tablespoons mango chutney

1. Slice the croissants lengthwise and layer on the turkey, roasted peppers, and onion slices. Top with the remaining croissant half.
2. Wrap in tinfoil and place in a 350°F oven for about 2 minutes.
3. Remove from the oven and carefully lift the croissant top. Put slices of Brie and the mango chutney on top, then add the other half of the croissant. Serve immediately.

MAKES 2 CROISSANTS

Courtesy of Groupe Lactalis, Belmont, Wisconsin.

Brie Raspberry Salad with Balsamic Vinaigrette

A garden's bounty is fit for a king and queen when Wisconsin Brie joins the royal taste court.

Balsamic Vinaigrette

3 tablespoons balsamic vinegar

2 tablespoons fresh lemon juice

¼ cup hazelnut oil

¼ cup olive oil

Salt and pepper to taste

1. Whisk all the ingredients together.

Salad

8 cups Boston lettuce

½ cup raspberries

½ cup chopped walnuts

I wheel (7 ounces) President Brie, cut into pieces

2 tablespoons chopped fresh mint leaves

1. Toss the lettuce with the vinaigrette. Divide it among eight plates.
2. Top with the raspberries, walnuts, Brie pieces, and fresh mint, and serve.

SERVES 8

Courtesy of Groupe Lactalis, Belmont, Wisconsin.

Wisconsin Camembert with Hazelnuts and Dried Apricot Compote

Chef Todd Downs, who created this mouthwatering dish, is with Rondelé Specialty Foods in Merrill, Wisconsin. With more than twenty-five years in the culinary industry under his belt, he focuses now on creating recipes with Rondelé's many award-winning soft and spreadable cheeses.

12 pieces (each 2 inches square) Wisconsin Camembert cheese, rind trimmed off

2 cups hazelnuts, toasted, skinned, and chopped

4 cups dried apricots, cut into ¼-inch strips

3 cups Gewürztraminer wine

½ cup sugar

2 vanilla beans, split and scraped

1. Coat the cheese squares evenly with the chopped hazelnuts. Reserve at room temperature, covered, until the cheese softens.
2. In a saucepan, combine the apricots, wine, sugar, and vanilla beans. Simmer until the apricots are soft and the compote is thickened, about 20 minutes.
3. Place a piece of Camembert on each of twelve small plates. Top with a heaping spoonful of compote. Serve.

SERVES 12

Courtesy of the Wisconsin Milk Marketing Board, Inc.

Baguette with Wisconsin Brie and Berries

Picnic like the French with a basket filled with a baguette, sausage to slice, and a ripe Camembert wheel. Add some cherries, grapes, cherrystone tomatoes, black olives, and fresh radishes. Don't forget a blanket, knives, plates, napkins, glasses, and, of course, a corkscrew. On a hot summer's day, a bottle of dry French rosé makes for a perfect lazy afternoon.

I wheel (6 ounces) Wisconsin Brie, rind cut off

⅓ cup orange marmalade

I pint fresh raspberries

⅓ cup chopped pecans

French or sourdough baguette

Salad greens including arugula, watercress, and/or spinach

1. Bring the Brie to room temperature. Cut into small pieces.
2. Add the orange marmalade, then fold in the raspberries and pecans.
3. Slice the bread in half horizontally. Hollow out the bottom half, leaving a ¾-inch shell. Spread the Brie mixture on the bottom half. Top with enough salad greens to cover the Brie and fill the inside of the sandwich. Replace the top of the bread. Cut into individual servings.

SERVES 6

Recipe courtesy of the Wisconsin Milk Marketing Board, Inc.

Neufchâtel

Neufchâtel originated in the town of Neufchâtel (no surprise there) in Normandy; it dates back to the sixth century. In France it often comes in a heart-shaped form. There, Neufchâtel is a soft, slightly crumbly, unripened cheese. It resembles Camembert with its white, edible rind, but it has more of a sharp and somewhat salty taste.

The Neufchâtel made in the United States bears little resemblance to its French progenitor. Here it's similar to cream cheese, but lower in fat because it's made with whole milk rather than cream. It has a mild flavor and is usually sold in brick form.

West Bend's Level Valley Creamery, now owned by Schreiber Foods, has won many awards for its Neufchâtel. In addition to plain, the firm makes more than thirty flavors, including berry, strawberry, pineapple, chive, onion, herb, and smoked salmon

Salmon and Dill Wisconsin Brie Torte

This torte can be made with any size wheel of Brie, and with plain or herbed cheese. For larger wheels, adjust the ingredients accordingly.

I wheel (8 ounces) Wisconsin Brie

3 tablespoons Neufchâtel or cream cheese, softened

4 slices smoked salmon

Fresh dill

I tablespoon capers

Red pepper strips, for garnish

1. Carefully cut the Brie into halves horizontally.
2. Spread softened cream cheese on the cut surfaces of each side. Place the smoked salmon, dill, and capers neatly on the bottom half; carefully replace the top.
3. Garnish with more fresh dill and with red bell pepper strips.
4. Chill well and cut the Brie into pie-shaped wedges for serving.

SERVES 8 AS AN APPETIZER

This recipe was inspired by the Wisconsin Milk Marketing Board, Inc.

with roasted garlic. It advertises its Neufchâtel cream cheese as being "lite," with 23 percent butterfat, high in moisture and soft in texture.

Neufchâtel can be substituted for any recipe calling for cream cheese. It's great in dips, frosting, and cheesecake recipes—not to mention the ubiquitous bagels and lox. You can also serve it in sandwiches with jam or jelly, or on fruit and nut breads. Delicious! It pairs well with fruity white wines such as Riesling.

Muenster (Munster)

Historians believe that Muenster originated in Alsace, France, although others give the credit to Germany. The name comes from the term *monasterium* or *monastery*—it was originally made by monks.

The Silver-Lewis Cheese Co-operative has been operating in the same location in Monticello since 1897, with the third generation of the Lewis family supplying the milk from their nearby farm. The co-op, known for its Brick and Muenster cheeses is currently operated by Josh and Carla Erickson. Pictured is their daughter, Lonna Slack.
Photo by Bill Wyss

In Wisconsin, Muenster was first made in the late 1800s by European immigrants. Americans took a liking to its mild taste, and its firm texture made it ideal for slicing in sandwiches. Muenster is recognizable by its often orange surface and creamy white interior. When young it is very mild, although with age it becomes creamier and has more aroma and a savory taste. Cheesemakers across the state have been honored for their Muensters.

Muenster is made in a variety of styles. You can find it with cranberries, hot peppers, and caraway seeds, as well as in low-sodium and kosher varieties. It's delicious in sandwiches. How about sliced Muenster with avocado, tomatoes, and mayonnaise? Or try sausage and mustard on a hearty bread with slices of Muenster and pickles on the side. You can also add Muenster to your mashed potatoes, or melt some shredded cheese on any vegetable casserole. It pairs well with Gewürztraminer and lager beers.

Muenster can be difficult to slice unless it's firm and well chilled. You can always spray your cheese slices with a nonstick vegetable spray to keep them from sticking together.

Corn-Stuffed Tomatoes with Wisconsin Muenster Cheese

Wisconsin sweet corn and fresh tomatoes, along with Wisconsin Muenster, make for a fabulous trio of tastes.

8 medium tomatoes

I tablespoon butter

¼ cup sliced green onions

⅓ cup diced green pepper

2 ½ cups fresh corn kernels (4–5 ears),
    cut from the cob

2 tablespoons water

I tablespoon fresh thyme leaves *or*
    ¼ teaspoon dried thyme

6 slices chopped cooked bacon

2 tablespoons mayonnaise

I ½ cups shredded Wisconsin Muenster
    cheese

1. Slice the tops from the tomatoes. Carefully scoop out the pulp, leaving a shell. A serrated grapefruit spoon or melon baller works well for this. Turn the tomatoes upside down and drain them on paper toweling.

2. Preheat the oven to 400°F. Lightly grease a pizza pan or other baking sheet. Set aside.

3. Heat the butter in a 9- or 10-inch skillet. Add the green onions and sauté over medium heat for about 3 minutes. Add the green pepper and sauté for 2 to 3 minutes longer. Add the corn kernels, water, and thyme. Bring to a boil. Cover and cook at a gentle boil until the corn is tender, about 5 to 7 minutes. Remove the pan from the heat and drain.

4. Stir in the bacon pieces and mayonnaise. Fill each tomato with one-eighth of the mixture. Bake for 10 to 15 minutes, until the tomatoes are almost cooked but still hold their shape.

5. Remove the tomatoes from the oven and top each with some Muenster. Bake for 3 to 5 minutes more, until the cheese melts. Or place the cheese-topped tomatoes under a hot broiler, broiling just until the cheese melts and browns slightly.

SERVES 8

Courtesy of the Wisconsin Milk Marketing Board, Inc.

Wisconsin Cheese Steak Sandwich

Move over, Philly: Here comes the Dairy State. Using Wisconsin ingredients in this recipe earns kudos from die-hard sandwich lovers.

Steak and Marinade

¾ cup vegetable oil

¼ cup red wine vinegar

¼ cup prepared chili sauce

2 teaspoons Worcestershire sauce

½ teaspoon salt

2 tablespoons fresh lemon juice

2 teaspoons seasoned salt

3 cloves garlic, minced

4½ pounds beef flank steak

1. In a bowl, combine all the marinade ingredients except the steak. Place the steak in a nonmetal baking dish and pour the marinade atop.
2. Cover and marinate overnight in refrigerator, turning occasionally. Let the steak come to room temperature before grilling. Remove the steak from the marinade and drain off any excess.

Cheese Bread

½ cup (I stick) butter, softened

4 cloves garlic, minced

2 loaves French bread, split lengthwise

4 cups (I6 ounces) shredded Wisconsin Muenster cheese

1. Combine the butter and garlic and spread on the cut bread. Sprinkle each half with 1 cup of the cheese.
2. Cut two sheets of heavy foil to wrap the two sandwich halves, coating each sheet with cooking spray. Wrap the halves, loosely, side by side in foil, two halves per packet.
3. Preheat the broiler. Place the steak in a broiler pan 2 to 3 inches from the top of the oven. Broil for 6 minutes on each side. Remove the steak and let it rest for 10 minutes.
4. Put the bread onto the middle rack of the oven. Broil for 8 minutes or until the cheese melts.

5. Slice the steak thinly, across the grain.
6. Remove the bread. Top the grilled bread with sliced beef, serving open faced.
7. Cut each loaf into six pieces and serve immediately.

SERVES 6

Courtesy of the Wisconsin Milk Marketing Board, Inc.

"A cheese may disappoint. It may be dull, it may be naïve, it may be over sophisticated. Yet it remains, cheese, milk's leap toward immortality."

—Clifton Fadiman (1904–1999), American writer, editor, and *New Yorker* magazine reviewer, from *Any Number Can Play,* 1957

CHAPTER 9

HISPANIC CHEESES

ALTHOUGH THERE WERE HISPANICS IN WISCONSIN as early as the eighteenth century, the state's more contemporary Spanish-speaking population dates to around 1910, when Mexican refugees settled here after the revolution in their homeland. While there were only about 1,000 individuals of Hispanic descent permanently living here in the mid–twentieth century, thousands more were migrant workers. As the need for farm laborers grew during World War II, additional Hispanics flocked to Wisconsin, primarily from Mexico.

Many stayed after the war and became citizens. They were eventually joined by Puerto Ricans and natives of other Latin countries. By 1970 more than 40,000 Hispanic residents considered Wisconsin their home. As of this writing, some 194,000 Hispanic Americans live in our state.

They have naturally brought their cuisine, and their cheeses, with them. Today Hispanic varieties have moved beyond ethnic kitchens and restaurants to become favorites in the wider community. Food fans love working with Hispanic cheese because of the wide range of serving and cooking possibilities. There are three primary styles: fresh, melting, and hard.

Fresh Cheeses

Fresh cheeses are mild and crumbly in texture. What sets them apart from other Hispanic cheeses is that they don't melt when heated. They become warm and soft, but don't lose their shape. This is an important factor in many dishes, such as enchiladas and chiles rellenos, where the cheese is used as a stuffing and needs to maintain its form without getting soupy. White in color, fresh varieties include Queso Blanco, Panela, and Queso Fresco. They were originally produced by local cheesemakers and had a shelf life of less than a week. Today they are fine for up to three or four months. These cheeses are often eaten as a snack with fruit. They are also often crumbled on salads or used as a recipe's base ingredient.

Queso Blanco, or "white cheese," is a variety that browns when melted, but holds its shape. It can be crumbled on enchiladas, chiles rellenos, and other Mexican dishes. With a mild, fresh, slightly salty taste, fried Queso Blanco cubes make great croutons in salads.

Queso Blanco is a favorite of Mexican chefs, as well as home cooks, who pair it with white wine, sangria, or any of the Wisconsin-brewed darker lagers and bocks such as Steven Point Bock, a New Glarus Brewing Company Uff-Da Bock developed by brewmaster Dan Carey, a Huber or Bergoff bock from the Huber Brewery, or perhaps a Louie's Demise ale from the Milwaukee Ale House for a change of pace. Queso Blanco complements guava, mango, and pineapples.

A variation of Queso Blanco is Queso Blanco con Frutas, or "white cheese with fruit." With its fruit pieces, this cheese is 25 percent lower in fat. It can be cubed and pan fried or skewered on a shish kebab and grilled.

Panela, one of the most popular cheeses in Mexico, is a fresh cheese with a mild taste and crumbly texture. When heated it becomes soft with a creamy taste but—like other fresh cheeses—does not lose its shape; this makes it an excellent frying cheese. It can also be grilled and served with salsa. Or you can easily serve a slice on a hot corn tortilla.

Authentic refried beans include shredded Panela, which is mixed in during the cooking process to add texture. Panela can be deep-fried and served as an appetizer with salsa. Dipped in powdered sugar, it becomes a delicious dessert.

Queso Fresco: *Fresco* is the Spanish word for "fresh." Queso Fresco is wonderful when crumbled over tacos, enchiladas, salads, and refried beans. You can also slice it into thick slabs and sauté it to a golden brown.

> **"Won't you come in? We were just about to have some cheese."**
>
> —Wallace and Gromit, Wallace speaking, from *A Close Shave* (1995)

Couscous and Wisconsin Queso Blanco

When these Middle East and Hispanic ingredients mingle, taste buds come out the winner.

I package (10 ounces) couscous mix

1½ cups chicken broth

½ cup water

10 asparagus spears, cut into 1-inch pieces
   (3 per spear)

2 tomatoes, chopped

I cup canned chickpeas, rinsed and
   drained

3 green onions, thinly sliced

½ red bell pepper, cut into julienne strips

⅓ cup dried currants or raisins

1½ cups (6 ounces) crumbled Wisconsin
   Queso Blanco

Dressing

Juice of ½ lemon

⅓ cup olive oil

⅛ teaspoon ground cumin

⅛ teaspoon curry

I drop Tabasco sauce

Pinch garlic powder

Salt and pepper to taste

1. Prepare the couscous according to package directions, omitting any butter. Fluff the prepared couscous lightly with a fork. Let it stand for 5 minutes.
2. Meanwhile, place the asparagus on a microwave-safe plate; sprinkle with 1 tablespoon of water. Cover loosely with plastic wrap and microwave on high for 2 minutes; set aside.

1. In a small bowl, whisk together the dressing ingredients.
2. In a large bowl, combine the prepared couscous with all of the other ingredients. Toss well with the dressing.
3. Cover and chill for at least 1 hour before serving.

SERVES 6

Recipe inspired by the Wisconsin Milk Marketing Board, Inc.

"Inside Out" Grilled Cheese with Red Onion Jam

You can prepare these sandwiches ahead of time, if you like. Simply rewarm them in a 350°F oven just before serving.

Red Onion Jam

2 red onions, julienned

¼ cup salad oil

½ cup rice vinegar

¼ cup grenadine syrup

Juice of 1 lemon

½ cup golden raisins

1 tablespoon fresh thyme leaves

Freshly ground black pepper to taste

1. Sauté the red onions in the oil, cooking slowly.
2. Add the remaining jam ingredients. Cook for about 20 minutes, until thickened.

Grilled Cheese

12 slices sunflower seed bread, cut into 2-inch squares ⅛ inch thick

Melted butter

24 slices Wisconsin Queso Blanco con Frutas, cut into 2-inch squares ¼ inch thick

1. Brush the bread slices on both sides with melted butter. Toast until golden brown.
2. Heat a large, nonstick skillet over medium-high heat. Lightly grill the cheese squares until they're golden brown on both sides.
3. Place twelve of the cheese squares on a serving platter or individual plate. Top each with a teaspoon of Red Onion Jam and then a slice of the toasted sunflower bread.
4. Top the bread with another teaspoon of Red Onion Jam.
5. Top each sandwich with a slice of the remaining Queso Blanco con Frutas cheese. Press the sandwiches together.

MAKES 12 SMALL SANDWICHES

Courtesy of the Wisconsin Milk Marketing Board and Todd Downs, a chef-ambassador for the Wisconsin Milk Marketing Board, Inc.

Wisconsin Queso Blanco Fruit Compote

This berry-good dish is wonderful for summery dining.

¼ cup fresh blueberries

¼ cup fresh raspberries

¼ cup sliced fresh strawberries

¼ cup diced apples

¼ cup diced fresh pineapple

3 tablespoons blackberry jam

6 ounces Wisconsin Queso Blanco
    Cheese, sliced into 12 strips

I ounce sunflower seeds, shelled and
    salted

1. Combine the fruits and jam in a medium bowl. Gently mix.
2. Heat a nonstick frying pan over a medium-high flame and fry the Queso Blanco for 30 seconds on each side. Remove the pan from the heat.
3. Divide the fruit mixture among six salad plates, topping each with two fried Queso Blanco strips.
4. Top each with sunflower seeds and serve immediately, while the cheese is still warm.

SERVES 6

Courtesy of the Wisconsin Milk Marketing Board, Inc., and John Esser.

Sundance Salad

Fresh mixed greens and fruits take on extra zing with Salsa Dressing, enhanced by the addition of Wisconsin Queso Fresco.

Salsa Dressing

⅔ cup mild or medium garden-style salsa

¼ cup red wine vinegar

I tablespoon vegetable oil

¼ teaspoon chili powder

1. In a medium bowl, combine the salsa, vinegar, oil, and chili powder; chill until serving time.

Salad

6 cups torn curly-leaf lettuce

I avocado, peeled and cut into I2 wedges

I papaya, peeled, seeded, and cut into I2 wedges

½ pineapple, peeled and cut into I2 wedges

I tomato, cut into I2 wedges

I small red onion, thinly sliced

I cup (4 ounces) crumbled Wisconsin Queso Fresco

1. Arrange the lettuce on six individual plates. Top with the avocado, papaya, pineapple, tomato, onion, and cheese.
2. Toss with Salsa Dressing and serve.

SERVES 6

Courtesy of the Wisconsin Milk Marketing Board, Inc.

WINNING AND WORTHY WISCONSIN HISPANIC CHEESES

Paul Rufener from Swiss Heritage Cheese took top honors for his Queso Blanco at the 2006 World Championship Cheese Contest. At the World Dairy Expo, the Wisconsin Cheese Group of Monroe won first and second prizes for its Michoacano, Queso Blanco, and Fresco Wheel.

Hans Lehner from Valley View Cheese Coop won best of class for his Queso Quesadilla at both the World and US Championships.

At the World Championship Cheese Contest in 2006, Jamie White from Torkelson's Prairie Hill Cheese Plant won top prize for his Panela. Steve Stettler of Decatur Dairy captured third for his Asadero.

CHULA VISTA CHEESE

Chula Vista Cheese Company in Browntown, Wisconsin, is a regular vendor at Madison's farmers' market. The firm produces a variety of Hispanic specialty cheeses including its Chihuahua cheese (a Brick–Monterey Jack combination), Queso Blanco, and Brick. More than a hundred area farms supply the milk to make over 40,000 pounds of cheese every day.

SPECIALTY CHEESE

Specialty Cheese Company has four plants in Wisconsin making more than thirty-five varieties of ethnic cheese from milk provided by some sixty small family farms. Many are Hispanic varieties sold under the La VacaRica brand. The firm has ten Wisconsin licensed cheesemakers who produce numerous award-winning cheeses.

Cheesemaker Jim Meives of the Chula Vista Cheese Company proudly wears his "Dangerously Cheesy" T-shirt while at the farmers' market on Madison's Capitol Square.

Photo by Martin Hintz

Melting Cheeses

Hispanic melting cheeses melt without separating into solids and oil. They are generally mild tasting and make marvelous snacks. Often used in quesadillas and tacos, they're also great on pizza, in grilled cheese sandwiches, on burgers, and on tortillas and taco chips because they aren't greasy and have a richly cheesy taste.

Asadero is a flavorful cheese with a smooth texture and slightly tangy flavor that enhances many Mexican dishes. In Spanish, *asadero* means "baking."

Add shredded Asadero to tostadas or tacos along with your favorite fillings: lettuce, diced onions, tomatoes, cilantro, chile peppers, and meats such as chicken, beef, or pork. (The same fillings make for a great Mexican pizza!) Asadero also matches up nicely with fruits such as mangos, papayas, nectarines, peaches, and melons. For a delicious dessert, fill an enchilada with diced fruit, top it with Asadero, and sprinkled with cinnamon, sugar, and nutmeg. Beverages that pair well with Asadero include Chardonnay, sangria, margaritas, Peck's Pilsner from Madison's Great Dane brewpub or a Point Special Lager from the Stevens Point Brewery. The latter brew is not very hoppy, making it a perfect complement to spicier Hispanic foods. Making that "point," Point brewmaster John Zappa says he loves the combination of flavors.

Queso Quesadilla: This milder version of Asadero originated in northern Sinaloa, a Mexican state along the Pacific Ocean. It's smooth, creamy, and mild, and was used in the original quesadillas—hence the name for this popular American dish. (Quesadillas are basically tortillas, topped with shredded cheese, and either folded in half and grilled or topped with a second tortilla and cooked on both sides.) Queso Jalapeño is a variation on Quesadilla, with bits of real jalapeño peppers added to the cheese for spice.

Queso Quesadilla is ideal for enchiladas, burritos, chiles rellenos, and nachos. We've found that it makes excellent grilled cheese sandwiches. Serve it on a Mexican pizza with chorizo—or a taco pizza with taco meat, salsa, Quesadilla, tomatoes, olives, peppers, and whatever else you can think of!

Wisconsin Tamale Pie

This dish can be made anywhere from mild to spicy, depending on your choice of salsa and green chilies. If you opt for a hotter version, be sure to have a big glass of Wisconsin milk on hand to quell the fire!

Graphic courtesy of Maple Leaf Cheese

2 tablespoons butter

I large onion, chopped

1½ pounds ground beef

3 cups tomato salsa

I small can green chilies, drained

I cup corn, drained

I tablespoon cumin

I tablespoon chili powder

½ teaspoon ground cinnamon

½ cup chopped fresh cilantro

1⅓ cups water

I cup chicken stock

2 teaspoons baking powder

1½ teaspoon salt

⅓ cup vegetable or canola oil

3 cups yellow cornmeal

2 large eggs

1½ cups (6 ounces) shredded Wisconsin Asadero or Queso Quesadilla cheese

1. Make the filling: Melt the butter in a heavy frying pan. Cook the onion and ground beef in the butter until browned. Drain.
2. Add the salsa, chilies, corn, and spices. Stir and simmer for 10 to 15 minutes. Remove the pan from the heat and add the cilantro. Set the filling aside.
3. Make the crust: Bring the water and chicken stock to a boil and remove from the heat.
4. Whisk together the baking powder, salt, and oil. Stir in the cornmeal. Add the chicken stock and let this mixture sit for 5 minutes. Mix in the eggs.
5. Prepare the pie: Grease a 13x9-inch casserole dish. Preheat the oven to 400°F.
6. Spread 2 cups of the cornmeal mixture on the bottom and sides of the dish. Cover with the beef filling. Sprinkle with the cheese.
7. Stir the reserved cornmeal mixture with ½ cup of hot water and spread this carefully over the cheese.
8. Bake the pie for 25 minutes until browned. Let it stand for 15 minutes and serve.

SERVES 8

Recipe inspired by many friends.

Huevos Rancheros

Suggested beverage pairings for Huevos Rancheros: Riesling, White Grenache, sangria, and margaritas. This is great for Sunday brunch.

¼ cup olive oil, divided

4 tortillas

½ teaspoon chili powder

4 eggs

2 green onions, including the green portion

I tomato, peeled and chopped

I teaspoon oregano

I small can jalapeño peppers

Salt to taste

I tablespoon chopped fresh cilantro

I cup shredded Wisconsin Queso
    Quesadilla

1. Brush 2 teaspoons of the oil over one side of tortillas. Sprinkle with the chili powder.
2. Beat the eggs with a whisk.
3. Heat the remaining olive oil and add the onions. Sauté them until golden brown.
4. Add the tomato and cook until soft. Add the oregano and jalapeño peppers and stir.
5. Pour the eggs into the pan and mix with the sauce. Add salt and stir the eggs until they are cooked. Remove from heat and sprinkle with fresh cilantro.
6. Quickly sauté the tortillas in a buttered skillet until golden brown. Cook until crisp and golden brown on each side.
7. Transfer the tortillas to two serving plates. Top each with some egg mixture and ¼ cup of the cheese.

SERVES 2

Inspired by a Wisconsin Milk Marketing Board recipe.

CHEF NOTE:

There are many ways to make huevos rancheros. For instance, you can spread a cup of heated canned refried beans over the tortillas before adding the eggs. Or garnish with diced ripe avocado, if you like. We prefer our eggs to be well mixed, but others put the unbeaten eggs directly into the tomato mixture and scramble them together. Fried eggs are another option.

Hard Cheeses

Hispanic hard cheeses have a strong flavor and a dry crumbly texture; they're used for grating. Traditionally they were salted and aged in the outdoor heat for up to a year.

Cotija, also called Queso Anejo, is often referred to as the Parmesan of Mexico. It's used profusely in Mexican dishes, not only as a cheese but also as a spice. Its taste is sharp and somewhat salty. Cotija is grated onto enchiladas, tostadas, rellenos, tacos, salads, soups, and refried beans. It's also mixed directly into casseroles or recipes to enhance the flavor. It pairs well with margaritas, Zinfandels, and lager beers. For the latter, Mart suggests the award-winning, dangerously delicious and smooth Bavarian Lager from Madison's Capitol Brewery.

Enchilado or **Anejo Enchilado** is another hard cheese created in Mexico; *anejo* means "aged cheese" in Spanish. This variety was originally used to make *antojitos* (appetizers) and enchiladas. Its taste is milder than Cotija's, and it's softer and less crumbly, but it's often rolled in paprika or chili powder to give an extra kick. The warning is the bright reddish orange exterior.

Enchilado is delicious when crumbled over fresh salads, enchiladas, tacos, and soups. When added to casseroles and lasagnas, it provides extra color and zest. As a snack, it's a fine complement to fruit, salsa, and chile peppers.

Spectator 1: I think it was, "Blessed are the cheesemakers."

Mrs. Gregory: Ahh, what's so special about the cheesemakers?

Gregory: Well, obviously it's not meant to be taken literally; it refers to any manufacturer of dairy products.

—Monty Python troupe, *The Life of Brian* (1979). (Unable to hear clearly, spectators at the back of a crowd misinterpret Jesus Christ sermonizing on "Blessed Are the Peacemakers.")

Pork Enchiladas

Serve your enchiladas with sangria, margaritas, pilsner beers, or Chardonnay.

4 dried Anaheim or New Mexico chilies

½ cup boiling water

I cup orange juice

I teaspoon salt

½ teaspoon ground cumin

¼ teaspoon dried oregano

2 cloves garlic

1½ pounds boneless pork, cut into 3 or 4 chunks

3 tablespoons butter, divided

I cup milk

I can (4 ounces) diced green chilies

2 tablespoons flour

2 cups (8 ounces) shredded Wisconsin Queso Quesadilla or Cheddar cheese, divided

8 burrito-size (about 10 inches) flour tortillas

1. Remove the stems and seeds from dried chilies.
2. In bowl, pour the boiling water over the chilies. Let stand for 20 minutes to soften.
3. In an electric blender or food processor, puree the softened chilies, orange juice, salt, cumin, oregano, and garlic. Set aside.
4. In large saucepan, brown the pork in 1 tablespoon of the butter. Add the chili sauce; heat to a boil. Cover. Reduce the heat and simmer for 1½ to 2 hours, or until the pork is tender.
5. Preheat the oven to 350°F.
6. Shred the pork using two forks. Return the meat to the saucepan; set aside.
7. In an electric blender or food processor, puree the milk and green chilies. Set aside.
8. In a small saucepan, over medium heat, melt the remaining 2 tablespoons of butter. Stir in the flour and cook for 1 minute. Gradually stir in the milk mixture. Cook and stir until the mixture thickens and begins to boil.
9. Add 1 cup of the cheese, stirring until cheese melts.
10. Spread 1 cup of the cheese sauce in the bottom of a greased 13x9x2-inch baking pan. Set aside.
11. Spoon ½ cup of the pork mixture down the center of each tortilla; roll up and place seam-down in the baking pan.

12. Pour the remaining cheese sauce over the filled tortillas. Sprinkle with the remaining cheese.
13. Cover and bake for 30 minutes.
14. Uncover. Bake for 15 minutes more or until hot and bubbly.

SERVES 8

Courtesy of the Wisconsin Milk Marketing Board, Inc.

Seared Sea Scallops with Orange-Parsnip Puree, Hazelnut Butter, and Wisconsin Granqueso

Aged for six months, GranQueso is a Manchego-style cheese, which means it's made from cow's milk rather than sheep's. It has an interesting flavor, a sweetness-with-a-bite. We've discovered that this cheese is delicious grated on soups and salads or as a stand-alone.

Scallops

½ **cup olive oil**

¼ **cup fresh orange juice**

I **crushed bay leaf**

½ **teaspoon toasted coriander seeds, ground**

½ **teaspoon crushed sea salt**

¼ **teaspoon cracked black pepper**

I6 **large sea scallops**

1. In glass dish or plastic bag, mix the olive oil, orange juice, bay leaf, coriander, sea salt, and black pepper. Add the scallops.
2. Cover the glass dish or marinate in the bag for 1 hour in the refrigerator.

Orange-Parsnip Puree

I pound parsnips, peeled and cut into
    2-inch pieces

Juice and zest of I orange

½ cup (I stick) butter

Salt and pepper to taste

1. Cook the parsnips in boiling water until tender, 10 to 15 minutes. Drain.
2. While they're still hot, combine the parsnips with juice and zest of 1 orange, butter, salt, and pepper. Process in a food processor until smooth. Keep this mixture warm.

Hazelnut Butter

I cup toasted hazelnuts

2 tablespoons sugar

I teaspoon salt

I ½ cups shredded Wisconsin GranQueso
    Cheese

1. In a food processor, combine the hazelnuts, sugar, and salt. Process until a very smooth paste forms, at least 5 minutes. (The mixture will be quite thick.)
2. Preheat the broiler to high.
3. Heat a large ovenproof sauté pan over high heat. Drain the sea scallops and sear them in the pan, about 3 minutes per side. Cover with the cheese.
4. Place the pan under the broiler until the cheese is bubbling, about 1 minute.
5. Serve two scallops per plate with parsnip puree and hazelnut butter.

MAKES 8 TAPAS

Courtesy of the Wisconsin Milk Marketing Board, Inc., and chef James Campbell Caruso, El Farol, Santa Fe, New Mexico.

Avocado, Jicama, and Grilled Shrimp Salsa on Black Beans with GranQueso Nachos

The original directions for this delicious dish suggested serving it at room temperature. We chose to heat the chips, beans, and cheese, but either way the unique combinations of tastes and textures make this a winner.

12 large shrimp (10–15 count), grilled and chopped

Salt to taste

1 tablespoon minced garlic

3 tablespoons minced jalapeño (seeds optional)

⅓ cup minced sweet onions

1 avocado in ¼-inch dices

½ cup ¼-inch-diced jicama

⅓ cup ¼-inch-diced red tomato

⅓ cup ¼-inch-diced yellow tomato

1 tablespoon grated fresh ginger

2 tablespoons chopped fresh cilantro

1 tablespoon chopped fresh basil

3 tablespoons fresh lime juice

3 tablespoons Spanish olive oil

2 dozen triangle-shaped tortilla chips

1 cup cooked black beans, pureed to make a paste

1 cup grated Wisconsin GranQueso

1. Preheat the oven to 400°F.
2. Season the shrimp with salt and grill over medium heat until they're cooked.
3. Let the shrimp cool, then chop them and combine them with veggies, herbs, lime juice, and oil, adding more salt to taste. Set aside.
4. Spread the tortilla chips on heatproof platter and top each with a dollop of black bean paste. Then sprinkle the cheese on top.
5. Heat in the oven for about 10 minutes. Place shrimp salsa on top and serve.

SERVES 8

Courtesy of the Wisconsin Milk Marketing Board, Inc., and Dean Fearing, chef at the Mansion on Turtle Creek and chef-ambassador for the WMMB.

Chiles Rellenos (Stuffed Peppers)

For a chunkier salsa, limit how much you blend the ingredients after oiling. Serve with Mexican beer or orchata, a chilled rice–cinnamon drink that can be purchased in stores specializing in Hispanic foods.

4 peppers (poblano, jalapeño, or habanero)

2 cups grated cheese (Queso Fresco, Cheddar, or Monterey Jack)

½ cup flour

4 egg whites

½ cup vegetable oil

1. Roast the peppers individually over the open flame of a gas stove or under the broiler of an electric stove. Peel off the skins and scrape out the seeds from inside the peppers.
2. Stuff the peppers evenly with the cheese of your choice. Roll them in the flour.
3. Whip the egg whites until they form peaks, then roll the peppers in the whites.
4. Heat the vegetable oil in a pan until hot. Slow-cook the peppers in the oil until they turn a golden color, turning often.
5. Remove the peppers and place them on paper towels to soak up any excess oil.
6. Spoon salsa (recipe follows) over the chiles rellenos and serve.

Salsa

4 cups water

4 large tomatoes

1 small yellow onion

1 clove garlic

2 whole jalapeños

¼ cup chopped fresh cilantro

Sprinkle of black pepper (optional)

Salt to taste

1. Bring the water to boil, then add the tomatoes, onion, garlic, and jalapeños.
2. Bring to second boil and cook for 7 to 10 minutes, until the ingredients soften.
3. Put the mixture into a blender and add the cilantro, black pepper, and salt.

SERVES 4

Courtesy of chef Lupe Ferrer, Poco Loco Restaurant, Milwaukee, Wisconsin.

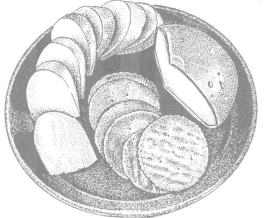

CHAPTER 10

MORE WISCONSIN CHEESES

WISCONSIN HAS RIGHTFULLY EARNED ITS TITLE AS the nation's Cheese State, given its extensive history of cheesemaking, the skill of its producers, the quality of its products, and the extensive selection of cheeses made, sold, and celebrated here. In addition to the cheeses outlined in previous chapters, Wisconsin has numerous niche varieties. Each can be the basic ingredient for still more delicious recipes.

Brick

Brick cheese is a Wisconsin original, created in 1877 by John Jossi, a Swiss-born American cheesemaker. In 1857, when Jossi was twelve, he came to America with his family and settled in upstate New York before moving to Richwood, Wisconsin. Two years later, at age fourteen, Jossi was managing a Limburger factory in the village. He eventually married the daughter of a local cheesemaker. In 1873 they moved back to New York for a few years, where he worked in a larger Limburger plant. There he began to envision the cheese that was later to become Brick.

Jossi wanted a cheese with a drier curd and less smell than Limburger. He also came up with the idea of forming the cheese into the shape of bricks as well as using bricks to press the moisture from the cheese . . . hence the name. The Jossis moved back to Wisconsin in 1877 and started producing Brick cheese, which quickly became successful as he shared his Brick-making knowledge with others. Jossi died in Milwaukee in 1902.

Today there is a difference between handmade Brick—a washed-rind, surface-ripened cheese made with a smear that gives it its full, earthy flavor—and other factory-made Bricks that lack the traditional distinctive flavor.

Widmer Cheese Cellars is still making its award-winning Brick the old-fashioned way in its plant in Theresa, Wisconsin, not far from Jossi's original factory. Wisconsin Master Cheesemaker Joseph Widmer is a third-generation Widmer cheesemaker. His grandfather John O. Widmer came from Switzerland and started the company in 1922. Young Joe still sticks to the traditional method, carefully transferring the curds by hand from the vat to the cheese molds, hand turning them three times during the first day, pressing them with the same bricks his grandfather used, and then putting them into a brine solution with salt and the necessary bacteria cultures before aging them.

Other Wisconsin companies make Brick in mild, medium, and aged varieties, plain or flavored with caraway and hot peppers, as well as organic and kosher varieties. Award-winning Brick cheeses are produced by Klondike Cheese, the Deppeler Cheese Factory, and the Chalet Cheese Cooperative, all in Monroe; Zimmerman Cheese in South Wayne; the Silver-Lewis Cheese Factory Cooperative in Monticello; and Blaser's Premium Cheese in Comstock.

A young Brick has a mild and sweet flavor with a touch of nuttiness. As it ages, it becomes pungent and tangy. Joe Widmer of Widmer Cheese likes his Brick ripened for ten to twelve weeks. He suggests creating a sandwich with Brick cheese, sweet onions, strong mustard, and a slice of Milwaukee-made Usinger's liverwurst, all served on rye, pumpernickel, or dark bread. Or try an open-faced sandwich on Italian bread with asparagus, ham, and Brick. When broiled until brown, Brick is also delicious. Don't forget the gherkins! A glass or two of beer, either a pale ale, draft beer, or dark, makes a hearty beverage complement. A mild Brick also pairs well with light red wines such as Beaujolais.

Orange Rosemary Pound Bread

You'll have an easier time cutting the Brick cheese called for in this recipe if you chill it first. Also note that the washed rind is bitter and should not be eaten.

I cup (2 sticks) unsalted butter, softened

I cup granulated sugar

2 tablespoon light honey

5 large eggs

2 cups cake flour

I cup (4 ounces) shredded Wisconsin Brick or Monterey Jack cheese

I tablespoon orange juice

I tablespoon chopped fresh rosemary leaves

Grated peel of I orange

I½ teaspoons orange flower water

1. Preheat the oven to 350°F. Grease and lightly flour a 9x5x4-inch loaf pan.
2. In a bowl, cream together the butter and sugar until they're very light and fluffy.
3. Stir in the honey and add the eggs, one at a time, beating well after each addition.
4. Add the flour, ½ cup at a time, mixing after each addition.
5. Gently stir in the cheese, orange juice, rosemary, orange peel, and orange flower water.
6. Spoon the batter into the prepared pan. Bake for 1 hour, or until the bread is golden brown on top and a cake tester comes out clean.
7. Cool the loaf for 15 minutes, remove it from the pan, and cool completely before serving. Let it stand, wrapped, overnight, before serving for best results. Serve with orange-flavored whipped cream, vanilla ice cream, or macerated fresh berries.

SERVES 12

Courtesy of the Wisconsin Milk Marketing Board, Inc.

Cottage Cheese

When Little Miss Muffet sat on her tuffet, she could have actually been eating cottage cheese, similar to her famous curds of bedtime story fame. Drained and washed to remove the acidity, today's cottage cheese is not pressed. Subsequently, some of the whey remains. Cottage cheese is a fresh, mild-tasting variety with about a week's shelf life. Originating in Eastern and Central Europe, it became popular in colonial America. The name stems from the fact that families made small batches of this cheese in their cottages.

Healthwise, cottage cheese is a dieters' delight, made in both fat-free and low-fat forms. Bodybuilders also love its low fat and carbohydrates, as well as its high content of casein protein.

Historically, cottage cheese was produced by simply putting the raw milk in a pot and keeping it in a warm place. After several days the action of the bacteria in nonpasteurized milk would turn into a soft white curd. This was then sliced, warmed to about 100°F for several hours, and drained. This cheese had a sour taste, but it could also be drained without cooking. If the curds were pressed after cooking, it was called farmer's cheese.

Cottage cheese is an original comfort food, a standard dish complemented with peaches or other fruit. It's a delicious addition to many salads, and a must for lasagna. Cottage cheese is used in numerous dips and desserts because it comes in a variety of styles, including large curd, small curd, and dry curd. Wisconsin cheesemakers produce quality cottage cheese flavored with ingredients such as pineapple or chives.

Top a baked potato with cottage cheese, chopped dill, and salt and pepper.

Make a smoothie with half a cup of cottage cheese, half a cup of milk (low fat is great), a tablespoon or two of sugar, a teaspoon of vanilla extract, and half a cup of frozen fruit. Blend in a mixer.

> **"A small garden, figs, a little cheese, and, along with this, three or four good friends; such was a luxury to Epicurus."**
>
> —Friedrich Wilhelm Nietzsche (1844–1900), German philosopher and classical scholar, from *The Wanderer and His Shadow* (1879)

Carrot and Raisin Wisconsin Cheese Spread

This is the perfect healthy treat for both kids and adults.

⅔ cup cottage cheese

¼ cup peanut butter

I tablespoon honey

¼ cup shredded carrots

2 tablespoons raisins

1. Combine the cottage cheese, peanut butter, and honey. Mix until well blended. Stir in the carrots and raisins.
2. Spread on rice cakes, crackers, toast, or bagels.

SERVES 4

Courtesy of the Wisconsin Milk Marketing Board, Inc.

Super Whipped Potatoes

Ahhh, comfort food at its finest.

I pound (about 5 medium) russet potatoes, peeled and cut into cubes

¼ cup (½ stick) butter

2 cloves garlic, finely chopped

¼ cup milk

I cup cream-style large-curd cottage cheese

1. In a large saucepan, cook the potatoes in salted boiling water for 15 minutes, or until tender. Drain.
2. Melt the butter in the same saucepan, and sauté the garlic for 3 minutes. Add the milk.
3. When this mixture is hot, return the potatoes to the pan. Remove from the heat.
4. Whip the potato-garlic mixture until it's light and fluffy. Beat in the cheese.
5. Serve hot with additional butter, if desired.

SERVES 4

Courtesy of the Wisconsin Milk Marketing Board, Inc.

German Baked Cheese Torte

Scott Stroessner is the chef at Turner Hall Ratskeller Restaurant in Wisconsin's Cheese Central, Monroe. This recipe is from his grandmother, Rose Stroessner.

Crust

20 graham crackers

½ cup granulated sugar

½ teaspoon ground cinnamon

¼ cup shortening

1. Preheat the oven to 350°F.
2. Place the crackers in a plastic bag with a zip top. Remove any air inside and close the bag. Using a rolling pin, roll over the crackers until they become fine crumbs.
3. Remove the crumbs from the bag and place them in a bowl. Add the sugar, cinnamon, and shortening, and mix thoroughly.
4. Butter a torte or springform pan and line it with the crumb mixture, reserving 1 cup for a topping.

Filling

2 pounds cottage cheese

I cup sugar

2 tablespoons flour

4 eggs, beaten

I can (I4 ounces) sweetened condensed milk

I teaspoon vanilla extract

1. Put the cottage cheese through a ricer or food mill. Add the sugar and flour and mix well. Add the eggs, sweetened condensed milk, and vanilla, again mixing well.
2. Pour the filling into the crust and sprinkle the top with the remaining crumbs.
3. Bake for about 1 hour, until set but not hard.

SERVES 8

Courtesy of chef Scott Stroessner, Turner Hall Ratskeller Restaurant, Monroe, Wisconsin.

Cream Cheese

Cream cheese was created in 1872 by William A. Lawrence, a dairyman from Chester, New York. He and other cheesemakers were trying to create a cheese similar to France's Neufchâtel, substituting cream for milk to make it richer. Cream cheese is meant to be consumed fresh and not aged. Other ingredients are often added to the base product, such as herbs, pepper or garlic, onions, chives, dill, or olives. Even sweet flavors, including berries, are popular. Mmmm, good, when served with lox and your favorite bagel.

> "Remember, I beseech thee, that thou hast made me as the clay; and wilt thou bring me into dust again? Hast thou not poured me out as milk, and curdled me like cheese?"
>
> —Job 10:9–10

Cream cheese gained national popularity in 1880 when New York cheese distributor A. L. Reynolds began marketing it in tinfoil wrappers. He called his product Philadelphia Brand because Philadelphia had a reputation as a "gourmet" town, especially when it came to dairy products. Another milestone was the invention of pasteurized cheese in 1912 by James L. Kraft. He then developed pasteurized Philadelphia Cream Cheese, which remains the most popular cheese used for making cheesecake.

Layered Pumpkin Torte

This is a perfect alternative to Thanksgiving pumpkin pie.

Crust

2 cups graham cracker crumbs (about 24
squares)

½ cup (1 stick) butter, melted

¼ cup sugar

¼ cup chopped pecans

1. Preheat the oven to 350°F.
2. In a medium bowl, combine the graham cracker crumbs, melted butter, and ¼ cup sugar.
3. Remove ¼ cup of the crumb mixture; stir in the chopped pecans, and set aside. Press the remaining crumb mixture onto the bottom of an ungreased 13x9x2-inch baking pan.

Cream Cheese Filling

1 package (8 ounces) cream cheese

¾ cup sugar

2 eggs, beaten

1. In a small mixing bowl, combine the cream cheese, ¾ cup sugar, and beaten eggs. Beat until well mixed.
2. Pour this over the crumb mixture in pan and bake for 18 to 20 minutes. Cool on a wire rack.

Pumpkin Topping

⅓ cup sugar

1 envelope unflavored gelatin

2 pasteurized egg yolks, lightly beaten

½ cup milk

½ teaspoon ground cinnamon

¼ teaspoon salt

1 can (16 ounces) pumpkin

2 pasteurized egg whites

¼ cup sugar

1. In a medium saucepan, combine ⅓ cup sugar and the gelatin.
2. Stir in the egg yolks, milk, cinnamon, and salt. Cook and stir over medium heat until bubbly; stir in the pumpkin.
3. Transfer the mixture to a large mixing bowl and let it cool.
4. In a small mixing bowl, beat the egg whites until soft peaks form. Gradually add ¼ cup sugar, continuing to beat until stiff peaks form.
5. Gently fold the egg whites into cooled pumpkin mixture.

6. Spoon over the cooled crust and filling in the baking pan.
7. Cover. Chill for at least 4 hours or until pumpkin mixture is firm. Just before serving, sprinkle the reserved crumb mixture on top.

SERVES 16

Courtesy of the Wisconsin Milk Marketing Board, Inc.

Feta

Feta is a firm, crumbly cheese with a tart, salty taste. It was first made in Greece from sheep's or goat's milk. In Wisconsin producers usually make feta from cow's milk, although more cheesemakers are now using goat's milk as well. Feta is often described as "pickled" because it's put in a brine solution of salt and water after it's formed. This brine lengthens the shelf life of the cheese, helping it last for about six months longer than other fresh cheeses. A less salty feta can be created by rinsing the cheese in cold water or milk. Wisconsin cheese lovers also enjoy trying various flavors, including tomato, basil, black pepper, garlic, herbs, or dill. This is an extremely versatile cheese; it can even be sautéed, since it browns well and does not melt.

Feta is essential in Greek salads. Mix romaine lettuce, calamata olives, red onions, tomatoes, and chopped red and green peppers. The dressing is easy to prepare: Mix six tablespoons olive oil, one teaspoon dried oregano, one juiced lemon, and ground black pepper to taste. Toss everything in a large bowl to create a salad fit for Alexander the Great.

For a contemporary dish, you can make a delicious Greek pizza with red and green peppers, tomatoes, calamata olives, and crumbled feta.

Shrimp and Wisconsin Feta Salad

This salad could be served with a fine white Greek wine such as a fruity Assyrtiko or the pinkish Moshofilero, whose German counterpart is the always popular Gewürztraminer. But the real feta lover will keep some Retsina on hand, reveling in its unique piney taste. For good reason this wine, produced for more than 2,700 years, is called the Wine of the Gods. The Greeks' top deity and renowned cheese fan, Zeus, probably demanded his wines be served with Wisconsin cheese products when planning those fabled parties atop Mount Olympus.

I pound medium shrimp, cooked and deveined

I cup (4 ounces) crumbled Wisconsin feta cheese

I cup cream-style cottage cheese

8 green onions, thinly sliced

2 tomatoes, cored and coarsely chopped

I ½ teaspoons dried oregano, crushed

2 ½ teaspoons pepper

8 ounces spaghetti (or the pasta of your choice), cooked and drained

1. Combine all of the ingredients except the pasta in a large bowl. Mix well.
2. Add the pasta and toss, then serve immediately.

SERVES 6

Courtesy of the Wisconsin Milk Marketing Board, Inc.

THE GREAT WISCONSIN CHEESEBURGER

Genghis Kahn may claim that his hordes invented the hamburger in the thirteenth century, but the residents of Seymour, Wisconsin, have had their day in court. A mock trial, "The Hamburger Hearings," was held at the National Hamburger Festival in Akron, Ohio, in August 2006 to determine who actually dreamed up the idea of flattening ground meat into a patty.

Four American cities, including Seymour, claimed the honor, and each community stated its case in front of a judge and a jury called the "Burger Commission." Alas, the august body could not come up with a decision, so hizzoner set up a two-week online vote to determine the rightful claimant. The winner? Seymour, which won the nod over Akron; New Haven, Connecticut; and Athens, Texas. According to the Wisconsinites, Seymour resident Charlie Nagreen served the world's first hamburger at the Seymour Fair of 1885. "Hamburger" Charlie squished a meatball and placed it between slices of bread so folks could stroll and eat at the same time. There's a towering statue in Seymour of Hamburger Charlie, invention in hand.

There are at least five tales of how the first cheeseburger was created. The one with the most credence singles out a cook named Lionel Sternberger of the Rite Spot Restaurant in Pasadena, California. In the mid-1920s Sternberger was serving burgers to a group of homeless men. One allegedly asked for a slice of cheese added to his order. Sternberger then added this twist to his menu—and thus was the cheeseburger launched. National Cheeseburger Day is held every September 18.

Seymour still has the most elaborate celebration of anything to do with the hamburger and its cheeseburger cousin. It annually hosts a Hamburger Festival the first weekend in August, featuring a Bun Run, Ketchup Slide, parade, hot-air balloon ascensions, and plenty of burgers. In 1989 the fest served the world's largest hamburger, tipping the scales at 5,520 pounds and feeding 13,000 persons. A concrete replica of Seymour's world-record pattie and bun looks almost good enough to eat.

WHERE TO GET SOME OF WISCONSIN'S BEST CHEESEBURGERS

- Avenue Bar, Madison.
- Bear Trap Inn, Saxon.
- Blue Moon Bar & Grill, Madison.
- Clearwater Harbor, Chain O'Lakes.
- Dotty Dumplings Dowry, Madison.
- Elsa's on the Park, Milwaukee.
- Great Dane Pub & Brewing Co., Madison.
- Hershleb's, Wisconsin Rapids.
- Kewpee Sandwich Shop, Racine.
- Krolls, Green Bay.
- Late's, Manitowoc.
- Monty's Blue Plate Diner, Madison.
- Petersen's Hamburger Stand and Ice Cream Parlor, Jefferson.
- Tofflers, New Glarus.

Wisconsin Turkey Pizza Burger

I tablespoon butter

I cup diced celery

3 cups finely chopped cooked turkey

I can (8 ounces) tomato sauce

I teaspoon salt

I teaspoon dried oregano

½ teaspoon pepper

4 hamburger buns (8 halves), toasted and
buttered

8 slices (I ounce each) Wisconsin Provolone
cheese

1. Preheat the oven to 300°F.
2. Melt the butter in large skillet. Sauté the celery slowly until it's tender. Add the turkey and cook until warmed. Add tomato sauce and seasonings; simmer.
3. Place the bun halves on a baking sheet; spoon about ½ cup of the turkey mixture over each half. Top each with a slice of cheese and bake for 5 minutes or until cheese melts.

Courtesy of the Wisconsin Milk Marketing Board, Inc.

Wisconsin Two-Cheese Burger

I pound ground beef

2 teaspoons finely chopped onion

½ teaspoon salt

¼ teaspoon pepper

8 slices (I ounce each) Wisconsin Swiss
cheese

I cup alfalfa sprouts

8 slices (I ounce each) Wisconsin Cheddar
cheese

4 hamburger buns, sliced

4 lettuce leaves

4 slices avocado (optional)

1. Combine the meat, onion, and seasonings; mix well. Shape into four 4-inch patties. Grill or broil the burgers to your desired doneness. Top each burger with two slices of Wisconsin Swiss cheese; remove from the heat when the cheese is melted.
2. Place alfalfa sprouts and two slices of Cheddar on the bottom half of each of four hamburger buns. Add the hamburger patties, additional alfalfa sprouts, lettuce, avocado (if you like), and finally the bun tops.

Courtesy of the Wisconsin Milk Marketing Board, Inc.

Wisconsin Mooburger

1½ pounds ground beef

¼ cup dry bread crumbs

1 egg

¾ cup (3 ounces) shredded Wisconsin
cheese; choose either crumbled
Wisconsin Blue Cheese, crumbled
Pepper Jack Cheese, crumbled
Wisconsin Basil & Tomato Feta
Cheese, or other shredded
Wisconsin cheese

6 hamburger buns, sliced

6 slices tomato

6 lettuce leaves

1. In a large mixing bowl, combine the beef, bread crumbs, and egg; mix well, but lightly. Divide the mixture into 12 balls. Flatten each on waxed paper to 4 inches across.
2. Place 1 tablespoon of shredded cheese on each of six patties. Top with the remaining patties, carefully pressing the edges to seal.
3. Grill the patties 4 inches from hot coals, turning only once, for 6 to 9 minutes on each side, or until no longer pink. To keep the cheese between the patties as it melts, do not flatten the burgers with your spatula while grilling.
4. Place the burgers on their buns and top with tomato and lettuce.

Courtesy of the Wisconsin Milk Marketing Board, Inc.

Open-Faced Cowboy Cheeseburgers

1 pound ground beef

½ cup diced celery

1 tablespoon butter

⅓ cup tomato sauce

½ cup tomato ketchup

Onion salt

2 large hamburger buns, split

6 slices (1 ounce each) Wisconsin Mild
Cheddar, Brick, or Colby cheese

4 slices carrot

4 slices cucumber

4 frilled celery stalks

2 green pepper rings, halved

1. Preheat the broiler.
2. Sauté the ground beef and skim off the fat. Set aside.
3. In a saucepan, sauté the celery in the butter. When it's tender, add the ground beef, tomato sauce, and ketchup. Season slightly with onion salt.
4. Put 2 slices of cheese atop each split bun. Place under the broiler just long enough to melt the cheese. Remove from the broiler and spoon on the ground beef mix.
5. Arrange "eyes" and "mouths" made from the remaining cheese slices atop the ground beef mix.
6. Return the burgers to the broiler to slightly melt the cheese. Place the sandwiches on plates and arrange cucumber–carrot "ears," a celery "crown," and green pepper "collars."

Courtesy of Widmer Cheese Cellars.

Fontina

Fontina originated in the 1400s, first being produced high in the snowcapped Italian Alps near the French and Swiss borders. Mont Fontin and the nearby village of Fontinaz inspired the name *Fontina*—or *Fontina Val d'Aosta*, as it's called in Italy. Because of its versatility as a cooking and table cheese, numerous countries and international chefs have adopted this dense, smooth, elastic cheese. In addition to Italian-style Fontina, there are also Swedish and Danish varieties. Wisconsin cheesemakers make all three versions.

Both the Danish- and Swedish-style Fontinas have a tongue-tickling tartness, a nutty, mild, and earthy flavor that ranges from mellow to sharp, depending on the age. Colors range from pale ivory to a straw yellow. Each is coated in a special red wax. The Swedish-style has straight corners, while the Danish is rounded. Mild Italian-style Fontina has a smooth, supple texture with tiny holes, its coloring ranging from a beautiful ivory to pale gold. The taste is earthy and buttery; it's made either with a brown rind or rindless.

Monroe's Roth Käse makes a variety of Fontinas, with its Mezza Luna Fontina winning many national and international awards. This handcrafted cheese is cured for six to eight weeks to develop its richly complex flavor. Since it melts easily, Fontina is often used in Italian cooking. Subsequently, Roth Käse suggests a high-end Verdicchio or Pinot Grigio to complement Fontina's tart, yeasty finish. The company also makes Krönenost Fontina, nicknamed "the original melting cheese." This is a full-bodied wonder, recognizable by its signature red wax casing.

Other award-winning Wisconsin Fontinas include Carr Valley's Smoked Fontina and the Alto Dairy Cooperative's Fontina.

Fontina is great any time of day. For breakfast, we have added it to egg dishes and used it in crepes. It's also good with fruit and bread. Or try putting slices of Fontina between two slices of polenta. Top with a marinara sauce and bake until the cheese melts and the dish is warm.

Fruity wines are perfect with Fontina, especially light reds such as Gamay Beaujolais or Pinot Noir. Whites like Riesling or Gewürztraminer are just as distinctive.

Tuscan Bruschetta

For other lip-smacking Fontina sandwiches, place some slices of this cheese on a crusty bread along with prosciutto or Genoa salami. Or try using focaccia bread for sandwiches layered with pesto, roasted red peppers, and Italian salami.

3 medium tomatoes, seeded and julienned

½ medium orange sweet pepper, julienned

½ cup wild mushrooms, sliced

⅓ cup red wine vinegar

I cup olive oil

2 cloves garlic, minced

I tablespoon lemon juice

Salt and pepper to taste

¼ cup pitted and sliced black olives

½ cup fresh basil chiffonade

2 tablespoons chopped fresh mint

I baguette, sliced diagonally and toasted

I½ cups shredded Sartori Foods Fontina

1. Combine the tomatoes, pepper, and mushrooms in a large bowl.
2. Whisk together the red wine vinegar, olive oil, and garlic.
3. Toss the vinaigrette with the vegetables. Add the lemon juice and season with salt and pepper. Fold in the black olives, basil, and mint. Marinate for 1 hour or overnight.
4. Top the baguette slices with a heaping tablespoon of the veggie mixture and sprinkle with the Fontina.
5. Serve immediately or place under a broiler for 2 to 3 minutes until the cheese is melted.

SERVES 8 AS AN APPETIZER

Courtesy of Sartori Foods, Plymouth, Wisconsin.

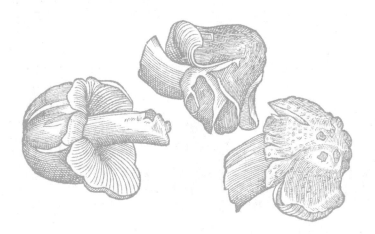

Edam and Gouda

Both Edam and Gouda are creamy Dutch cheeses originating in villages of the same names more than 800 years ago. According to legend, Edam was originally shaped in balls for easy rolling up a gangplank for storage in a ship's cargo hold. Edam is part skim milk and has a firmer texture than Gouda, which is made with whole milk. Edam is known for its red wax covering, while Gouda's wax shade varies. If it's red, the cheese is mild. Yellow or clear wax suggests aging or flavoring. Black wax or brown rind indicate a smoked cheese.

Wisconsin Edam is produced in smoked, caraway, aged, organic, and reduced-fat varieties. Wisconsin Gouda also comes in many varieties: plain, caraway, smoked, and reduced fat.

Wisconsin Gouda is a consistent award winner on the national and international stages. Favored varieties come in plain or in exotic styles. Particularly popular is the Smoked Peppercorn Gouda made by Danish-based Arla Foods, which took over White Clover Dairy in 2006. The dairy, in Kaukauna, was started by a group of area farmers in 1897. Other top tasties include the Roth Käse Vintage Van Gogh, Carr Valley Gouda, and Bass Lake Cheese Smoked Gouda.

Slices of both Gouda and Edam are perfect for both grilled and cold sandwiches. Versatile, they also melt well; they can be shredded over baked vegetable dishes, frittatas, and twice-baked potatoes, or even diced in salads. Creamed pasta dishes such as fettuccine Alfredo are enhanced with shredded Edam.

A great gouda!
Photo courtesy of Maple Leaf Cheese

Gouda Pear Crisp

For an even simpler Gouda dessert, layer fresh apples or pears and hearty slices of Gouda in a baking dish. Then sprinkle with a sugar–cinnamon crumb mixture and bake.

2 pounds (about 5) Bosc or other winter pears, cored and sliced thinly

½ cup dark or golden raisins

¼ teaspoon ground nutmeg

3 tablespoons lemon juice

½ cup packed brown sugar

¾ cup oat bran

⅛ teaspoon salt

¼ cup (½ stick) cold butter, cut into bits

I cup (4 ounces) shredded Wisconsin Gouda

1. Preheat the oven to 350°F.
2. Arrange the pear slices in a buttered 8x8-inch pan. Sprinkle with the raisins, nutmeg, and lemon juice.
3. Mix the sugar, oat bran, and salt. Cut in the butter until the mixture resembles coarse cornmeal. Stir in the cheese. Sprinkle this mixture over the pears.
4. Bake until the pears are just tender and the top is lightly brown, about 35 minutes.

SERVES 6

Courtesy of the Wisconsin Milk Marketing Board, Inc.

Photo courtesy of Maple Leaf Cheese

Carr's Aged Gouda, Artichoke, and Leek Tart With Crisp Apple, Gouda, and Tarragon Salad

This dish was created by Sanford D'Amato, chef-owner of Sanford, the Coquette Café, and the Harlequin Bakery, all in Milwaukee, Wisconsin. D'Amato has won the AAA Four Diamond Award, Mobil's Four-Star award, and the highest rating for food (29) given by the Zagat guide. He is also a contributor to the James Beard Winning Styles cookbook, and was personally chosen by Julia Child to cook for her eightieth birthday. Although this wonderful recipe is labor intensive, it is definitely worth the time and effort. We've served it at dinner parties, and our guests were ecstatic.

Tart Shell

One 11-inch-diameter by 1½-inch-high removable-bottom tart pan

6 ounces (about 1 cup) flour, divided

2 ounces Carr's aged Gouda cheese, cut into small dices

2 ounces cold unsalted butter, cut into small dices

½ whole egg (beat 1 large egg and measure off half)

2 ounces chilled water

¼ teaspoon kosher salt

1 egg white, lightly beaten

1. Place ¼ cup of the flour and the Gouda cheese in a food processor. Process until the cheese is fine.
2. Add the remaining flour and butter and pulse ten to fifteen times, until the butter is pea size.
3. Mix the egg, water, and salt. Turn on the processor and quickly pour in this mixture. When a ball just starts to form, stop the processor; do not overmix. Remove the dough from the processor, dust it lightly with flour, and form it into a 5x2-inch-thick disk. Cover with plastic wrap and refrigerate for at least 1 hour or overnight.
4. When the dough is properly chilled, roll it out with a light dusting of flour into a circle about 15 inches in diameter. The dough should be about ¼ inch thick. Make sure there are no holes in it.
5. Dust off any excess flour and place the dough in the tart pan, pushing it into each corner.
6. Refrigerate the shell for at least 15 to 20 minutes.
7. Preheat the oven to 375–400°F. Remove the shell from the refrigerator, trim any excess dough from the edges, and cover the shell with a piece of aluminum foil (lightly pressed into the corners). Top with dried beans or rice to weigh down the foil.

8. Bake for 10 to 12 minutes, until the sides are set and just starting to color.

9. Remove the foil with the beans or rice inside, reduce the oven temperature to 350°F, and continue to bake for 8 to 10 more minutes, until the shell is lightly golden and cooked but not too brown. If the dough starts to puff, press it down lightly with a clean cloth every 3 minutes.

10. Before the last 2 minutes of baking, brush the inside of the tart shell with the beaten egg white. (You don't have to use all of it.) Reserve at room temperature.

Aged Gouda, Artichoke, and Leek Filling

8 ounces Carr's aged Gouda cheese, diced small

2 large artichokes (5–6 ounces each), leaves removed, bottoms and stems trimmed, and choke scooped out; place trimmed bottoms and stems in water with a squeeze of lemon in it

2 tablespoons extra-virgin olive oil, divided

Kosher salt and fresh black pepper to taste

2 tablespoons dry white wine

I leek (8 ounces), trimmed, split lengthwise, dirt washed out, and cut on the bias into ¼-inch-thick pieces

I clove garlic, chopped fine

4 whole eggs

2 egg yolks

I cup heavy cream

I cup whole milk

I¼ teaspoons kosher salt

¼ teaspoon fresh-ground black pepper

⅛ teaspoon ground nutmeg

1. Dry the artichokes, cut their bottoms in half, and cut each half into ¼-inch slices. In a 10-inch sauté pan over high heat, add 1½ tablespoons of the oil.

2. When the oil is hot, add the artichokes and season with salt and pepper to taste. Cook for about 4 minutes.

3. Add the white wine and cook for 1 minute, until the wine evaporates. Add the remaining ½ tablespoon of oil and the leeks. Season the leeks lightly and cook for 1 minute. Add the garlic and toss for 30 seconds.

4. Remove the mixture to a plate and refrigerate to cool.

5. Meanwhile, in a bowl, add the eggs and egg yolks, whipping until well blended. Add the cream, milk, 1¼ teaspoons salt, ¼ teaspoon pepper, and ⅛ teaspoon nutmeg to form the custard.

6. Preheat the oven to 375°F.

7. When the artichokes and leeks are cool, finish assembling the tart by placing the shell (still in its tart pan) on a cookie sheet.

8. Scatter half of the artichoke–leek mixture on the bottom of the shell, then scatter over half of the cheese.

9. Add half of the custard mixture, then the remaining artichoke–leek mixture and cheese.
10. Place the cookie sheet with the tart shell on top on an oven rack and pour in enough custard to come up to the top of the tart's edge; do not overfill.
11. Bake for 20 to 25 minutes, until just set.
12. Let rest outside the oven for at least 15 minutes and serve with Crisp Apple, Gouda, and Tarragon Salad (recipe follows). If you like, the tart can be reheated before serving in a 325°F oven.

Crisp Apple, Gouda, and Tarragon Salad

1 tablespoon grape seed oil

2 teaspoons walnut oil

1½ teaspoons sherry vinegar

½ teaspoon lemon juice

¼ teaspoon kosher salt

⅛ teaspoon fresh-ground black pepper

1 large Granny Smith apple (about 5 ounces)

1 large Ida Red or other tasty red apple (about 5 ounces)

2 cups packed small arugula leaves, cleaned and dried

5 ounces Carr's aged Gouda, cut into julienne

¼ cup loose-packed fresh tarragon leaves

About 15 minutes before you'll be serving the tart, prepare the salad.

1. In a large bowl, place grape seed oil, walnut oil, sherry vinegar, lemon juice, salt, and pepper. Mix.
2. Cut the two apples in half from stem to bottom. Remove the cores. Slice the apples ¼ inch thick and cut into julienne (leave the skin on). Add the apples to the bowl.
3. Place the arugula, tarragon, and Gouda on top of the apples and toss together just before serving. Adjust the seasoning with salt and pepper. Serve this salad on the side of each slice of Aged Gouda, Artichoke, and Leek Tart.

SERVES 8–10

Courtesy of Sanford D'Amato, chef-owner of Sanford, the Coquette Café, and the Harlequin Bakery, all in Milwaukee, Wisconsin.

Havarti

Havarti was created in Denmark in the 1880s by Hanne Nielsen, who carefully studied numerous European cheesemaking methods. She then developed the cheese on Havarti, her experimental farm. Hence the name.

Wisconsin cheesemakers produce Havarti, similar to the pale Denmark original, as an interior-ripened, rindless cheese that is semi-soft with tiny holes known as eyes. Havarti can range from mild to tangy, strong, and aromatic, with the taste intensifying as it ages.

The Center for Dairy Research at the University of Wisconsin–Madison has created a special Wisconsin-style Havarti with a firmer, more buttery texture. Another variety is produced with extra cream. For the weight-conscious cheese lover, a low-fat Havarti is available. Creative Wisconsin cheesemakers flavor their Havarti with caraway, dill, jalapeño, pesto, or hot peppers.

There are many award-winning Wisconsin Havartis. At the 2006 World Championship Cheese Contest, Ron Buholzer from Klondike Cheese Company in Monroe won the top prize. Other Wisconsin-winning Havartis have come from Decatur Dairy, Edelweiss Town Hall, Arla Foods, and Cedar Grove Cheese. Klondike and Decatur have taken prizes for their Dill Havarti; Edelweiss and Decatur, for Havarti Pepper. Roth Käse has also captured awards for its Reduced Fat Havarti and Horseradish Havarti.

Fruity wines such as Riesling or Beaujolais Nouveau are notable sipping companions for this cheese. Creamy Havarti may be hard to slice, so be sure that the loaves are well chilled to make cutting easier.

Photo by Martin Hintz

Salmon Gravlax on Wisconsin Havarti Crostini with Dill Mustard

This recipe makes about 24 pieces and is an excellent hors d'oeuvre that can be passed or set on a buffet. In any case, we guarantee that it will disappear quickly.

Dill Mustard

½ cup Dijon mustard

I ounce white wine

I tablespoon chopped fresh dill

½ teaspoon black pepper

1. Mix all the ingredients well.

Crostini

I long multigrain baguette

8 ounces Wisconsin Havarti cheese

I pound salmon gravlax (smoked salmon may be substituted), sliced paper thin

I bunch fresh dill for garnish (optional)

1. Cut the baguette on the bias about ½ inch thick. Lightly toast the slices in the oven and cool.
2. Thinly slice the Havarti into triangles approximately the size of the crostini.
3. Spread Dill Mustard on each piece of toast. Next, place a slice of Havarti on top of the mustard, followed by a slice of gravlax or smoked salmon. Garnish with a small sprig of fresh dill as an added option.

SERVES 8 FOR APPETIZERS

Courtesy of the Wisconsin Milk Marketing Board, Inc.

Kasseri

Kasseri is a Greek cheese usually made from sheep's or goat's milk. But in Wisconsin cow's milk, or a blend of cow's milk (75 percent) and sheep's milk (25 percent), is most often used. The texture varies, with some Kasseris slightly crumbly while others are firm with a natural rind. These grate well and are used in cooking. The taste is mild with a slight tartness. Kasseri remains solid when cooked, retaining its shape.

This cheese can also be grilled alone on skewers. For an extra Old World treat, wrap a piece of Kasseri in a grape leaf, secure it with a toothpick, and grill. Serve with Greek olives and pita bread. A late-harvest Gewürztraminer or red wines such as Chianti go well with it.

Saganaki

When lighting the saganaki, Greeks customarily yell "Opa!" In Greek, this could mean something like, "My eyebrows are ablaze." But in German opa means "grandfather," so it could also mean that Grandpa is on the hot seat. And of course OPA is the acronym for the Ontario Power Authority. The choice of meaning is yours.

For Each Serving:

4 ounces Kasseri cheese

Flour, for dusting

3 tablespoons olive oil or butter

Juice of ½ lemon

Splash of cognac or Ouzo

1. Cut the Kasseri into slices ¼ to ½ inch thick. Chill the slices in ice water, pat them dry, and dust them with flour.
2. Melt the olive oil or butter until it sizzles but does not brown. Add the cheese slices and sauté quickly on both sides.
3. Squeeze the juice of ½ lemon into the skillet and sprinkle with a few drops of Ouzo or cognac. (Some chefs prefer to squeeze the lemon as the final step.)
4. Ignite. Serve after the flames have died down.

Limburger

Limburger, often mislabeled as a stinky German cheese, actually originated in Belgium. It was first made by Trappist monks in the Liege region and sold in the city of Limburg. As such, it remains the most famous Belgian cheese, despite the fact that the Germans produce more of it.

The Chalet Cheese Co-op in Monroe has the distinction of being the only Limburger-producing cheese plant in the United States. This small factory rests atop a ridge in the rolling, green hills of southwest Wisconsin's Green County. A farmer-owned co-op, Chalet was founded in 1885. In 2004 the firm acquired Deppeler Cheese, another top-quality cheese company in Monroe. Both facilities have won numerous honors for their high-quality cheeses.

Chalet's specialty is the butt of many jokes, receiving its "stinky cheese" nickname from the pungent smell. There is a cheese eaters' myth that the monks who created Limburger originally stomped the milk and curds with their bare feet, but Master Cheesemaker Myron Olson, Chalet's general manager, assures us that this is not the case. The odor is in fact caused by a bacterium called *Brevibacterium linens* or B-linens.

Olson still makes Limburger the old-fashioned, labor-intensive way. His Limburger is a surface-ripened cheese, kept in a cool, moist cellar for a week. It is then hand washed with a B-linens bacterial solution called a smear and turned twice. The individual bricks are hand wrapped in parchment and waxed paper before selling. At this point, the young Limburger is firm, crumbly, and salty, much like feta. Over the next six months, Limburger goes through more transformations than a movie star with Botox treatments. After about six weeks, the cheese begins

Photo by Martin Hintz

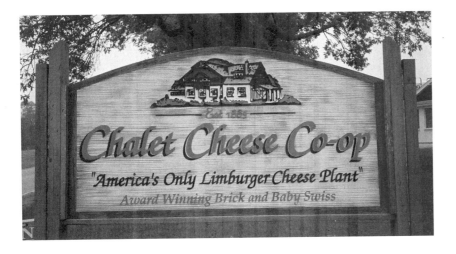

REAL MEN DO EAT LIMBURGER

Chalet Cheese Limburger makes for a popular sandwich at Baumgartner's Cheese Store & Tavern in Monroe, one of Wisconsin's longest continuously operating cheese outlets. The dark-paneled Old World store, which opened in 1931, is located on Monroe's main square. There's truth to a sign inside: THROUGH THIS PORTAL, YOU CAN GET THE BEST CHEESE SANDWICHES IN THE WORLD.

Hearty slabs of Limburger, topped with slices of raw onion, are layered on rye bread to create a premier menu item. A glass of locally brewed Huber beer and a bowl of industrial-strength homemade chili round out a lunch worth trekking miles to enjoy. The chili is billed as the world's second best because "Mom's is always best."

Limburger was the draw for Baumgartner's owners, Chris Soukup and his brother Tyler, who purchased the tavern in 2005. As youngsters, their computer engineer father drove them all the way from Freeport, Illinois, about 20 miles to the south, just for these husky manwiches.

Chris Soukup, owner of Baumgartner's in Monroe, has a long-standing love affair with the place. He and his brother Tyler used to visit Baumgartner's as kids to enjoy limburger sandwiches and chili.

to soften at the edges; soon it becomes smooth and creamy. At around three months it has developed Limburger's signature odor. A suggested "eat-by" date is stamped on the traditional silver foil wrapping, indicating a six-month window after its production for retaining the best flavor. Longer means the package might need to be buried. Deep. At any rate, it's time to purchase a fresh one.

Limburger is best eaten the traditional way in a sandwich made of dark rye bread topped with a hearty slab of raw onion. Mart's accompanying beverage of choice is a champion Berghoff bock made by the century-plus-old Huber Brewery in Monroe, or a tankard of Spotted Cow from nearby the New Glarus Brewery. Limburger is also good with other dark breads, crackers, pretzels, mustards, and the ubiquitous, cheese-friendly gherkins.

Wisconsin Limburger Pizza

Limburger rind is bitter and is usually trimmed prior to eating. After cutting, be sure to clean your cheese cutting board before exposing it to other cheese. The mold and bacteria readily transfer to other cheeses.

I package (7 ounces) **Chalet Limburger cheese**

I 12-inch prepared bread shell or frozen pizza crust

I cup finely sliced new potatoes

6 fresh asparagus spears, cut into I-inch pieces, sliced in half lengthwise

¼ cup chopped red onion

I garlic clove, minced

I tablespoon fresh thyme or I teaspoon dried thyme

¼ teaspoon salt

2 tablespoons olive oil

Red pepper flakes to taste

1. Preheat the oven to 425°F.
2. Cut away a ¼-inch rind from all sides of the cheese. Discard the rind. Shred the remaining cheese. Spread the pizza shell with ¾ cup of this cheese. Set aside.
3. Boil the potatoes, then slice and peel them. Boil the asparagus until al dente, about 2 minutes.
4. Combine the potatoes, asparagus, onion, garlic, thyme, and salt. Sprinkle the olive oil over the mixture and toss lightly.
5. Spread the vegetables evenly over the pizza. Sprinkle the remaining ¾ cup of cheese over the vegetables. Sprinkle with the red pepper flakes.
6. Place on a baking sheet and bake for 18 to 20 minutes.

MAKES I (12-INCH) PIZZA

Recipe adapted from Agri-View *newspaper, May 27, 1999.*

Monterey Jack

Monterey Jack is a California creation first made by the Franciscan monks and called queso del pais. It was popularized in the 1890s by David Jacks, a Scottish businessman who came to America in 1849. While amassing land and a fortune, Jacks seized the chance to mass-market this mild white cheese. First termed "Jack's Cheese," the name was eventually changed to the more memorable Monterey Jack.

Graphic courtesy of DCI Cheese Company

Monterey Jack is a semi-soft, creamy white cheese that, when mixed with Colby, becomes Cojack. Chunks of fiery chile pieces are added to make Pepper Jack. Monterey Jacks come in dozens of other flavors, spiced with dill, garlic, peppercorns, roasted garlic, morels, leeks, onions, and chives. Hispanic flavors are produced with jalapeño or habanero peppers and salsa. Fruit-flavored Monterey Jacks are sweetened with blueberry, apple, and cinnamon. Wisconsin cheese is also available in kosher, raw milk and organic varieties.

Jacks are great for sandwiches and extremely popular for creating Mexican dishes such as quesadillas or for including in casseroles and on pizzas. Riesling, Colombard, Rhine, or related fruity wines are fine counterpoints to the more spicy Jacks. Mart likes his lager beers or Belgian-style ales when Jack-snacking.

Meister Cheese Company is a leader in award-winning Monterey Jack cheese. The firm dates back to 1923, when grandfather Joseph Meister began making cheese in Muscoda—a snug village in the Wisconsin River Valley area in the southwest corner of the state. The firm's Great Midwest line of Jack is famous for unique flavors. Meister won top honors for its Great Midwest Ranch Monterey Jack at the 2006 American Cheese Society competition. And at the World Cheese Awards that same year, its Great Midwest Smokey Jack won the gold. Also honored are Great Midwest Roasted Red Pepper Monterey Jack, Farmstead Jack, Habanero Jack, Pesto Jack, and Morel and Leek Jack.

A fun way to check out the Meisters' cheese, especially their award-winning Wild Morel and Leek Jack Cheese, is visiting the annual Morel Mushroom Festival. The popular event is held in Muscoda the weekend after Mother's Day each year.

Cherry Jack Empanada

Kids love Monterey Jacks because of their smooth taste, especially when served with fruits such as apples or—as in this recipe—cherries.

½ cup slivered almonds

I package (15 ounces) refrigerated
    piecrust rounds (2 crusts)

I can (16 ounces) tart red cherries, well
    drained, *or* 2 cups pitted fresh
    cherries

½ cup diced dried apricots

¼ teaspoon almond flavoring

½ teaspoon ground cinnamon

I tablespoon packed brown sugar

1½ cups (6 ounces) shredded Great
    Midwest Salsa Jack cheese

I egg, beaten

I tablespoon milk

3 tablespoons coarse sugar

1. Preheat the oven to 400°F.
2. Toast the almonds on cookie sheet in the oven for 6 to 8 minutes, until golden. Let them cool; leave the oven on.
3. Unfold both piecrusts on a separate baking sheet.
4. In a bowl, combine the toasted almonds, cherries, apricots, almond flavoring, cinnamon, brown sugar, and Salsa Jack. Mix well.
5. Spoon half of the mixture onto half of one piecrust, within 1 inch of edge, leaving the other half uncovered. Fold the pastry over the filling; crimp the edges to seal. The finished empanada should resemble a semicircle.
6. Repeat with the remaining crust and filling.
7. In a small bowl, combine the egg and milk. Brush the empanadas with this egg mixture and sprinkle with the coarse sugar.
8. Cut four small slits in top of each empanada. Bake for 20 to 25 minutes, until the pastry is golden brown.

SERVES 12

Courtesy of the DCI Cheese Company.

MARVELOUS TO MAGNIFICENT: STILL MORE WISCONSIN CHEESE

BUTTERKÄSE

Butterkäse originated in Germany and remains extremely popular there and in neighboring Austria. Although this cheese contains no butter, the name literally means "butter cheese," describing its butter-like texture. Butterkäse is a melt-in-your-mouth variety, creamy, mild, odorless, and semi-soft in texture. It ripens in about a month.

Robert Wills from Cedar Grove Cheese in Plain, Wisconsin, is a Wisconsin Master Cheesemaker for Butterkäse, as well as for Cheddar. Visitors can tour the family-owned company and sample its many styles of specialty cheese. Cedar Grove, one of the state's earliest organic cheesemakers, has won numerous gold medals for its products.

A traditional German sandwich comprises Butterkäse with ham or salami and mustard on a hard roll, with pickled vegetables on the side. Because Butterkäse is mild and melts well, it also makes a great cheeseburger or grilled cheese sandwich. It won't overpower other tastes, so put it atop vegetables. Butterkäse is a taste marriage made in heaven when combined with fruits such as grapes and melons, and sausages or cured meats. It's excellent served with dry or semi-sweet wines like Semillon, Chardonnay, or Rhine. Pilsner or other light lagers work nicely as well.

COLD PACK

Like Brick and Colby, cold pack is a Wisconsin original—a smooth, spreadable cheese blended without heat. It's sometimes called club or crock cheese because it was packed in cheese crocks.

Cold pack is different from most cheese spreads in that it's regulated by the FDA and cannot have any added water. In addition, it has less than a 44 percent moisture content and must have the same amount of moisture as the cheese used to make it. It's similar to the natural cheese from which it's made, such as Cheddar, Swiss, or blue.

Pine River Pre-Pack cheese company of Newton has captured World Champion honors for its Cold Pine River Pre-Pack. The firm uses a nine-month-aged Cheddar as a base and adds herbs, spices, and other dairy ingredients. Pine River's other award winners are Sharp Cheddar, Garlic & Herb, Port Wine, Swiss & Almond, French Onion, and Horseradish. The company also makes Smokey Bacon, Jalapeño, and an Almond Cheese Log.

Although Cold Pack cheese was created to spread on crackers or bread, we find it superb on baked potatoes. In addition, you can make a delicious cheese sauce simply by melting the cheese and adding cream or milk. We suggest using eight ounces of cheese to a quarter cup of milk. For a zingy appetizer, melt Jalapeño Cold Pack cheese (eight ounces) with two tablespoons of milk and then pour over corn chips. A dollop on an omelet results in an entirely new taste treat.

STRING CHEESE

Wisconsinites love their string cheese—salty, cylindrical-shaped snacks about 6 inches long and 1 inch in diameter. String cheese is best munched by pulling strips of cheese from the cylinder along its length and eating the strings. It's a great nibble for road or airplane trips, as well as a hiking pick-me-up. The Baker Cheese Factory, in St. Cloud since 1916, is one of Wisconsin's primary producers of string cheese. For three decades its factory has produced a quality mozzarella cheese that's stretched into strings and then sliced into various sizes.

Wisconsin State Fair string cheese winners have included Rob Stellrecht and Bruce Willis (no, not *that* Bruce Willis), both of the Burnett Dairy Co-op in Grantsburg; and George Crave, Crave Brothers Farmstead Cheese, Waterloo.

Note that if you put string cheese in a microwave oven for thirty seconds, its structure will change and it will lose its ability to form strings.

CHEESE CURDS

Cheese curds are as Wisconsin as, well, milk. These always popular snacks usually consist of fresh young Cheddar cheeses before being processed into blocks and aged. Unlike aged cheese, juvenile curds lose their desirable qualities if refrigerated or not eaten for a few days. If they get too old, the noticeable squeak heard when eaten disappears, and the chunks become dry and salty. Thus it's best to purchase the springy, chewy curds directly from a dairy plant or specialty cheese store; supermarket curds are often several weeks old and have lost their punch. But desperate souls have been known to microwave their tired curds for a couple of seconds. This briefly revitalizes the pieces. Fresh is still best.

Some die-hard fans love their curds prepared in a beer-based batter and deep-fry them. The resulting crusty outsides and gooey interiors are then dipped into a ranch or other style of dressing.

FARMER'S CHEESE

There are two types of farmer's cheese (also spelled *farmers* or *farmers'*). One is basically a pressed cottage cheese, which becomes drier and more crumbly. The other is a firmer, semi-soft cheese that is cured for a short time and can be cubed or shredded. This type is similar to Havarti, but lower in fat and has a buttery flavor with a hint of acidity. Around the world farmer's cheese is made from the milk of cows, goats, and sheep.

Like many cheeses, farmer's cheese is delicious in potato dishes, in macaroni and other casseroles, or with vegetables such as green beans. We've added it to pastrami-on-rye sandwiches, served with a sharp mustard. It's a great snack, lower in fat than other cheeses. Kids love its soft, buttery taste.

The Cedar Grove Cheese Company has won awards for its farmer's cheese in the Light/Lite & Reduced Fat Cheeses category (25 to 50 percent reduction in fat per serving). Farmer's cheese also comes in many distinct flavors: caraway, dill, jalapeño, garden vegetable, garlic and dill, smoked, and tomato basil.

CHEESE CURD CAPITAL OF WISCONSIN

The Ellsworth Dairy Cooperative located in Ellsworth was established in 1910 and proclaimed the *"Cheese Curd Capital of Wisconsin"* by Governor Anthony S. Earl in 1984. The cooperative, now with 521 dairy farm family owners, began making cheese in 1966 and two years later started selling packaged curds. Each June on the Pierce County Fair Grounds there is an annual Cheese Curd Festival that features lots of fresh and deep fried cheese curds, a parade, the Cheese Curd Run, a cheese curd–medallion hunt, a cheese curd eating contest, and lots of music and other activities. It also has a retail outlet in the town.

GLOSSARY

affinage: Process of aging a cheese.

aged: Generally describes a cheese that has been cured longer than six months. Aged cheeses are characterized as having more pronounced and fuller, sometimes sharper flavors than medium-aged or current-aged cheeses.

bandaging: A traditional English process that involves wrapping cheese in cheesecloth.

bloomy rind: The descriptive term for an edible cheese rind, or crust, that is covered with harmless *Penicillium candidum* mold to produce flavor.

blue veined: Cheese with blue or green streaks of harmless, flavor-producing mold throughout its body.

brushing: During curing, washed-rind cheese varieties are "brushed" with liquids. Brine, beer, wine, or brandy produces a moist rind to promote earthy flavors. Hard cheeses such as Parmesan are often brushed or rubbed with a vegetable oil.

cheddaring: This step in Cheddar-style cheese production takes place after heating, when the curd is cubed to drain the whey; the cheese is then stacked and turned.

creamy: A term used to describe cheese texture or taste. Creamy textures are rich, soft, spreadable, and, potentially, runny. The term also refers to color.

flaky: Cheese that breaks into flakes when cut, typical of Parmesan, Romano, Asiago, and Cheddar aged more than ten to twelve months.

fresh: This classifies cheeses that have not been cured, such as mascarpone, cottage cheese, cream cheese, and ricotta. Feta and some other varieties that have been cured for short periods may also be called fresh.

hard (firm): Cheese varieties with a relatively inelastic and unyielding texture, including Cheddar and Swiss.

hard grating: Cheeses used primarily in cooking; examples include Parmesan, Romano, and Asiago, all well aged and easily grated.

medium aged (mellow): Generally semi-firm, firm, or hard cheeses that have been cured for three to six months. Medium-aged cheeses are usually mellow and smooth textured. The term is frequently used to describe Cheddars.

mild (young): Cheeses with light, unpronounced flavors; also refers to briefly aged Cheddars.

natural rind: A rind that develops naturally on the cheese exterior through drying while ripening without the aid of ripening agents or washing. Most semi-firm or hard cheeses have natural rinds; these may be thin, like that of bandaged Cheddar, or thick as in Parmesan, pecorino Romano, and wheel Swiss (Emmentaler).

pasta filata: Italian for "to spin paste or threads," this term refers to the process of heating curds, which can then be elongated or molded into the desired shape. The resulting cheese stretches whenever cooked or melted. The *pasta filata* family includes mozzarella, provolone, and string cheese.

pasteurized process cheese: A blend of fresh and aged natural cheeses that have been shredded, mixed, and cooked, along with emulsifier salt. Following this process, no more ripening occurs.

rindless: As you might expect, cheese without a rind. Brick and Colby are cured in a protective coating, such as in plastic film, to prevent rind formation. Other cheeses, such as feta, don't have rinds because they aren't allowed to ripen.

ripening: The chemical and physical alteration of cheese during the curing process.

salting: A step in cheesemaking in which salt is either added while the cheese is in curd form or rubbed on the cheese after pressing. Salt helps preserve cheese as well as enhancing its flavor. Brining occurs when cheese is soaked in a salt solution.

semi-hard: A classification based on a cheese's body. Cheddar, Edam, and Gouda all fall into the semi-hard category.

semi-soft: A wide variety of cheeses that are made with whole milk and melt when cooked. These include Monterey Jack, Brick, Muenster, Fontina, and Havarti.

sharp: This refers to the sharp, tangy flavor of aged cheeses, such as Cheddar.

silky or satiny: This refers to the texture of soft, spreadable cheeses. A satiny texture is characteristic of nicely ripened Brie.

smoked cheese: Methods for smoking cheese include the addition of liquid smoke to the brine or smoking over wood chips. Smoked Cheddar, Swiss, and provolone have unique flavors.

soft-fresh: Cheeses with a high moisture content, including cottage cheese, cream cheese, Neufchâtel, feta, mascarpone, ricotta, and Queso Blanco.

soft ripened: A classification of cheese based on its body. Brie and Camembert are soft-ripened cheese varieties.

surface ripened: This cheese ripens from the exterior when mold, yeast, or bacteria is applied to its surface. Brie, Camembert, and Limburger are surface-ripened cheeses.

Swiss-type: Cheese with holes or eyes in their interior. The eyes develop during the curing process when gas, formed through fermentation, is trapped and expands. Various-size holes result, ranging from the pea-size holes in Baby Swiss to the larger pockets in aged Swiss.

terroir: The special geographic characteristics that give a food product its individuality; the overall sense of place as expressed in food.

variety: The generic name of a cheese by which it is most commonly identified, such as Cheddar, Colby, or blue.

washed rind: A cheese rind that has been washed periodically with brine, whey, beer, cider, wine, brandy, or oil during ripening. The rind is kept moist to encourage the growth of an orange-red bacteria. The bacteria may be scraped off, dried, or left to further rind development. Washed-rind and bloomy-rind cheeses make up what's termed the soft-ripening (surface-ripened) classification. Limburger is a washed-rind cheese.

wheel: A round of cheese.

Definitions courtesy of the Wisconsin Milk Marketing Board, Inc.

SAMPLE WHEEL OF WISCONSIN CHEESE COMPANIES

Alto Dairy Cooperative
N3545 Highway EE
Waupun, WI 53963
(920) 346-2215
www.altodairy.com
www.blackcreekclassic.com
Alto Dairy, a 110-year-old farmer-owned cooperative, makes more than 500,000 pounds of cheese per day. Their Black Creek Classic cheeses, including a Naturally Aged Black Creek Cheddar and a Pasture Grazed White Cheddar, have won many awards.

Babcock Hall Dairy Plant
1605 Linden Drive
Madison, WI 53706
(608) 265-2726
http://foodsci.wisc.edu/store
Babcock Hall is the home of the Department of Food Science, as well as the Walter V. Price Cheese Research Institute and the Center for Dairy Research at the University of Wisconsin-Madison. The plant's Gouda and its Manchego, which is made from sheep's milk, have won awards.

Baker Cheese Factory
N5279 County Highway G
St. Cloud, WI 53079
(920) 477-7871
www.bakercheese.com
Baker Cheese is proud of being the "String Cheese Specialists." The family-owned string cheese manufacturer was founded in 1916.

Bass Lake Cheese Factory
598 Valley View Trail
Somerset, WI 54025
(800) 368-2437
www.blcheese.com
Established in 1918, Bass Lake makes a variety of cheeses, many with added flavors ranging from herbs and spices to cranberries and even olives. In 1991, Master Cheesemaker Scott Erickson and his wife Julie purchased the company and the accompanying store where they sell their cheese.

Beechwood Cheese Company
N1598 West County Road A
Beechwood, WI 53002
(920) 994-9306
www.beechwoodcheese.com
Beechwood is one of the five remaining cheese factories in Sheboygan County, once considered the "Cheese Capital of the Nation." Beechwood is a small, family-run operation known for its Almost Famous Cheese Curds and other cheeses, including Uncle Charlie's Chicken Soup Cheese, Screamin' Mimi Triple Pepper Cheese, Chipotle Ole, Garden Dilly Jack, and Chuckwagon Cheddar. All are sold at the firm's retail shop.

BelGioioso Cheese, Inc.
5810 County Road NN
Denmark, WI 54208
(920) 863-2123
www.belgioioso.com
BelGioioso Cheese, founded by Errico Auricchio, is famous for its classic Italian cheeses that have won many prestigious awards over the last two decades. Among BelGioioso's award-winners are American Grana, fresh mozzarella, a crumbly Gorgonzola, a Creamygorg, Tiramisu Mascarpone, provolone, Parmesan, and Vegetarian Parmesan.

Blaser's Premium Cheese
P.O. Box 36
Comstock, WI 54826
(715) 822-2437
www.blasersusa.com
Since 1948, Blaser's Crystal Lake Cheese Factory has been making premium specialty cheeses. Among its products are various flavored cream cheeses, goat's milk fetas and chèvres, and Italian cheeses.

Bleu Mont Dairy
3480 County Road F
Blue Mounds, WI 53517
(608) 767-2875
www.cheeseforager.com/bleumont
Bleu Mont Dairy, owned by cheesemaker Willi Lehner, is famous for its artisan cheese using certified organic milk and rotationally grazed cows. Lehner's award-winning Bandaged Cheddar and various washed-rind cheeses have earned the company international recognition.

Brunkow Cheese of Wisconsin
17975 Highway F
Darlington, WI 53530
(608) 776-3716
www.pcmli.com/cw_bk.htm
Founded in 1899, Brunkow is owned by some thirty dairy families. Visitors are welcomed at the plant in Darlington where Brunkow makes Cheddar, Monterey Jack, Colby, CoJack, and flavored cheeses such as Garden Salad, Garlic Cheddar, and Pepper Jack as well as raw milk Cheddar spreads and a variety of organic cheeses.

Burnett Dairy Cooperative
11631 State Road 70
Grantsburg, WI 54840
(715) 689-2468
www.burnettdairy.com
Burnett Dairy Cooperative was formed in 1966 and is now owned by 230 local dairy farmers. The co-op's award-winning Alpha's Morning Sun is a combination of Cheddar, provolone, and Swiss. Burnett's also make a variety of unique string cheeses.

Butler Farms
W13184 Sjuggerud Road
Whitehall, WI 54773
(715) 983-2285
Butler Farms is a licensed Grade A sheep dairy, one of the first in the United States. It is known for Camembert, aged Tomme, and fresh Brebis.

Cady Cheese Factory, Inc.
126 Highway 128
Wilson, WI 54027
(715) 772-4218
www.cadycheese.com
The Cady Cheese Factory produces many different varieties and flavors of longhorn cheese, which is a mild Cheddar or Colby made into a long, orange cylinder. Cheesemakers here believe cheese is better and more flavorful when made in smaller form.

Capri Cheesery
P.O. Box 102
Blue River, WI 53518
(608) 604-2640
www.capricheesery.com
Cheesemaker Felix Thalhammer uses goat's milk to make Capri cheeses in small batches, using traditional artisan techniques. He specializes in various fetas as well as some of his own creations, including Govarti, a combination of Gouda and Havarti. His Bear Cheese is made with traditional Muenster techniques.

Carr Valley Cheese Company
S3797 County Trunk Highway G
La Valle, WI 53941
(608) 986-2781

www.carrvalleycheese.com
Carr Valley Cheese is a fourth-generation company, doing business for more than a century. The owner, certified Master Cheesemaker Sid Cook, has won hundreds of top awards in national and international competitions, more than sixty in the last three years. The company's Cocoa Cardona, aged Cheddars, and Canaria, a firm, Parmesan-like cheese, are among his award winners.

Cedar Grove Cheese
E5904 Mill Road
Plain, WI 53577
(800) 200-6020
www.cedargrovecheese.com
Cedar Grove has been making cheese since 1878. The firm produces organic cheese, various cow's milk cheeses, and a sheep's milk cheese called Dantes, along with Mona and Farko, which are mixed sheep's and cow's milk cheeses.

Chalet Cheese Cooperative
N4858 Highway N
Monroe, WI 53566
(608) 325-4343
www.wisdairy.com/BuyWICheese/
CompanyDetail
Chalet Cheese was founded in 1885 by five dairy farmers. Today, Chalet has twenty-nine members. The plant is the only producer of Limburger in the United States, yet also specializes in many award-winning Brick and Baby Swiss cheeses. The company's retail brands are Deppler Cheese Factory, Country Castle, and Castle.

Chippewa Valley Cheese Corporation
50901 Francis Street
Osseo, WI 54758
(715) 597-2366
www.chippewavalleycheese.com
*Chippewa Valley is owned by more than
fifty family dairy farmers from around
Wisconsin. It makes quality farmer's
cheese, mozzarella, Colby, Colby Jack,
Pepper Jack, and Monterey Jack.*

Chula Vista Cheese Co.
2923 Mayer Road
Browntown, WI 53522
(608) 439-5211
*Chula Vista is co-owned by Master
Cheesemaker Jim Meives. The company
specializes in making Chihuahua cheese,
producing more than 40,000 pounds
each day.*

Crave Brothers Farmstead Cheese
W11555 Torpy Road
Waterloo, WI 53594
(920) 478-4887
www.cravecheese.com
*Brothers Charles, George, Thomas,
and Mark Crave own this operation
that makes farmstead classics, including
mascarpone, fresh mozzarella, farmer's
cheese, rope part-skim mozzarella, and
Les Frères.*

DCI Cheese Company
3018 Highway 145
Richfield, WI 53076
(262) 677-3407
www.dcicheese.com
*DCI supplies premium DCI-owned
or exclusively held brands including*

*Salemville Cheese, Black Diamond,
Great Midwest, Timber Lake, Organic
Creamery, Black River, and others.*

Decatur Dairy, Inc.
W1668 Highway F
Brodhead, WI 53520
(608) 897-8661
www.decaturdairy.com
*Decatur Dairy is an award-winning
cheese producer from the Brodhead area.
Master Cheesemaker Steve Stettler
and his team are known for their
prizewinning Havarti and Muenster, as
well as the always popular fresh, squeaky
cheese curds.*

Dreamfarm
8877 Table Bluff Road
Cross Plains, WI 53528
(608) 767-3442
www.dreamfarm.biz
*Diana and Jim Murphy and their
family make delicious farmstead-fresh
goat cheese with milk from their goats.
Diana, a certified cheesemaker, produces
a variety of flavors such as plain, Garlic,
Garlic Dill, Peppercorn, French, Herb,
Herbes de Provence, and Italian Blend.*

Dupont Cheese, Inc.
P.O. Box 96
N10140 Highway 110
Marion, WI 54950
(715) 754-5424
*Dupont Cheese makes fresh curds, Colby,
Cheddar, Monterey Jack, Rainbow, and
other flavored cheeses. An observation
window at its retail outlet allows visitors
to watch cheese in the making.*

Eau Galle Cheese, Inc.
N6765 State Highway 25
Durand, WI 54736
(715) 283-4211
www.eaugallecheese.com
*Family-owned since 1945, Eau Galle is
noted for its hard organic Italian cheese.
It also makes numerous other styles, such
as a five-year-old private stock Cheddar.*

Edelweiss Creamery
W6117 County Road C
Monticello, WI 53570
(608) 938-4094
www.edelweisscreamery.com
*Edelweiss Creamery is a small, artisan
cheese factory employing state-of-the-art
technology. The firm was established in
1873 and is still at the original location.
Owner Bruce Workman is known for the
huge fondues he serves at the Wisconsin
State Fair and Monroe's Cheese Days
celebration. His Edelweiss Emmentaler
cheese is made with raw milk in a
traditional Swiss copper vat.*

Ellsworth Co-op Creamery
P.O. Box 610
232 North Wallace Street
Ellsworth, WI 54011
(715) 273-4311
www.ellsworthcheesecurds.com
*Ellsworth Dairy Cooperative was
proclaimed the "Cheese Curd Capitol
of Wisconsin" in 1984 by Governor
Anthony Earl. In 1966, they began
making cheese. Their 100% All Natural
Premium Chedder Cheese Curds are
sold nationwide, as well as at their on-
location store.*

Fantôme Farm
Route 1
Ridgeway, WI 53582
(608) 924-1266
www.fantomefarm.com
Fantôme Farm rests among the beautiful rolling hills of southwest Wisconsin. It is a small facility with a milk house for the goats and a factory where chèvre cheeses are made by hand.

FenceLine
22950 County Road Y
Grantsburg, WI 54840
(612) 521-0450
www.fencelinecheese.com
Lightly Aged Provolone and FenceLine Winter Sun, a cow's milk original, are among the award-winning cheeses made by FenceLine, based in northern Wisconsin's Burnett County. It also produces Italian country cheeses.

Foremost Farms USA Cooperative
P.O. Box 111
Baraboo, WI 53913-0111
(800) 362-9196
Foremost Farms is a dairy cooperative owned by about three thousand dairy farmers throughout the Midwest. It takes its name from a Guernsey bull named Langwater Foremost, owned by James Cash Penney Jr., founder of JCPenney Co. department stores.

Forgotten Valley Cheese
6519 Larson Road
South Wayne, WI 53587
(608) 439-5569
Forgotten Valley Cheese has been

operating since 1979, producing many international and national championship cheeses. Among the company's many products are farmer's cheese, Dill Havarti, Horseradish Havarti, Garlic Cheddar, Medium and Aged Cheddar, and Smoked Butterkase.

Franklin Cheese Co-op
W7256 Franklin Road
Monroe, WI 53566
(608) 325-3725
The Franklin co-op makes delicious Muenster, farmer's, and flavored cheeses in its facility located in Green County.

Gibbsville Cheese Company, Inc.
W2663 County Highway OO
Sheboygan Falls, WI 53085
(920) 564-3242
www.gibbsvillecheese.com
Located in east-central Wisconsin, the Gibbsville Cheese Company has been owned and operated by the Van Tatenhove family for more than sixty-five years. The plant produces Cheddar, Colby, Monterey Jack, and two-tone (Monterey Jack and Colby) cheeses.

Gile Cheese Company/Carr Cheese Factory
116 North Main Street
Cuba City, WI 53807
(608) 744-3456
www.gilecheese.com
Since 1946, Gile Cheese Company has been a champion Wisconsin cheesemaker, winning more than 200 awards for its products. The company produces Cheddar, Mild Colby, 50-50(Colby

Jack), Monterey Jack, Pepper Jack, Habanero Jack, and numerous other varieties.

Gingerbread Jersey
1025 West Lincoln Street
Augusta, WI 54722
(715) 667-5350
Virgil and Carolyn Schunk make their Colby, flavored Jacks, Cheddars, and curds from the milk of their own farm's herd. Fresh curds are available every Friday morning.

Grande Cheese Company
Dairy Road
Brownsville, WI 53006-0067
(920) 269-7200
www.grandecheese.com
Founded in the 1940s, in its early years Grande primarily produced Italian eating and grating cheeses such as provolone and Romano. It eventually capitalized on the country's pizza craze by manufacturing award-winning mozzarella that is shipped all over the United States.

Henning's Cheese
20201 Ucker Point Creek Road
Kiel, WI 53042
(920) 894-3032
www.henningscheese.com
Since 1914, Henning's has been a noted Wisconsin cheesemaker, receiving numerous awards for its Cheddar, Monterey Jack, and Colby. The company is known for its mammoth cheese wheels, which can weigh up to one thousand pounds or more for special orders.

Hidden Springs Creamery
S1597 Hanson Road
Westby, WI 54667
(608) 634-2521
www.hiddenspringscreamery.com
*Hidden Springs produces wonderfully
creamy cheese made from sheep's milk.
The family farm is located in the north-
central part of Vernon County in western
Wisconsin.*

Hoch Enterprises, Inc.
554 First Street
New Glarus, WI 53574
(608) 527-2000
www.wisconsindairyartisan.org/pdf/
directory.pdf
*Braun Suisse Käse Aged Cheddar is
among the award-winning cheeses
produced by Hoch Enterprises, which
uses milk from Brown Swiss dairy cows
to ensure a silky texture and a buttery
flavor for its cheeses, which also include
Baby Swiss, Aged Brick, and Aged
Cheddar.*

Hook's Cheese Company, Inc.
320 Commerce Street
Mineral Point, WI 53565
(608) 987-3259
www.cheeseforager.com/hooks.php
*Hook's Cheese Company was established
in 1976 by Tony and Julie Hook.
Through the years they have handcrafted
numerous international award-winning
varieties, including Colby and Cheddar.
Some of the latter has been aged as long
as ten years. The firm's tangy blue ranks
among its most popular styles.*

Klondike Cheese Company
W7839 Highway 81
P.O. Box 234
Monroe, WI 53566
(608) 325-3021
*The Buholzer family's Klondike Cheese
has gone through several permutations. It
had been a major manufacturer of Swiss,
then Cheddar, but since the mid-1990s
has become known for its feta. The cheese
is sold under a dozen different brands, as
well as the firm's own Odyssey label.*

Laack Brothers Cheese Company
7050 Morrison Road
Greenleaf, WI 54126
(920) 864-2815
*Established in 1986, the Laack Brothers
Cheese Company produces award-
winning cold pack and cheese spreads.
The fourth-generation family firm
specializes in Aged Cheddars.*

Lactalis USA, Inc.
218 Park Street
P.O. Box 347
Belmont, WI 53510
(608) 762-5173
www.presidentcheese.com
*Lactalis USA produces specialty
products such as feta, Roquefort, Brie,
Emmentaler, and goat's and sheep's milk
cheeses. It is the manufacturing and
marketing division of Lactalis American
Group, part of the French cheese and
dairy products producer Groupe Lactalis.
Its brands include Président, Sorrento,
Galbani, Société Roquefort, Valbreso,
and Rondelé.*

LaGrander's Hillside Dairy, Inc.
W11299 Broek Road
Stanley, WI 54768
(715) 644-2275
*LeGrander's Hillside Dairy has been
a family-run operation since 1960,
specializing in traditional longhorns
and daisy-style cheeses. It also produces
Cheddar, Colby, and Monterey Jack.*

Land O'Lakes
306 Park Street
Spencer, WI 54479
(715) 659-5910
www.landolakesinc.com
*Land O'Lakes, a co-op founded in 1921,
produces numerous varieties of cheese, as
well as many other dairy products. Its
Cheddars have garnered many awards
and its Web site offers numerous recipes
and many helpful hints about cheese and
its uses.*

LoveTree Farmstead Cheese
12413 County Road Z
Grantsburg, WI 54840
(715) 488-2966
www.lovetreefarmstead.com
*LoveTree Farmstead Cheese was
established in 1986 in the Trade Lake
area of northern Wisconsin. It produces
robust sheep's milk cheeses such as Trade
Lake Cedar, a natural rind cheese aged
on cedar boughs in a fresh air aging cave.*

Lynn Dairy, Inc.
W1929 US Highway 10
Granton, WI 54436
(715) 238-7129
www.lynndairy.com

Lynn Dairy, whose plant is managed by Wisconsin Master Cheesemaker David Lindgren, specializes in American-style cheeses such as Cheddar, Monterey Jack, Colby, farmer's cheese, and various flavored varieties.

Maple Leaf Cheese Cooperative:
N890 Twin Grove Road
Monroe, WI 53566
(608) 934-1234
www.wischeese.com
The Maple Leaf co-op was organized in 1910 and is still local farmer–owned, with some third-generation families still involved. Gouda, Cheddar, and Colby are among its specialties.

Meister Cheese Company
P.O. Box 68
Muscoda, WI 53573
(608) 739-3134
www.meistercheese.com
In addition to Wild Morel and Leek Jack, Meister Cheese's line of Great Midwest Monterey Jacks includes Jalapeno, Habanero, Salsa, Pesto and Caesar, Horseradish, Roasted Red Pepper, Ranch, and Buffaloblue Jack. It also has a Timber Lake label of flavored Cheddar cheeses, such as Chipotle and Tomato and Basil. The firm has been in business since 1923.

Mexican Cheese Producers, Inc. (MCP)
1625 10th Street, Suite 205
Monroe, WI 53566
(608) 325-3525
www.mexican-cheese.com

MCP was founded in 1994 by Miguel and Martina Leal, originally of Irapuato, Guanajuato, Mexico. The firm produces such excellent products as Cotija, the "Parmesan of Mexico"; Oaxaca; Colombian-style white cheese; and Para Freir for frying.*

Montchevré-Betin
336 South Penn Street
Belmont, WI 53510
(608) 762-5878
www.montchevre.com
Montchevré-Betin produces many styles of goat cheese, with numerous blue ribbons and best of class wins to its credit. Its plant is located amid the rolling hills of southwestern Wisconsin.

Mt. Sterling Cheese Cooperative
505 Diagonal Street
Mt. Sterling, WI 54645
(608) 734-3151
www.buygoatcheese.com
Mt. Sterling Cheese Cooperative is one of the country's largest goat's milk co-ops, located in southwestern Wisconsin. It is the last working cheese plant in Crawford County and makes raw milk cheeses, some no-salt varieties, and certified organic styles.

Mullins Cheese, Inc.
598 Seagull Drive
Mosinee, WI 54455
(715) 693-3205
www.mullinscheese.net
Mullins Cheese was established in 1970 and provides a range of products, including cheese gift baskets. The firm is

particularly noted for its excellent cheese curds.

Natural Valley Cheese
110 Omaha Street
Hustler, WI 54637
(608) 427-6907
www.cheeseforager.com/naturalvalley
Some eighty Amish dairy farmers, as well as sixteen dairy goat farmers, of whom eight are certified organic, supply milk to Natural Valley Cheese.

North Hendren Cooperative Dairy Company
W8204 Spencer Road
Willard, WI 54493
(715) 267-6617
North Hendren co-op manufactures about two million pounds of cheese yearly, mostly of the blue-veined variety under the Black River label. It has won numerous international awards for its quality products.

Northwoods Cheese Company LLC
800-B South Division Street
Waunakee, WI 53597
(608) 850-6870
www.northwoodscheese.com
Northwoods Cheese Company offers a wide variety of cheese, sausage, cutting boards, and gourmet snack products in gift packages. It has partnered with Greenco Industries to provide jobs for persons with disabilities.

Organic Choice
251 Industrial Drive
Mondovi, WI 54755
(715) 926-4788

www.nextgenerationdairy.com
Dairy products from Organic Choice are produced without the use of hormones, antibiotics, or steroids. Its Next Generation raw milk cheese is made from milk provided by member farms in west-central Wisconsin.

Organic Valley Family of Farms
One Organic Way
LaFarge, WI 54639
(608) 625-2602
www.organicvalley.com
Organic Valley was the first company in the country to offer organic cheese. Since 1988, it has been producing fine ricotta, feta, Colby, Cheddar, and numerous other varieties. More than 900 family farms provide milk to Organic Valley for its cheese production.

Park Cheese
P.O. Box 1499
Fond du Lac, WI 54935
(920) 923-8484
www.parkcheese.com
Park Cheese got its start as a cooperative making Brick cheese in the 1890s and began producing Italian cheeses in the 1940s. Its award-winning offerings, ranging from two-ounce containers to six-hundred-pound hunks of provolone, have even been praised by Bon Appétit *magazine.*

Pasture Pride Cheese (K&K Cheese LLC)
110 Eagle Drive
Cashton, WI 54619
(608) 654-7444

www.pasturepridecheese.com
Pasture Pride Cheese processes approximately 120,000 pounds of milk a day from over 250 family farms to make its cheeses, which include mild, medium, and sharp Cheddars, Colby, Muenster, and other varieties. The firm was started by the Old Order Amish to provide an economic outlet for their community.

Rondelé Specialty Foods
8100 Highway K S
Merrill, WI 54452
(715) 675-3326
www.rondele.com
Rondelé Specialty Foods, part of Lactalis USA, is known for its spreadable and reduced-fat cheeses that have captured numerous international awards.

Roth Käse
657 Second Street
Monroe, WI 53566
(608) 328-2122
www.rothkase.com
The Roth family began making cheese in 1863 in Switzerland and eventually imported European cheeses to North America. In 1991, the firm started making cheese in the Little Switzerland region of south-central Wisconsin, specializing in Gruyère and other cheeses of Alpine origin.

Sargento Foods Inc.
One Persnickety Place
Plymouth, WI 53073
(920) 893-8484
www.sargentocheese.com
Founded in 1953, Sargento Foods is

one of the country's leading packagers of shredded, sliced, and snack cheese. Among the largest privately-held firms in the United States, the company is owned by the Gentine family.

Sartori Foods
201 Morse Street
P.O. Box 503
Antigo, WI 54409
(715) 623-2301
www.sartorifoods.com
The Sartori family came to the United States in the early 1930s from the small town of Valdastico in northern Italy. Since the company's founding, its blue-veined and Italian cheeses have been consistent award winners. Sartori's flavor-infused Xtreme Cheeses, such as a parsley-horseradish cream cheese, are becoming popular.

Seymour Dairy Products
124 Bronson Road
Seymour, WI 54165
(920) 833-2900
www.seymourdairyproducts.com
The Seymour Dairy Products plant is fifteen miles west of Green Bay, crafting premium blue-veined cheeses in Danish, German, and Italian styles. Many of its labels have won major prizes in international competitions.

Silver Lewis Cheese Co-op
W3075 County Road EE
Monticello, WI 53570
(608) 938-4813
Built in 1897, the Silver Lewis Cheese Co-op plant produces farmer's, Brick,

and Muenster cheese. The Green County firm serves loyal customers from as far away as the East Coast and Texas who've learned about it via word-of-mouth.

Specialty Cheese Company
Box 425
430 North Main Street
Reeseville, WI 53579
(800) 367-1711
www.specialcheese.com
Specialty Cheese Company has four production plants, including one that has been continuously in operation since around 1839. Among its labels, the Rich Cow brand emphasizes cheese from the Middle East, such as the popular Ackawi and Jibneh Arabieh, and Hispanic varieties.

Sugar River Cheese Company
1342 Dartmouth Lane
Deerfield, IL 60015
(847) 267-0595
www.sugarrivercheese.com
Sugar River produces numerous varieties of kosher cheese, including interesting styles such as White Cheddar with Chipotle. All of its cheeses are certified by the Chicago Rabbinical Council.

Suttner's Cheese Curds and More
N14505 Sandhill Avenue
Curtiss, WI 54422
(715) 223-3338
Located in Clark County, Suttner's is one of the best outlets in northwestern Wisconsin to buy cheese. The store specializes in offering fresh, squeaky curds

that are popular both with locals and tourists.

Swiss-American, Inc.
4200 Papin Street
St. Louis, MO 63110
(800) 325-8150
www.swissamerican.com
Swiss-American was established in 1938 and is now a leading importer and distributor of cheese and deli items. The firm provides more than three hundred varieties of cheeses for thousands of outlets each week. Ninety percent of its domestic cheese is from Wisconsin.

The Swiss Colony
1112 7th Avenue
Monroe, WI 53566
(608) 328-8400
www.swisscolony.com
Entrepreneur Ray Kubly started The Swiss Colony mail order cheese operation from the basement of his home in 1926. After expanding into gift baskets, the firm now has grown to seven affiliated companies offering everything from furniture to collectibles . . . and always cheese, of course!

Swiss Valley Farms
W3959 County Highway D
Mindoro, WI 54644
www.swissvalley.com
Swiss Valley Farms dairy cooperative manufactures grand champion Swiss; blue-veined cheese in wheels, wedges, and crumbles; and creamy, shredded, string, and chunk product varieties. The company is the sixteenth largest dairy

cooperative in the United States, with seven hundred employees and sales of $425 million dollars. It utilizes 1,100 dairy producers in four states.

Trega Foods
P.O. Box 223
Little Chute, WI 54140
(920) 788-2115
www.tregafoods.com
More than three hundred employees contribute to making Trega Foods a worldwide supplier of award-winning cheese products, with plants in Weyauwega, Little Chute, and Luxemburg, Wisconsin. Its signature variety is a crisply sharp Cheddar.

Union Star Corp.
7742 County Road II
Fremont, WI 54940
(920) 836-2804
www.unionstarcheese.com
Master Cheesemaker Dave Metzig is certified in Cheddar and makes it in a variety of ages. The company also makes flavored Muensters, Colby, string cheese, and cheese curds.

Uplands Cheese
5023 State Road 23
Dodgeville, WI 53533
(608) 935-5558
www.uplandscheese.com
Award-winning Pleasant Ridge Reserve, made from the non-pasteurized milk of one herd of Wisconsin cows, has the marvelously smooth texture of French Gruyère. Uplands Cheese is owned and managed by Mike and Carol Gingrich

and Dan and Jeanne Patenaude, who began farming together in 1994.

White Clover Dairy (now owned by Arla Foods, Inc.)
489 Holland Court
Kaukauna, WI 54130
(800) 243-3730
www.arlafoodsusa.com
White Clover Dairy was formed in 1897 by a small group of farmers in Kaukauna, north of Milwaukee. The firm's internationally award-winning cheeses have included Gouda, Havarti, and feta.

Widmer's Cheese Cellars
214 Henni Street
P.O. Box 127
Theresa, WI 53091
(920) 488-2503, (888) 878-1107
www.widmerscheese.com
Owner Joe Widmer is a certified Master Cheesemaker, handcrafting small batches of award-winning Brick, Cheddar, and Colby. His grandfather, John Widmer, emigrated from Switzerland to start the family company in the 1920s.

Wisconsin Dairy State Cheese Company
Box 215
Rudolph, WI 54475
(715) 435-3144
Noted for its squeaky-good cheese curds, Wisconsin Dairy State Cheese offers guided tours of its plant and has an observation window to watch the cheesemaking process.

Wisconsin Farmers Union Specialty Cheese Company
303 East Highway 18
Montfort, WI 53569
(608) 943-6771
Wisconsin Farmers Union was founded in 1930 and now produces prize-winning Montforte Blue Cheese, Montforte Gorgonzola, Aged Cheddar and Swiss, and numerous other varieties. The plant is located an hour's drive west of Madison in central Wisconsin.

Wisconsin Organics
302 West Stanley Street
Thorp, WI 54771
www.wiorganics.com
Wisconsin Organics cheeses come in eight-ounce, two-pound, and five-pound sizes, in addition to forty-pound blocks for the truly hungry. The company is famous for its mild and sharp Cheddar, Pepper and Monterey Jacks, and white Colby, plus other varieties of cheese, along with delicious milk and butter. Launched in the late 1990s, the company has grown into one of the Midwest's largest producers of organic dairy products.

Wisconsin Sheep Dairy Cooperative
N50768 County Road D
Strum, WI 54770
(715) 695-3617
www.sheepmilk.biz
The fifteen farms in the Wisconsin Sheep Dairy Co-op make it a top producer of artisan sheep's milk cheese and the largest single outlet of quality sheep's milk in the country.

Wiskerchen Cheese
5710 East County Road H
Auburndale, WI 54412
(715) 652-2333
www.wiskerchencheese.com
Wiskerchen is a premier manufacturer of blue cheese and feta, producing quality cheese since 1936. Located in central Wisconsin, the company produces cheeses for several large food companies under their national brand names.

Zimmerman Cheese, Inc.
N6853 Highway 78
South Wayne, WI 53587
(608) 968-3414
www.wisconsinmade.com/zimmerman/
Known for its outstanding Baby Swiss, the third-generation Zimmerman firm distributes its cheese products nationally under a variety of labels. The company is located in Wisconsin's lush Lafayette County.

APPENDIX B:

FOR MORE READING

Allen, Terese. *Bountiful Wisconsin: 110 Favorite Recipes.* Middleton, Wis.: Trails Media Group, 2000.

Allen, Terese, and Harva Hachten. *The Flavor of Wisconsin.* Madison, Wis.: Wisconsin State Historical Society Press, 2008.

Allen, Terese. *Wisconsin's Hometown Flavors: A Cook's Tour of Butcher Shops, Bakeries, Cheese Factories, and Other Specialty Markets.* Middleton, Wis.: Trails Media Group, 2003.

Carroll, Ricki, and Laura Werlin. *Home Cheese Making: Recipes for 75 Delicious Cheeses.* North Adams, Mass: Storey Publishing, 2002.

The Fondue Cookbook. London: Hamlyn Press, 2002.

Herbst, Sharon Tyler and Ron. *The Cheese Lover's Companion: The Ultimate A-Z-Cheese Guide.* New York: William Morrow, 2007.

Hintz, Martin. *Backroads of Wisconsin.* Stillwater, Minn.: Voyageur Press, 2002.

Hintz, Martin, and Daniel Hintz. *Day Trips from Milwaukee* (second edition). Guilford, Conn.: The Globe Pequot Press, 2002.

Hintz, Martin, and Pam Percy. *Off the Beaten Path: Wisconsin* (ninth edition). Guilford, Conn.: The Globe Pequot Press, 2007.

Hintz, Martin, and Stephen Hintz. *Wisconsin: Fun with the Family Wisconsin* (sixth edition). Guilford, Conn.: The Globe Pequot Press, 2006.

Rath, Sara. *The Complete Cow: An Entertaining History of Dairy & Beef Cows of the World.* Stillwater, Minn.: Voyageur Press, 1998.

Scavarda, Marylou, and Kate Sater. *Vin et Fromage.* Santa Rosa, Calif.: Sonoma County Citizen Advocacy, 1981.

Setting the Pace: Wisconsin Holstein History, 1890-1990. Baraboo, Wis.: The Wisconsin Holstein Association, 1990.

Stuttgen, Joanne Raetz, and Terese Allen. *Cafe Wisconsin Cookbook.* Madison, Wis.: The University of Wisconsin Press, 2007.

RECIPE INDEX

INDEX

ABOUT THE AUTHORS

DEVOTED CHEESE FANS AND ALL-AROUND FOODIES, Pam Percy and Martin Hintz live on five acres in River Hills, a suburb of Milwaukee, along with Tom, their Maine coon cat, and Thelma and Louise, their two Saanen dairy goats. Percy and Hintz also raise vegetables, chickens, and quail.

Percy has written a highly acclaimed coffeetable art book called *The Complete Chicken*, as well as the detailed *The Field Guide to Chickens*. In addition to her considerable cooking and hostessing skills, she has also organized festivals, managed a theater company, and produced an award-winning variety program that enjoyed an eight-year broadcast run on Wisconsin Public Radio. Percy also was the owner of Creme, a high-end import bath and beauty product boutique, which she operated with her daughter, Katie.

Hintz has three multiple-edition Globe Pequot guidebooks on Wisconsin to his credit, as well as some ninety additional nonfiction works for other publishers. A long-time member of Milwaukee County's North Shore Library Board, he is also active in numerous professional journalism associations. Among them, Hintz is a past president of the Society of American Travel Writers and is currently the association's Freelance Council chair. Hintz also writes for numerous newspapers and magazines and publishes *The Irish American Post*, a journal of Irish and Irish-American affairs.

In addition, as Boris and Doris on the Town, this husband-wife team cover Milwaukee's social scene as gossip columnists for *The Shepherd Express* weekly newspaper.